INTRODUCTION TO DERIVATIVE FINANCIAL INSTRUMENTS

INTRODUCTION TO DERIVATIVE FINANCIAL INSTRUMENTS

Options, Futures, Forwards, Swaps, and Hedging

DIMITRIS N. CHORAFAS

New York   Chicago   San Francisco   Lisbon   London
Madrid   Mexico City   Milan   New Delhi
San Juan   Seoul   Singapore   Sydney   Toronto

The McGraw·Hill Companies

1 2 3 4 5 6 7 8 9 0   DOC/DOC   0 9 8

ISBN   978-0-07-154663-8
MHID 0-07-154663-4

M

This publication is designed to provide accurate and authoritative
information in regard to the subject matter covered. It is sold with the
understanding that neither the author nor the publisher is engaged in
rendering legal, accounting, futures/securities trading, or other professional
service. If legal advice or other expert assistance is required, the services of a
competent professional person should be sought.
>   —*From a Declaration of Principles jointly adopted by a Committee*
>   *of the American Bar Association and a Committee of Publishers*

McGraw-Hill books are available at special quantity discounts to use as
premiums and sales promotions, or for use in corporate training programs.
To contact a representative, please visit the Contact Us pages at
www.mhprofessional.com.

This book is printed on acid-free paper.

Library of Congress Cataloging-in-Publication Data

Chorafas, Dimitris N.
   Introduction to derivative financial instruments : options, futures,
forwards, swaps, and hedging / by Dimitris N. Chorafas.
     p. cm.
   ISBN-13: 978-0-07-154663-8
   ISBN-10: 0-07-154663-4
1. Derivative securities.   2. Options (Finance).   3. Portfolio management.
4. Risk management.   I. Title.
HG6024.A3C489 2008
332.64'57—dc22

                                                                2008000297

CONTENTS

PART THREE

OPTIONS

Chapter 7

The Use of Options   149

Chapter 8

The Pricing of Options   179

Chapter 9

Option Traders, Buyers, and Writers   203

PART FOUR

RISK CONTROL FOR OPTIONS

Chapter 10

The Greeks: Delta, Gamma, Theta, Kappa, Rho   227

Chapter 11

Credit Risk and Market Risk with Options   243

PART FIVE

FUTURES, FORWARDS, AND SWAPS

Chapter 12

Futures and Forwards   271

Altogether the circumstances seem to me as dangerous and intractable as any I can remember, and I can remember a lot, wrote Paul Volcker, the former Federal Reserve chairman, in the *Washington Post* in April 2005. Two years later, in May 2007, Jean-Claude Trichet, president of the European Central Bank, said there are reasons to believe that traders and investors underestimate the risk that they are taking.

A great deal of this risk comes from leveraging, and just as much from *derivative financial instruments*—this book's theme. Derivatives can be friends or foes depending on how we design them, price them, use them, and control the exposure we are assuming with them. In a comprehensible, easy-to-follow manner, this is the message the text brings to the reader.

The book is introductory, written for professionals who start their career working in the treasury department of industrial companies, merchandising firms, banks, and other financial institutions. It is also written in a way to be understandable by the educated person outside the field of finance who cares about his or her investments—a fast-growing breed.

Derivatives are a product of our time. Many people think that while computers, TV sets, automobiles, and other wares are subject to rapid innovation, financial instruments remain practically the same. This is not true. There exists plenty of innovation in finance, and a great deal of it is accomplished through derivatives.

Starting some time in the early 1990s, and largely induced by the desire to make financial instruments flexible and adaptable to end-user needs, a structural change took place within the financial industry such that it rapidly became more visible and fast paced. As an old adage has it, whenever competitive conditions are altered,

- New windows of opportunity open up.

- Market niches grow in dimensions.
- The more agile companies refocus their plans to take advantage of the innovation.

Innovation in finance through derivative instruments is the subject of Part 1. Chapter 1 brings to the reader's attention the evolving field of service science where, over the last few years, many worthwhile developments have been recorded. Chapter 2 explains, in a comprehensible way, what is meant by *vanilla derivatives*, as well as *exotic derivatives* and *synthetic* and *structured financial products*.

Chapter 3 presses the point that because derivatives are useful and powerful instruments, they must be employed in a way that promotes strategic objectives. And because one of their main uses is for hedging, Chapter 4 outlines for the reader the better hedging practices, types of hedging instruments, rules for hedge accounting, and the meaning of right and wrong hedges.

Part 2 brings to the reader's attention the perils of an uncontrolled exposure and its effect on the entity's liquidity. Liquidity and solvency are two different concepts, but as Dr. Gerald Corrigan, then chairman of the New York Fed, said in October 1987 to Dr. Alan Greenspan: in a panic, illiquidity morphs into insolvency. Chapter 5 explains why this is so, and Chapter 6 suggests what should be done to avoid this happening.

Part 3 introduces to the reader the concepts underpinning options, one of the most ancient, popular, and powerful derivative financial instruments. The use of options is the theme of Chapter 7, and how options are priced that of Chapter 8. Chapter 9 discusses who are the traders, buyers, and writers of options.

Part 4 addresses itself to risk control tools and methods, connected to options. Chapter 10 explains "the Greeks" as tools for measuring risk and return, and Chapter 11 makes the point that there is both credit risk and market risk with options—and for both of these exposures, the devil is in the detail of the ways and means employed for their management.

Other by-now traditional derivative instruments are futures, forwards, and swaps, which is the message Part 5 brings to the reader. Chapter 12 looks at what futures offer to investors, as well as what distinguishes futures from forwards. Another one of its themes is price discovery.

Swaps, swaptions, credit default swaps, and other swap flavors are the subject of Chapter 13, along with practical examples of risks assumed with swaps.

Chapter 14 presents to the reader tools and methods for interest rate risk management by means of derivative instruments, including the synergy that exists between interest rates and currency rates. This choice has been deliberate because the interest rate is a factor that practically affects every citizen, whether he or she has taken a mortgage, bought an auto on credit, made an investment in bonds, has traded in securities, or has managed assets. Interest rate risk must be managed, but we must realize that without fully understanding the behavior of interest rates, risk control is meaningless.

Moreover, no matter which method we use, the day will come when we will have to confront stiff credibility tests on the way we have handled interest rate risk. Appreciation of this fact encourages the use of innovative approaches and of rigorous risk control measures.

The message the preceding paragraphs bring to the reader is valid for individual investors, small firms, and big firms. Eventually, no company can avoid the law of large numbers, which means slowing revenue as it grows in size and complexity and as the market that it addresses tapers off—unless the company is able to reinvent itself and its products without losing track of the exposure that it assumes.

ACKNOWLEDGMENTS

I am indebted to a long list of knowledgeable people and organizations for their contribution to the research that made this book feasible. I am indebted also to several executives and experts for their constructive criticism during the development of the manuscript into its current form.

Let me take this opportunity to thank Jeanne Glasser for suggesting this project, Jane Palmieri for seeing it all the way to publication, and Marci Nugent for the editing work. To Eva-Maria Binder goes the credit for compiling the research results, typing the text, and making the camera-ready artwork and index.

Dr. Dimitris N. Chorafas
December 2007
Valmer and Vitznau

INTRODUCTION TO DERIVATIVE FINANCIAL INSTRUMENTS

PART ONE

Innovation in Finance through Derivative Instruments

CHAPTER 1

Financial Innovation

SERVICE SCIENCE

Banking and finance are service industries that for many centuries have been characterized by tradition, regulation, and a relatively slow innovation. This contrasts to the science-based characteristics of manufacturing, which, since the late nineteenth century, have evolved rather rapidly. Not until the early twenty-first century did we examine the theoretical background of the service industry at large, as well as that of some of its multiple sectors.

To appreciate the message conveyed by the above paragraph, we should start with a most basic query: What is meant by *service*? An orderly way of answering this question will look at fundamental issues underpinning the notions of conception, design, organization, and provision of a service, including its

- Nature
- Product characteristics
- Market offering
- Execution
- Profitability
- Feedback control

As it has been the case with manufacturing, an analytical approach to the notion of services will address both their consistency and the development of practical fields where they can be put to work. It will also include the effective management of a service or services, and not only that of service products. A couple of practical examples can help in guiding the reader's mind.

In 1882, journalists Charles Dow, 31, Edward Jones, 27, and Charles Bergstresser, 24, started Dow Jones & Company—a service industry. Its object was to pick up news and gossip and peddle them to brokers, bankers, and speculators. Seven years later, in 1889, Dow Jones launched the *Wall Street Journal* (WSJ), another service product, which started as a four-page stock-and-bond paper priced at 2 cents.

Information technology (IT) is a more recent example of a service industry's development, which took place in the second half of the twentieth century. Originally confined to number crunching and accounting, today IT brings the concept of service orientation to the boardroom, by combining the best features of a technological evolution ongoing for six decades. Modern basic ingredients are

- Modeling
- Experimenting
- Using knowledge artifacts
- Employing IT to continuously improve business policies and processes

Take as an example the science of logistics, which has been known since the time of Alexander the Great, more than 2,300 years ago. Blending IT with logistics, and most particularly the Internet, has delivered the benefits of supply chain management accomplished online, in real time, in a way involving both the real and virtual worlds. Many experts look at this present-day version of logistics as the forerunner of *service science*, a twenty-first-century term.

Technology alone, however, though necessary is not enough. Also in Alexander's time, Demosthenes, the great orator and politician of ancient Athens, said that "business is built on trust." Trust is confidence, and it is foremost in all sorts of financial operations from lending and trading to investing; therefore, it is a pillar of service science.

- Etymologically, *trust* means reliance, faith, conviction, and certitude.
- In credit terms, *trust* is used to describe the reliability of a partnership, as well as the credibility and trustworthiness that should go along with it.

Down to basics, innovation in finance and banking—therefore in the service industry—started with the notion of credit itself and the laws that guaranteed dependence on a counterparty's credit-worthiness. The origin of these laws dates back to the early seventeenth century BC, under the reign of Hammurabi, the great Babylonian emperor and legislator.

It needs no explaining that trustworthiness is pivotal in banking and finance—all the way from extending credit to exercising trustee functions. For example, service science connected to securities management integrates the meaning of *custody, care, charge, guardianship, protection*, and *safekeeping*. But the term *trust* is also used to describe a monopoly or cartel—as in the expression "an international trust controls the market in diamonds."

A pillar of service science, next to trust and technology, is learning. As Buddha said: "We should live as if it is the last day of our life, and we should learn as if we live forever." Learning and being able to manage change correlate. Change never manifests itself as a single significant event, and (with the exception of revolutions) it rarely comes in big discrete packages.

Rather, change usually makes itself known in a series of "small" events connected to learning, trust, and technology, as well as in steady step-by-step developments based on what we learn. "Men accept change only through necessity," said Jean Monnet, the French banker who with Dillon tried to rest control of Bank of America out of the hands of Amadeo Giannini—and lost—"and they see necessity only in crisis."

MOTIVATION FOR FINANCIAL INNOVATION

Financial innovation is the art and science of developing new products and processes that promote service science by promoting credit, enhancing investment, facilitating trading, and bringing under wider perspective other activities which were not present or popular prior to an innovative initiative. One of the earliest examples of financial innovation is the use of paper money first in China, then in the Western world (more on this later). Another example is derivative financial instruments, which exploded 20-fold in the last 15 years of the twentieth century. (More on derivatives, underlyings, and notional principal in Chapter 2.)

"Clothes and automobiles change every year," Paul M. Mazur, of Lehman Brothers, once suggested: "But because the currency remains the same in appearance, though its value steadily declines, most people believe that finance does not change. Actually, debt financing changes like everything else. We have to find new models in financing, just as in clothes and automobiles, if we want to stay on top. We must remain inventive architects of the money business."[1]

One of the first persons on record known to have mastered the concept of financial innovation—and with it the art of trading risk—was John Law, the Scottish gambler and financier who repeatedly made and lost a big fortune. He is said to have gotten his insight about risk by calculating the odds, and he became known for having invented and used his tools and findings in public lotteries, assuring the odds were in his favor. These exploits led John Law to one of the main branches of service science: analytical finance. He is also credited as the first European who publicly issued paper money[2]—a new product for the early eighteenth century, which was Law's time.

Just as they are today, in the late seventeenth and early eighteenth centuries, economics, finance, and gambling were intermingled. Then, as now, new developments caught the public eye. For instance, in 1694 Thomas Neale, Master of the Mint and groom porter to the King of England, invented a government lottery to provide a 16-year loan for the crown. Since then, government lotteries have become taxation's alter ego—and a source of profits for those who know how to take advantage of them.

In 1728 Charles Marie de la Condamine, a mathematician and philosopher, discovered that the French royal authorities had made a major blunder in setting the terms of a new state lottery. To promote the tickets, they undertook to subsidize the lottery's prizes— but the prizes they were offering were greater than the maximum revenue the state could obtain from ticket sales.

In an early-eighteenth-century version of analytics aiming to unearth market anomalies, together with other intellectuals,

---

[1] Joseph Wechsberg, *The Merchant Bankers*, Pocket Books/Simon and Schuster, New York, 1966.
[2] Janet Gleeson, *The Moneymaker*, Bantam Books, London, 1999.

Condamine and Voltaire, the philosopher, author, and poet, found the way to make a guaranteed large but entirely legal fortune. For at least a year, month after month they cornered the royal lottery market by buying up all lottery tickets.[3]

Innovation in finance and economics, however, predated Law, Voltaire, and Neale by 22 centuries. Options were invented in ancient Greece by Thales, a mathematician and philosopher, though they really became part of the strategy of financial institutions in the 1970s, after the Black-Scholes algorithm made possible a model for pricing them (more on options in Part 3).

The first research ever to be established as organized service science rather than issued as one-man efforts like those of Thales, Thomas Neale, or Thomas Edison, saw the light in the late nineteenth century. History books say that credit for it goes to Werner von Siemens, the founder of the company under the same name that is today Germany's largest and most powerful electronics and electrical engineering firm.

In 1953 when I was studying at UCLA, the top three laboratories in the world were the famous Bell Labs of AT&T, the General Electric (GE) Laboratory in Schenectady, and the General Motors (GM) Laboratory in Detroit. Of these, only GE's labs still claim leadership.

In the late 1950s, 1960s, and 1970s, organized laboratory effort was not known in finance. By the 1980s, however, Tier 1 banks had developed facilities resembling small Bell Telephone Laboratories equipped with analysts, mathematicians, physicists, and engineers—the rocket scientists. One of the first examples was the Advanced Systems Group (ASG) at Morgan Stanley.

Over the years, these small analytical labs have gained strategic significance and have become important product development units. Largely based on Wall Street and in London's City, they have focused their work on engineering financial innovation. Insurance companies have followed the banks along this road of research and development (R&D) by creating a new class of financial instruments designed to transfer insurance risk to the capital markets. This offers several advantages to the insurers, three of the most

---

[3] Ian Davidson, *Voltaire in Exile*, Atlantic Books, London, 2004.

important being these:

- Diversification of funding sources for major insurance contracts
- Reduction of counterparty risk for insured parties
- Somewhat higher risk-adjusted returns for investors

Shortly after being invented, in the short span of the last three years of the twentieth century, an estimated $13 billion of these risk transfer instruments were issued worldwide. About two-thirds of the securitized insurance products concern property catastrophe reinsurance in the form of bonds, swaps, and options (see Chapter 2). Of the balance, the majority are contingent capital and life insurance securitizations. Notice that none of these existed prior to the mid-1990s.

Both Wall Street and the City have followed the Silicon Valley's lead (see the following section, "The Technology Side of Service Science") in understanding that research and development are cornerstones to competitiveness and therefore to corporate survival. Without new products a company will find itself out of the market in the span of a few years. As competitors introduce new financial instruments at a rapid pace, a bank, insurance firm, hedge fund, or other entity has to run fast to make profits and stay in business.

The reader should, however, notice that part of Silicon Valley's and Wall Street's favorable climates for steady innovation are the hire and fire labor laws in America. The United States has relatively few obstacles to employment, the starting of new companies, raising private capital, or going public. Reducing bureaucratic obstacles to innovative companies is far different from the generous subsidy programs paid by the heavy-handed continental European and Japanese governments, which are desperate for a dynamic economy but unable to change their prevailing negative cultures.

THE TECHNOLOGY SIDE OF SERVICE SCIENCE

Silicon Valley provides an excellent example on how innovation works and what may be its aftermath. The great experience of Silicon Valley started in the 1950s with a plan by Frederick Terman, then dean of Stanford University's Engineering School, to create an industrial park on Stanford land. A few companies accepted the offer, but the area really took off in the 1970s with the explosive growth of semiconductors and microprocessors, followed by the enormous demand for software and the Internet.

A large number of the intellectual resources that feed this formidable machine are nearby. Faculty and graduates of the science and engineering departments from Stanford, the University of California, and other local area institutions of higher learning have been leaders in forming the start-ups. In turn, these renowned scientists have attracted high-quality labor in the Valley's large pool of engineers, physicists, mathematicians, and software experts.

Statistics on the concentration of brain power that has developed as a by-product of the innovation culture are most impressive. More than 1 million people are currently working in the Silicon Valley, and almost 40 percent of them have at least a bachelor's degree. About 35 percent of them are foreign born, having been attracted to working in the Silicon Valley for one or more of the following reasons:

- Imaginative projects
- Well-paid jobs
- Excellent career prospects
- Early access to high-tech frontier developments

The wheels of change have been moving fast, and this has dearly affected the Silicon Valley companies' business. How much each year's R&D output impacts on turnover, and how fast existing products lose market appeal, is dramatized in Figure 1.1 based on statistics provided in a meeting with Hewlett-Packard. For Hewlett-Packard and all other Silicon Valley companies, innovation has been a strategic decision.

Choosing Silicon Valley as a paradigm has been a deliberate choice because many financial experts today think that its pattern may one day characterize the banking industry, as smaller boutiques multiply. By all likelihood in the years to come the banking industry too will be characterized by start-ups and former start-ups that became giants—similar to the rise of Microsoft, Intel, and Apple in the field of information technology.

Some of these financial industry start-ups will supply innovative consulting and software services focused on product design

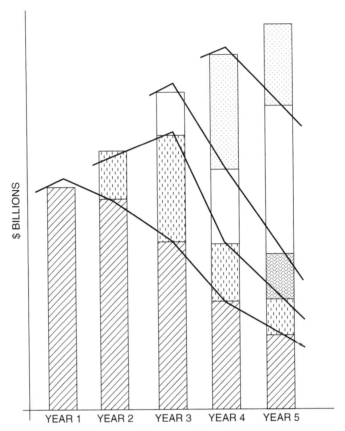

Figure 1.1 Rapid product life cycles: An example from Hewlett-Packard's product orders by year introduced to the market

and risk management technologies for new products. Innovative financial services will be at a premium because in banking, as in engineering, the able management of change distinguishes those who are fit to work in service science from those who aren't. Practically everything changes over time. In the broadest possible sense, areas of activity that would attract the most attention include

- Architectural concepts
- Functional details
- Planning of service offerings
- Organization of service provision

- Development of human resources
- Direction of execution activities
- Quality control of provided services
- Feedback from client satisfaction or dissatisfaction

Architectural concepts and functional details relate to the definition of services to be provided, sustained, or revamped. Answers to queries such as what, how, when, how much, and at which price should be provided after due analysis and experimentation—seconded by knowledge-enriched solutions aimed at assisting the service workers and at attracting customers because of

- Supervisor quality offerings
- Attractive, highly competitive prices

The planning of services, and organization of their provision, bring into perspective strategic prerequisites that address the structure of the services being offered and the quality of the service firm's personnel. Organizational and structural issues are as well very important regarding the relation of the service firm to its clients, looking at services as a concept that continues to evolve over time.

Additionally, an indispensable part of every design, production, and delivery process is the need for rules and feedback procedures focusing on quality management. It goes without saying that quality is a fundamental issue in the service industry, characterizing the service company's art and substance. The quality notion also relates quite closely to

- The client's perception of services being received
- Feedback on the client's appreciation of such services, including their cost-effectiveness

Therefore, all types of services—their background, performance quality, and competitiveness—should be the subject of steady examination. Metrics and methods must be available to permit dependable analysis of patterns of service, on which management can base corrective action. A thorough and critical examination is an integral part of the management infrastructure necessary for providing the stimulus for steady innovation and for the management of change.

By expanding the horizon of products offered to the market, technology and the advent of derivative instruments have given new perspectives to financial entrepreneurship. The currently predominant families of financial products are shown in Figure 1.2. A little-appreciated fact about derivatives is that they blur distinctions between instruments regulated by different authorities responsible for market discipline. This way, they virtually eliminate functional and other distinctions among

- Commercial banks
- Investment banks
- Insurance companies
- Pensions funds
- Nonbank financial institutions, such as hedge funds

New instruments can be created quickly for clients, in novel form, by the bank's origination and trading desks. Many of them are customized. They promote novelty without the need for complex documentation or extensive negotiation. Along with novelty, however, comes significant risk that the buyers (and sometimes the sellers) don't always appreciate.

ENTREPRENEURSHIP

Silicon Valley grew over time on its own initiative and enterprise, with little help and no subsidies from the U.S. government. To succeed, it capitalized on a great deal of trust its people had in the future of its products and services, as well as on their own ability to deliver. In fact, the distinguishing feature of Silicon Valley is not electronics but entrepreneurship. The same feature characterizes companies engaging in financial innovation.

Entrepreneurship succeeds when managers, engineers, financial experts, and other professionals are willing to invest an inordinate amount of time and effort in pursuing their goal while avoiding the beaten path. They must also communicate their ideas well enough to attract venture capitalists and enthusiastic collaborators. Successful entrepreneurship requires

- A great deal of insight
- The ability to grasp the opportunity

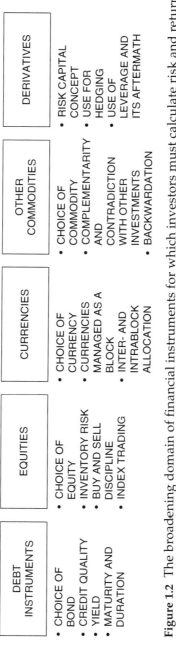

Figure 1.2 The broadening domain of financial instruments for which investors must calculate risk and return

DEBT INSTRUMENTS	EQUITIES	CURRENCIES	OTHER COMMODITIES	DERIVATIVES
• CHOICE OF BOND • CREDIT QUALITY • YIELD • MATURITY AND DURATION	• CHOICE OF EQUITY • INVENTORY RISK • BUY AND SELL DISCIPLINE • INDEX TRADING	• CHOICE OF CURRENCY • CURRENCIES MANAGED AS A BLOCK • INTER- AND INTRABLOCK ALLOCATION	• CHOICE OF COMMODITY • COMPLEMENTARITY AND CONTRADICTION WITH OTHER INVESTMENTS • BACKWARDATION	• RISK CAPITAL CONCEPT • USE FOR HEDGING • USE OF LEVERAGE AND ITS AFTERMATH

In 1954, Rockwood & Co., a chocolate firm in Brooklyn with a large inventory in cocoa beans, offered to redeem some of its stock. Warren Buffett calculated that trading the stock for beans and simultaneously selling cocoa beans on the commodities market would result in a huge profit because the market had soared. Taking advantage of price discrepancies in separate markets is the best example of benefit derived from insight.

Another basic characteristic of entrepreneurs is the readiness to challenge the "obvious" and therefore to experiment. Experimentation helps in accelerating the learning process, building know-how on the basis of day-to-day experiences. Experimenting in new ideas, methodologies, designs, and marketing strategies is what makes the entrepreneur keen in creating new markets and products—rather than protecting the status quo.

This sort of spirit sees to it that the entrepreneur does not have a unique method or technology that he or she keeps close to the chest but excels in what is known as the *first-mover advantage* in product or service innovation and in capturing market share. The first-mover advantage also helps in attracting venture capital for an infusion of cash and in building investor confidence. As explained in the preceding section, trust is a crucial factor in service science. In finance, the first-mover advantage has two aspects:

- Creation of new products and services that improve market share and the bottom line
- Rigorous risk management, because unlike companies that specialize in physical products, entities that deal in financial instruments take significant risks

As Figure 1.3 suggests, this is particularly true of those entities that are highly leveraged. Up to a point, but only up to a point, the gearing of equity makes the firm more efficient—though the risk increases. If not properly managed, successive layers of leveraging and exposure will eventually lead the company into trouble.

To appreciate the foregoing statement, the reader should understand that one of the characteristics of new financial instruments is the switch from dealing with assets to dealing with liabilities. Traditionally, bankers have been preoccupied with the assets side of business, which has underpinned the whole process of giving loans. But as of the late 1980s, it is the liabilities side that

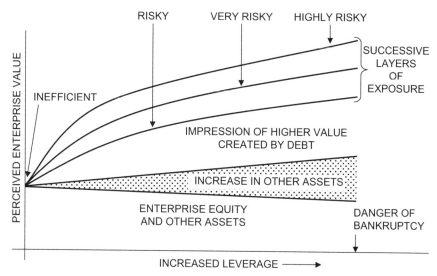

Figure 1.3 The limits of leverage beyond which exposure increases exponentially

is holding the upper ground. Money center banks provide this model by

- Buying money more cheaply in the marketplace rather than collecting deposits
- Placing emphasis on the monetization of debt and its resale through securitization

Securitized assets are somebody else's liabilities, credit derivatives being an example. From an entrepreneurial viewpoint, the new world of wholesale money markets has worked to the benefit of both the banks and their clients, particularly those more sophisticated. Just as a money center bank can sell certificates of deposit and securitized mortgages (or corporate loans) around the world, a big multinational corporation can circumvent the bank and sell promissory notes (or commercial paper), paying interest rates lower than those a bank demands for a loan.

Entrepreneurship has been instrumental in revamping intermediation, an age-old concept in banking. Contrary to what some people say, innovation does not weaken intermediation; if anything, it strengthens it by providing products and services more appealing than their predecessors. One example of restructured intermediation is when a bank designs a specific product for its customer(s) but executes the transaction through a third party—such as a special investment vehicle (SIV)—rather than directly:

- The bank's investment arm faces the intermediary as its counterparty.
- At the same time the intermediary deals with the client in an identical transaction.

Intermediation may as well occur if the arranging institution is unwilling to face the end client directly—for instance, for credit reasons such as when counterparty's credit limits are full. Restructured intermediation may also be employed for regulatory, tax, or other reasons.

The instruments of intermediation may be specially designed derivatives (Chapter 2) that enable participants to buy or sell an underlying asset at a predetermined forward price; options that grant the buyer the right, but not the obligation, to buy or sell an underlying asset at a predetermined price; or swaps and other customized over-the-counter (OTC) contracts. Today, these instruments are employed on a daily basis by

- Issuers
- Investors
- Financial intermediaries

Derivatives do more than allow taking risks or hedging risks. They permit the holder to virtually simulate any financial activity by redrawing assets and liabilities, separating and recombining different types of exposures, bypassing what regulators may prohibit, and changing the taxation profile of a client, investor, or company.

PAPER SHIPS: A CASE STUDY

Since the mid-1990s, one of the new instruments banks and securities firms have been offering is the *index certificate*. This is an investment product with a wide variety of characteristics, and its importance has significantly increased in the early years of the twenty-first century.

Tailored to meet a range of investment objectives, these instruments share the characteristic that banks establish for them bid-ask prices on each trading day:

If the certificate is based on a performance index,

Then on expiry of the period, interim earnings on the underlying asset can generally be collected as capital gains.

As advantages of index certificates, market participants cite that they have relatively low transaction costs and comparatively good liquidity; they require a low minimum capital outlay; and they provide a basis for risk diversification. From a legal viewpoint, index certificates are debt securities on which no interim dividends are paid. A single repayment is made when the certificate matures.

The downside is that investors must keep in perspective the ranking of the certificate in relation to the issuer's other liabilities, as well as the fact that many index certificates have become complex, and as such, they are neither transparent nor liquid. Moreover, critics say that lack of transparency also prevails in connection to their pricing.

True enough, pricing is most often a challenge with financial instruments, but the more complex they are, the more opaque they become. Basically, the value of index certificates, or *participation certificates*, is derived from their underlying. Generally the underlying is key domestic and foreign share indexes. Certificates also exist based on

- Sector indexes
- Baskets of indexes
- Exotic varieties with complex structures
- Other financial products all of which involve inherent risks

The last two fit the *paper ship index*—a new financial product. Shipowners who know how to play with the system could use it to hedge the future value of their assets, while speculators employ the paper ship index for profits. What this index provides is the ability to page the value of assets, but as with all hedges, there is the risk of a counterparty going bust (Chapter 4). A relatively recent example is that of a major Belgian company that was hit twice:

- First, from a wrong hedge through forward freight agreements (FFAs)
- Second, from time charges betting the wrong way in terms of market movement

That's the so-called double whammy. Leveraged bets have great risks because nobody really knows which way the market will switch. In the early years of the twenty-first century, with China's economic boom, the shipping market went to the stars. Experts had not really foreseen this, but while everybody has been jumping on the bandwagon, very few people have been questioning whether and when the shipping boom (which started in 2002) will end.

At the origin of the paper ship index is a brokerage firm: Clarkson Ship Brokers. Annoyed by the fact that insurance companies have not been providing residual value insurance, Richard Fulford Smith, one of its brokers, developed a derivative to fill the gap. Expert insurers say that dealing with the paper ship index is a game too complex for small ship owners, but it can be rewarding to those who truly understand its risk and reward profile.

People with a positive reaction to the paper ship index add that using this and similar instruments comes down to magnifying (read: gearing) one's assets. But what's the real cost? In all branches of finance, the major question to ask in terms of leveraging is on whose balance sheet this takes place:

- The shipowner
- The bank, or
- A special investment vehicle that lies between the bank and the shipowner

A key challenge is that of precalculating life-cycle risk, which is a prerequisite to realistic pricing of the paper ship index. As with any instrument, the pricing affects the issuer, the buyer, and the market as a whole. Still another challenge is that of arriving at a factual and documented answer to the question of how far the paper ship index is effective in laying off risk. As all derivatives, one of the counterparties will benefit and the other will lose.

This is tantamount to speculating, and some experts suggest that serious shipping companies should not be interested in the paper ship index. Another reason for this negative reaction is that a derivative shipping instrument cannot, and does not, have a commitment to high quality of services. Rather than hedging, some experts say, the answer to the shipping industry's problems is

- Greater consolidation
- More rational pricing of services being offered

This is equally true of shipping insurance. A crucial problem confronting the shipping insurance market is that it has not reached a level at which it incorporates an appropriate price for assumed risk. "[Today] insurance is a cheap product," said a Lloyd's insurer during our meeting, and "if you can buy cheap insurance, you don't need derivatives."

FORWARD FREIGHT AGREEMENTS AND THE MACROMARKETS

New financial instruments attract attention from several quarters: bankers, traders, assets owners, and investors. It comes therefore as no surprise that freight derivatives have interested not only investment banks but also shipowners, though the majority is still cautious about an instrument they know little about. Forward freight agreements (FFAs) are still relatively new in the market, even if experts suggest that with time they will become an inevitable part of shipping.

People careful about instrument design, as well as its risk and return, say that FFAs are not traditional forward contracts (see Chapter 2). Their handling needs a lot of sophistication that does not yet exist in the shipping sector, particularly among companies which are small- to medium-sized family-run organizations. There is as well the opinion that, as it has happened with other complex instruments, most markets are not ready to embrace FFAs. However, the new generation of shipowners seems open to the derivatives market and predisposed to understanding

- What hedging is
- How it can be done using forwards

Precisely for this reason, FFAs make a good case study. A conservative policy will involve agreements on a one-to-one ship and FFA ratio as a way to either increase or decrease the firm's exposure. Among issues to be kept in perspective are

- Counterparty risk
- The fact that FFAs are largely an unregulated market

To solve the counterparty risk problem, there should be an indexing system in which parties are rated for their exposure in the FFA market, accounting for the fact that a major counterparty collapse could have a devastating domino effect on many other paper ship holders. Of course, the physical ship market also carries risk, as owners can find themselves forced to renegotiate lucrative charter contracts to lower price levels, or they may face the counterparty's inability or unwillingness to pay.

Today, there is no forewarning system on credit risk, though there is an ongoing discussion that includes some of the parties involved in FFA transactions. Knowledgeable people suggest that a sound approach is to include all of the parties: shipowners, charterers, operators, and FFA brokers and the exchange(s). Critics, however, say the idea that brokers would draw up such a forewarning system poses an inherent conflict of interest.

Some experts advise that to help themselves calculate the odds, shipowners should make macroeconomic analysis and study macroopportunities. Many forward deals like currency exchange, stock indexes, bond futures, and several other derivatives have a macrodimension. The macromarkets are large enough to accommodate many investors, but those who have been searching for macro-opportunities appreciate that there is a significant difference between

- Maintaining momentum, and
- Gaining momentum after adversity.

Shipping is one of the industries where, after a profitless period or plain market downturn, each big player's size is hindered in regaining momentum. Moreover, momentum must be gained with profits commensurate to the risks being taken. The rate of return on "riskless" investments must be compared with the expected return associated with risky assets.

When the amount of exposure increases without a corresponding growth in returns, wise investors shift assets away from risky investments to those of less exposure. Risk and return sees to it that shipowners are more likely to use forward freight agreements when they labor to secure part of their new-building projects. For instance, in 2003 a Greek shipowner company was able to order up to five more units by carefully considering its timing in an FFA market that was on the rise:

- In September 2003, the spot charter market was showing signs of an increase,
- But shipyards were still quoting prices reflecting the lower charter levels that prevailed in previous years.

As Warren Buffett did with the Rockwood chocolate entity (as discussed under "Entrepreneurship"), through FFAs the Greek company "capitalized on the time lag of around three months before yards started to quote new building prices that reflected an increased charter market," Hajioannou said.[4] In December 2003, using derivatives a shipowner could order a Panamax (the largest-size ship that will fit through the locks of the Panama Canal) in the price range of $24 million to $25 million with delivery for 2006.

Deals in the futures and forwards markets (Chapter 2) stand or fall by the short- to longer-term balance between risk and reward. An analysis of the fundamental motivation for entering into a given type of transaction permits entrepreneurs and their risk managers to determine whether the transaction is suitable for the firm. Derivatives based on uninformed speculation are the sort of transactions that over the past decade have been the primary sources of losses for investors and intermediaries.

Being careful and analytically minded implies that one has to do his or her homework prior to commitment. Expert opinion helps, but one should not depend solely on experts. The way Frank Partnoy, a former investment banker and now a professor of finance, puts it, "The best piece of advice I ever received was from one manager who suggested I could become an expert in emerging markets by telling people I was an expert in emerging markets. Over time I would fill the gaps."[5]

---

[4] *TradeWinds*, September 24, 2004.
[5] Frank Partnoy, *F.I.A.S.C.O.: The Truth about High Finance*, Profile Books, London, 1997.

A principle one should learn is that

• New financial instruments tend to be complex by design.

This happens for many reasons, two of the most important being that novelty tends to have many unknowns and the fact that, in spite of that, clients always demand greater sophistication and inventiveness of features—which has inherent risks. Additionally,

• Many banks take double risks because they combine lending with trading.

Combining lending and trading with counterparties leads to risk correlation. A bank may give, for example, a $50 million loan to a client who uses it as a cash deposit for a derivatives deal. This and similar practices create concentric circles of credit risk and market risk, which will eventually lead to unexpected consequences.

RISK MANAGEMENT

Risk management is a very important integral part of service science. Innovation is always welcome, but to keep on beingahead of the curve, we must know the risks we are taking beforehand, not after the fact. Precisely for this reason, it has been a deliberate choice to introduce the reader to the concepts underpinning the control of risk in Chapter 1—even prior to the definition of derivative instruments, which is done in Chapter 2.

In today's economy, derivative instruments may be the motor of trading,

But risk control is the brake, and it is better to have a car without a motor than one with a motor but without brakes.

Risks assumed with financial instruments are by no means limited to derivatives. They can be found all over the debt market (junk bonds being an example) and in the equities market. In the go-go Internet company years (late 1990s), eBay, the auction house that uses its Internet site to match up buyers and sellers for all sorts of goods, went public through an initial public offering (IPO) on September 23, 1998—pricing shares at $18 each. At the close of 1998, eBay's shares were trading at $241 on the Nasdaq exchange—an increase of 1,200 percent in a quarter.

The stock of the virtual bookstore Amazon.com rose 966 percent; that of America Online, 586 percent; and of Yahoo!, 584 percent. In contrast, over the same period the equity price increase of many established industrial companies was mediocre or nil, with declines at Bethlehem Steel, Boeing, Caterpillar, DuPont, Lockheed Martin, and U.S. Steel. Less than two years later, at the end of March 2000, the curve of fast-rising equity prices of Internet companies bent:

- Many went into bankruptcy.
- Those who survived had their wings clipped.

The need for steady and rigorous watch over exposure is present, without exception, with every single investment. The added challenge in risk control with derivatives is that in an impressive number of cases,

- Their originators find it difficult to price them.
- Their exposure is nonlinear (Chapter 2).
- When reporting to regulators, they have to be marked to model, not to market, because for many of them there is no secondary market.

Compared to horse-and-buggy classical bonds and equities, complex derivatives are supersonic engines. Banks and investors who do not appreciate this difference, or people who don't have the training and experience required to be supersonic pilots, are living at the edge of an abyss where

- Risk and return equations are much more weighted on the risk side.
- Market bets turn sour with multi-billion-dollar losses, an example being Amaranth Advisors LLC, which in late 2006 lost $6 billion in one go by speculating on gas futures.

This section is not the only case in this book where emphasis is placed on risk management. Practically every chapter has something to say on the control of risk. Most particularly, Chapter 3 emphasizes the need for high technology; Chapter 5 takes a broader view of the types of risks assumed with derivatives; Chapter 10 explains "the Greeks"; Chapter 11 outlines why there is both credit risk and market risk with options; Chapter 13 does the same with credit default swaps (CDSs); and Chapter 14 informs the reader on the exposure associated with credit risk transfer (CRT) instruments and interest rate spreads.

The concept of risk management can be wide. On August 29, 2003, at the annual meeting of the Fed of Kansas, Dr. Alan Greenspan defined the Fed's role in interest rates as risk management. He said the term means a combination of judgment and analytics. In Greenspan's opinion, monetary policy and risk management correlate. The setting of interest rates by monetary authorities must account for

- Probable evolution in economic growth
- Improbable outcome in inflation, deflation, and (as an outlier) economic collapse

In reaching risk management decisions, the opinions of central bank board members and economists may differ because decision makers have different types of economic outlook and a variety of ways in identifying dangers associated to this outlook. Also, their projections on inflation and its aftermath, including inflation caps and floors, are not the same. Yet, they are all members of the same process of service science.

A similar statement is valid about risk control decisions made in connection to new and old financial instruments. No two people have the same appreciation of future volatility, market liquidity, and other critical factors that every day underpin market risk or are associated with a counterparty's creditworthiness. But a personal trait that distinguishes great risk managers from the average lot is the ability to say No! to a trade or investment—and stick to it.

In a shareholder meeting, Warren Buffett expressed his and his company's ability to hold the line: Well, we do have filters. And sometimes those filters are very irritating to people who check in with us about businesses—because we really can say no in 10 seconds or so to 90 percent of all of the things that come along, simply because we have these filters. (This reference appeared in a late 1990s Berkshire Hathaway stockholders' report.)

Filtering is a key word in finance. This is not a matter of always being negative but rather of using intelligence and good business sense. A crucial characteristic of a top trader or successful investor is that he or she wants businesses that he or she can understand. That is a cornerstone to every risk management action; sticking to it filters out a lot of things.

At that same shareholder meeting, Buffett also underlined the need to have some filters in regard to people: We want businesses that are being run by people who we're very comfortable with— which means people with ability and integrity. And we can assess that very fast. We've heard a lot of stories in our lives. Successful investors appreciate that in finance, as it is in science in everyday life, a chain of events can reach a point of crisis that magnifies small changes. As a popular verse has it,

> For want of a nail, the shoe was lost;
> For want of a shoe, the horse was lost;
> For want of a horse, the rider was lost;
> For want of a rider, the battle was lost;
> For want of a battle, the kingdom was lost!

Seen under this perspective, risk management is a metalevel (higher-up level) in a hierarchy of quality control missions and functions that guide the hand of professionals in regard to current and future exposure. Every quality control system can be analyzed into three parts:

- Monitoring and measurement
- Statistical analysis and reporting
- Decision making by variables or attributes

Between each two layers defined by these bullets lies a filter that can be thought of as passing the desired message stream but blocking the noise. (*Noise* is any unwanted or irrelevant input that alters the message.) In risk control, this noise may well be a psychological factor that alters the behavior of the trader, loans officer, investment advisor, or other professional.

In service science, filtering works in conjunction with the statistical decision system that is shown in Figure 1.4. The scope of quantitative and qualitative analysis is to sort incoming information elements into groups with the criterion being their deviation from specifications, limits, or tolerances. There is an analogy to this process in communications theory, when several types of messages are sent simultaneously over the same channel and are

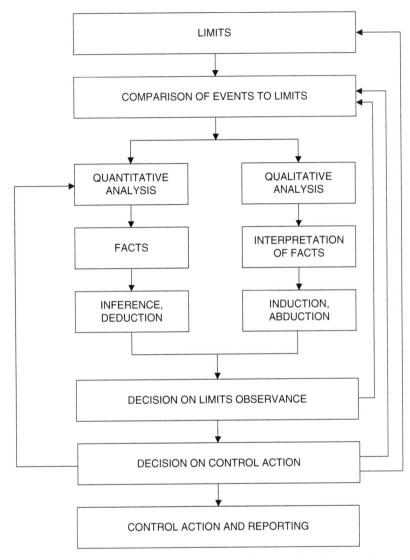

Figure 1.4 Successive steps characterizing risk control and corrective action

then unpacked, sorted out, and properly sequenced at the receiver.

In a similar way, incoming data streams can be analyzed to give answers to a potentially wide variety of problems involving compliance to, or alternatively lack of observance of, tolerances.

The principles of communications theory enable the controller to assume the proper perspective in evaluating the performance of the system under his or her supervision—and its produce.

At a metalevel, risk management may decide not to suppress errant impulses in the production process (trading, investments, loans, or activities) but to exploit them in order to unearth hidden trends. Or to exert tighter control, which requires continuously gauging not only trading and investment positions but also personal characteristics and attitudes. This should be made in a way that keeps business activities within established tolerances, but without creating a bureaucratic culture or killing individual initiative.

CHAPTER 2

Derivatives

DERIVATIVES DEFINITION BY THE FASB

Books and articles on financial history suggest that apart from the brilliant contribution of the motion of options by Thales, in ancient Greece, the existence of derivatives instruments and markets dates back to the seventeenth century, with equity shares bought and sold at a forward date, while share options were also traded. For instance, in the seventeenth and eighteenth centuries forward contracts in commodities, particularly rice, were traded in Japan.

Instrument features that today are considered to be characteristic of modern derivatives exchanges emerged during the second half of the nineteenth century on Chicago's commodities exchanges. There, for the first time in financial history,

- Quantities and prices were standardized.
- Margin calls were regulated.
- The possibility of fulfilling contracts by means of offsetting trades, rather than delivering the underlying, was introduced.

It is therefore not surprising that the large majority of early derivatives trades involved commodities rather than financial instruments. True enough, the first currency swaps appeared in the 1960s, but they were used mainly for circumventing British capital controls rather than for trading for profits. Financial derivatives, as we know them today, really started in the 1970s—with profits and losses written off-balance sheet (OBS).

In the late 1980s, the Financial Accounting Standards Board (FASB), an agency of the Securities and Exchange Commission (SEC), outlined 14 distinct classes that among themselves constituted the then available derivative financial instruments. There were commitments to extend credit; standby letters of credit; financial guarantees written (sold); options written; interest rate caps and floors; interest rate swaps; forward contracts; futures contracts; obligations on receivables sold; obligations under foreign currency exchange contracts; interest rate foreign currency swaps; obligations to repurchase securities sold; outstanding commitments to purchase or sell at predetermined prices; and obligations arising from financial instruments sold short.

Since then, however, the world of derivatives has undergone dramatic changes. Not only have the availability and trading of derivative financial instruments increased quite significantly but also products once considered as "exotic" have become commonplace—while novelty in product design has become a major competitive advantage, as Chapter 1 brought to the reader's attention. Other events, too, have had an impact, as we will see in this chapter.

Easily the most outstanding positive development of the 1990s and beyond has been the increased emphasis bankers and investors place on risk management. Both regulators and the better-governed firms have focused on ways and means for control of actual and potential exposure, with new legislation and regulation being instrumental in achieving this result.

Additionally, the booming trade in derivatives has seen to it that these instruments are no longer minor off-balance-sheet receivables and payables. They are integral parts of mainstream balance sheet (BS) activities, not only of banks and other financial institutions but also of a long list of other firms, including hedge funds, pension funds, and insurance entities, as well as manufacturing and service companies.

A real-life event helps in explaining this statement. When supervisory authorities reproached the chief executive officer of a British firm for its large off-balance-sheet exposure, he answered: "It is nonsense to look at an off-balance sheet. You should only control the balance sheet." A few months down the line, however, in the message the same CEO sent to his shareholders, he wrote: "Looking

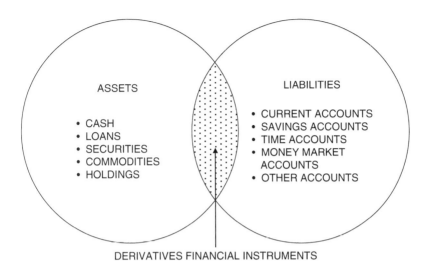

Figure 2.1 The original balance sheet taxonomy of assets and liabilities as enriched by a class of items that find a home only after their fair value has been established

at the balance sheet is not enough. You have also to appreciate the positions your company has off-balance sheet."

Among derivative instruments banks feature in their portfolio are fixed-rate loan commitments, futures, forwards, options, and swaps (see the sections "Options, Futures, Forwards, and Swaps in a Nutshell" and "Exotic Derivatives" later in this chapter), as well as a growing number of exotic derivatives (see the section "Synthetic Financial Instruments"). As Figure 2.1 suggests, the original binary balance sheet taxonomy of assets and liabilities—which dates back to the seminal work of Luca Pacciolo in the late fifteenth century[1]— has been enriched by a class of items that find a home in either the right side or the left side of the BS only after their fair value has been established. Thus the same instrument is

- On the assets side when the investor makes a profit with it
- On the liabilities side when he or she loses money because the instrument's market price moved south

[1] Dimitris N. Chorafas, *IFRS, Fair Value and Corporate Governance: The Impact on Budgets, Balance Sheets and Management Accounts*, Butterworth-Heinemann, London and Boston, 2005.

(For starters, *fair value* is the value agreed upon by a willing buyer and a willing seller, under other than fire sale conditions. Theoretically at least, fair value is market value. Practically, the two are not always equal because, among other reasons, market value is subject to panics and other extreme events.)

As innovation in the derivatives market went ahead by leaps and bounds, in 1998 the Financial Accounting Standards Board improved upon the definition of derivative financial instruments (brought to the reader's attention at the beginning of this section). Their changing nature and rapidly growing usage saw to it that existing distinctions among the many types of contracts had become blurred. In response, the Statement of Financial Accounting Standards 133 (SFAS 133) defined *derivatives* as financial instruments with the following characteristics:

- They have one or more underlying and one or more notional amounts (see "Notional Principal Amount and Underlying" later in this chapter) payment provisions or both.
- Usually, they require no initial net investment, and when this is needed, it is smaller than that called for with other instruments.
- They require or permit net settlements or provide for delivery of an asset that practically puts the buyer at a net settlement position.

For their part, regulatory authorities have called for the modernization of accounting and disclosure standards in order to address new financial products and new risk management techniques. They have as well cited serious deficiencies in disclosures, particularly connected to market risk exposure—an issue that the Basel Committee on Banking Supervision (BCBS) regulated through the 1996 Market Risk Amendment to the capital adequacy standards for credit risk of 1988, known as *Basel I* (Chapter 6).

Today, it is nobody's secret that bankers, treasurers, investors, regulators, and financial analysts are confronted by a rapidly growing complexity due to interrelationships and correlations embedded in practically all modern financial instruments. There is as well the issue that in many countries regulatory disclosures

- Are scattered throughout financial statement notes
- Are usually understood only by a relatively small sophisticated group of people

The majority of investors and professionals, including professional accountants, are mystified and frustrated by some of the effects derivatives have on the company's exposure, and therefore their impact on the company's on-balance sheets. It is not, therefore, surprising that both the FASB in the United States and the International Accounting Standards Board (IASB) in other countries, including the member states of the European Union, have established extensive disclosure requirements concerning derivatives and other financial instruments.

DERIVATIVES DEFINITION BY THE IASB

The international financial reporting standards (IFRS) by the London-based International Accounting Standards Board (IASB) defines *derivative* as a financial instrument whose value changes in response to a change in the price of an underlying, such as an interest rate, commodity, security price, or index. The definition also specifies that a derivative instrument typically requires no initial investment, or one that is smaller than would be needed for a classical contract with similar response to changes in market factors. Also part of the IASB definition is the fact that the derivatives contract is settled at a future date.

As the reader should appreciate that this IASB twenty-first-century definition of derivatives is neither quite different nor quite the same as the 1998 definition of derivatives by the FASB. This is regrettable because it leaves open to multinational companies the possibility to game the system.

In regard to the IASB's approach to reporting on financial instruments, the Basel Committee on Banking Supervision has addressed two areas of supervisory guidance closely connected to the International Accounting Standard 39 (IAS 39), which concentrates on hedging by means of derivatives products. One area includes what constitutes sound risk management policies and processes in relation to the fair value principle; the other, how a bank's use of fair value might affect supervisory assessment of the institution's

- Regulatory capital (see Chapter 6)
- Risk management system[2]

This is an area that lies in the junction of responsibilities by the FASB, IASB, and BCBS; and it concerns all financial instruments defined by the International Accounting Standards Board as contracts that give rise to a financial asset of one entity and a financial liability at the other entity in the transaction.

For instance, examples of financial instruments other than derivatives are cash (plain cash is a base commodity), demand and time deposits, commercial paper, leases, accounts, notes, loans receivable and payable, rights and obligations with insurance risk under insurance contracts, employers' rights and obligations under pension contracts, and debt and equity securities. As for derivative financial instruments, the most popular fall into two major classes:

- Interest rate products
- Currency exchange products

According to the IFRS, interest rate products include, but are not limited to, forward rate agreements (FRAs); interest rate swaps (IRSs); caps, floors, and collars; Eurodollar futures; Treasury bills and T-bond futures; options on Eurodollars; and options on T-bills and T-bonds. Accounting rules see to it that interest rate swaps, futures, forward rate agreements, and other interest rate instruments must be accounted for and revalued on an item-by-item basis. Gains and losses arising from derivative financial instruments must be

- Recognized and
- Treated in a similar manner to the more classical on-balance sheet instruments.

Typical currency products are futures, forwards, swaps, options, and options on futures. Interest rates, currencies, and equities are traded in spot positions and forwards and as options. Currencies and equities are often traded as spot positions. Foreign

---

[2] Basel Committee on Banking Supervision, "Supervisory Guidance on the Use of Fair Value Options under IFRS," Bank for International Settlements (BIS) Consultative Document, Basel, Switzerland, July 2005.

exchange forward transactions, forward legs of foreign exchange swaps, and other currency instruments involving an exchange of one currency for another at a future date must be included in the foreign currency position.

Derivatives disclosed as guarantees are issued in the ordinary course of business, generally in the form of written put options and credit default swaps (CDSs). An investment bank manages its exposure to these derivatives by engaging in various hedging strategies (Chapter 4). For some contracts, like written interest rate caps or foreign exchange options, the maximum payout is not easy to compute as interest rates or exchange rates could theoretically rise without limit.

Repurchase agreements (repos) are a popular derivative at which regulators look with great care. Securities lending indemnifications are arrangements in which the bank agrees to indemnify securities lending customers against losses accrued in the event that security borrowers do not return securities subject to the lending agreement and the collateral held is insufficient to cover the market value of the securities borrowed.

The IFRS accounting rules require that a repurchase agreement is recorded as a collateralized inward deposit on the liabilities side of the balance sheet. By contrast, the asset given as collateral remains on the assets side of the balance sheet. A reverse repurchase agreement (reverse repo) must be recorded as a collateralized outward loan on the assets side of the balance sheet for the amount of the loan.

NOTIONAL PRINCIPAL AMOUNT AND UNDERLYING

Widely used with derivatives, the term *notional principal amount* has been borrowed from the swaps market where it signifies the quantity of money on which is based the transaction. This money is never actually to be paid or received. For example, in interest rate swaps (Chapter 13) the notional principal amount is used as the basis for calculating the periodic payments of

- Fixed interest
- Floating interest

Also known as the *face amount*, the notional principal is specified by the contract. It may be a number of shares, currency units, kilos, bushels, or other metrics underpinning the derivatives contract. The obligations of counterparties are established on the basis of this notional principal amount—a concept that applies to a wide range of instruments. Examples are

- Caps and floors
- Forward rate agreements
- All types of forward contracts for Treasury bonds, guilds, and bunds

As these references suggest, the term *notional* is generic. The same is true with the term *underlying* in a derivatives transaction. This may be a specified commodity price, share price, interest rate, currency exchange rate, index of prices, or something else. It may also be a variable applied to the notional principal amount to determine the cash flows or other exchange of assets required by the derivatives contract.

In a general sense, the security involved in an option or other derivatives transaction is the underlying security. (More on options in Chapters 7 to 11.) Notice that while the underlying may be the price of an asset or liability, in itself it is not an asset or liability. Interest rates are the underlying of interest rate swaps; currencies are the underlying of currency swaps; gold is the underlying of gold futures.

The making of a derivative instrument whose value is based on an underlying has been a stroke of genius and a major step forward in financial engineering. In a way not unlike that of the physical sciences, innovation sometimes works through giant steps, but more often it works through steps that are smaller and that borrow on something already known. An example from the military is the original development of the tank, which eventually became a formidable weapon. As Figure 2.2 demonstrates, the original elements were a big wheel and a sliding track, just as the origins of modern derivatives were options and futures.

A very important concept in physics, engineering, and finance is that once a new product, be it a tank, a derivative, or something else, gets underway, it establishes its own market environment and operating conditions, which may have very little to do with those of its original components. Often, these conditions are more complex

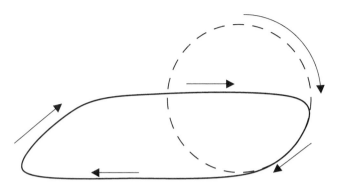

Figure 2.2 The big wheel and sliding track at the origin of modern tanks

than those of its components. For instance, it is a good bet that the relationship prevailing between the values of

- The underlying and
- The derivative

will be nonlinear. To explain this concept, Figure 2.3 provides an example of nonlinear behavior between variables *A* and *B*. As the

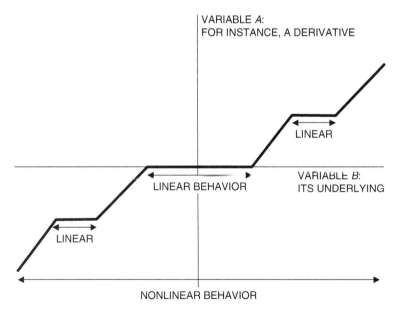

Figure 2.3 A nonlinear system characterizing the relationship between variable *A* and variable *B*

reader would notice, linear behavior is characterizing these two variables from time to time—this being a subset of nonlinear behavior, which is the wider case. The basic reasons for nonlinearities in market pricing are that

- The value of the derivative does not move mechanically in line with a given cash market.
- In many cases, the derivatives market itself actually determines prices in the underlying instruments.

Understanding nonlinearities is fundamental in appreciating the price functioning of products in derivatives markets, including risk, return, structure, cash flows, and obligations, as well as conditions at contract termination. Typically, the nonlinearities that characterize derivative financial instruments see to it that these require a much more rigorous review and evaluation than classical financial products.

The return mechanisms of a given instrument have to be properly analyzed in terms of their origin and sustenance.

Theoretically, profit elements may be derived from upfront fees, or upside potential of, say, an index. Practically, however, fees may be subject to discounts and upside profits are never guaranteed as they are dependent on the direction the market takes.

As the originator, trader, or market maker of derivative products, a bank's interest is in assuring a thorough understanding of assumed risks at all levels within the institution.

In Chapter 1, the "Risk Management" section made the point that this is a fundamental ingredient to the process of preventing losses and of gaining confidence that the bank will retain an active and interested clientele. If the bank is unable to understand and control exposure emanating from its own derivatives book, then it will eventually register major losses.

The reader should appreciate that this concept of nonlinearities, largely introduced with derivatives, is new in finance, and it is still far from being properly understood in all quarters. This has a precedence in the natural sciences. It was indeed disconcerting for physicists who had spent nearly three centuries having a love affair with linear systems to change culture and deal with nonlinearities—which practically meant that the whole is not equal to the sum of its parts.

The concept of linearities in underlying relationships is loved by many people because it makes it relatively easy to analyze risk. But neither Mother Nature nor complex financial instruments work that way. Sometimes, under the right circumstances, even tiny perturbations can grow in magnitude until the system's behavior becomes utterly unpredictable—which means chaotic.

This move from stability to chaos and then again to stability sees to it that even some very simple systems could produce astonishingly rich patterns of behavior; all that is required is nonlinearities. Eventually, the sequence would become so complex that events would seem to come at random. It needs no explaining that this has a most significant impact on the "right" pricing of derivative financial instruments.

If a given product carries unusually high or complex risk parameters,

Then the profit structure should reflect these characteristics, on a factual and documented basis, which is not easy.

In spite of difficulty and even adversity, the right pricing of a derivatives instrument is fundamental to the provision of a certain assurance that the issuer will be in charge of its exposure. Risks associated to projected profit payoffs must be well understood before the product is offered to the customer or launched in the market. It is highly unadvisable to guesstimate the return.

OPTIONS, FUTURES, FORWARDS, AND SWAPS IN A NUTSHELL

In their most basic form, all four types of derivatives in this heading have become institutionalized. An *option* is an agreement between a buyer and a seller that, when exercised, gives the former the right, but not the obligation, to require the option *writer* (seller) to perform certain specified obligations. For example, an option on an equity gives the buyer the right, but not the obligation, to purchase that equity from the writer during a stated period of time at a stipulated price:

- *If* the buyer decides to exercise his or her option to purchase, *then* the seller is obliged to turn over the equity at the agreed-upon price.

- In contrast, after an originally stipulated period of time, an option that is left unexercised expires as worthless.

The price a buyer pays to a seller for an option is its *premium*, meant to compensate the seller for his or her willingness to grant the option. The price at which the option can be exercised is the *strike price*. The last day on which an option can be exercised, or *offset*, is the *expiration date*.

An option is exercised at the sole discretion of the buyer who will tend to act only when it is in his interest to do so. For example, the buyer of an option to purchase Cisco Systems at $22 would be foolish to exercise his option if the market value of a Cisco share fell to $19. On the other hand, it would be to his advantage to exercise his right to acquire the equity if its value increased to $25. Generally, there are two types of options:

- A *call option* gives the buyer the right to purchase the underlying asset at the stated strike price, on or before the expiration date.
- A *put option* gives the buyer the right to sell the underlying asset at the strike price, on or before the expiration date.

The put option holder can make a profit if prices decline, while limiting his loss to the money paid as premium if the asset increases in value. If the $22 Cisco share price were connected to a put option, then the holder would have good reason to exercise it if the price tanked to $19, but no reason to do so if it zoomed to $25.

Futures and forwards are different types of instruments, as they may require the holder to buy or sell an underlying asset at some time in the future. Unlike an option, the holder cannot simply let the contract lapse.

Futures are current commitments that can be exercised, as their name implies, in the future. They are traded in exchanges and have a market, except of course in the case of panic. Futures take the form of contracts in which the quantity of the underlying and expiration date are standardized.

Forwards are not traded on exchanges; they are over-the-counter (OTC) instruments, essentially bilateral agreements that have no active market. Their specifications may or may not be standardized; quite often they are customized, agreed between buyer and seller on an ad hoc basis though the form of the contract may have some standard features.

While superficially they might seem similar to options, inasmuch as they entail the obligation to deliver or take delivery on a specified expiration date of a defined quantity of an underlying—and do so at a price agreed on the contract date—forwards and futures can involve major risks because of the leverage they make possible. Hence, they are suitable for only those investors who

- Have sufficient liquid assets
- Are familiar with this type of instrument
- Are able to absorb any losses that may arise, if the market moves in the opposite direction than the investor forecasted

Another type of derivative instrument provides the means for an agreement to exchange in the future a stream of cash flows, for instance by swapping floating-rate interest payments for fixed-rate interest payments, or vice versa. A standard *swap* involves

- Period receipt of a predetermined fixed amount
- Corresponding period payment of the spot value of a unit of the asset in reference

Swaps typically involve two parties that enter into an agreement that for a certain period they will exchange regular payments. In an interest rate swap, one counterparty pays the other a fixed rate of interest based on some variable rate of interest. The latter changes as market interest rates change.

Traders often look at the swap as a portfolio of forward contracts, one for a cash payment date and each written at the same forward price. For instance, a swap can be used to offset the risk of an uncovered position, seeing to it that there is a future cash flow that would move in the opposite direction to that of a hedged position.

At least theoretically, swapping cash streams from assets enables companies and investors to turn one type of asset or liability into a different one, as well as to execute a number of other bilateral transactions. In practice, however, swaps are not perfect hedges because one leg of the transaction may change much more than the other side (see Chapter 4). This statement is also valid for many other instruments.

Swaps are also made with commodities. Like the interest rate swaps, a *commodity swap* is a financial contract between two parties that effectively fixes the price of an asset for a period of time. The parties typically agree to the length of the swap, settlement period(s) within the swap, quantity of the commodity swapped per settlement period, and fixed price of the commodity. The commodity swap market differs from the interest rate swap market in at least two ways:

- Physical commodity swaps are more likely to be driven at the purchasing manager level than at the corporate treasurer level.
- The instruments available to the commodity swap dealer to use for hedging are usually limited to futures contracts that cover a period of up to one year at best, whereas an interest rate swap dealer has a large variety of instruments including 30-year bonds.

A market currently in the upside is that of credit risk swaps. A *credit risk swap* is a plain-vanilla version of credit derivatives[3] whereby the protection buyer pays the protection seller a fixed recurring amount in exchange for a payment contingent upon a future credit event; for instance, bankruptcy. In exchange for this premium:

If that event takes place,

Then the protection seller must pay the agreed compensation to the protection buyer.

Depending on the amount involved in the credit swap, this helps to cover part or all of credit loss pursuant to default. By transferring credit risk from protection buyer to protection writer, credit default swaps have opened up new opportunities for trading and other business transactions. These instruments, which as counterparty agreements involve their own credit risk, help in price discovery.

---

[3] Dimitris N. Chorafas, *Credit Derivatives and the Management of Risk*, New York Institute of Finance, New York, 2000.

Another interesting derivatives instrument is a *swaption*, which is an option on a swap. Options on caps, floors, and swaps give the purchaser the right, but not the obligation, to buy (or sell) the underlying instruments. Swaptions are basically options on other derivatives, also known as *compound options*.

EXOTIC DERIVATIVES

To most players, whether originators of derivative instruments or end users, the products introduced in the 1980s and early 1990s in the financial market have become commonplace. Forward rate agreements, interest rate swaps, currency swaps, stripped Treasuries (*strip* is an acronym for "separate trading of registered interest and principal of securities"), mortgage-backed securities (MBSs), asset-backed securities (ABSs), and other derivatives are now mainstream business.

Current and future challenges with derivative financial instruments are not so much associated to products that have become commodities but to the so-called exotics. The latter are innovative and complex instruments, very difficult to price the right way, and involve too many unknowns whose aftereffects are revolutionizing the banking industry.

Exotic derivatives are products of rocket scientists (Chapter 1) who see to it that the name and nature of these derivatives steadily change. Ten years ago exotic derivatives included all-or-nothing options, barrier and binary options, butterflies, complex choosers, compound (nested) instruments, discount swaps, down-and-out (or in) options, embeddos (embedded options), inverse floaters, knock-in/knock-outs, lookbacks, one-touch options, path-dependent issues, quantos (options in which two currencies are involved), step-lock options, and up-and-in (or out) options. Today,

- There is a great lot of "outperformance" products.
- There is almost every morning a new invention.

Therefore, for supervisors, bankers, and investors, a better way than naming the instrument itself is to classify a derivatives transaction as exotic by the fact that its price and underlying are linked by a nonlinear function. As we saw in the preceding section, this function may exhibit chaotic characteristics. Additionally, the payment streams of exotic derivatives tend to correspond to diverse underlyings. For example, they are

- Linked to different interest rates
- Expressed in different currencies

Still another characteristic of exotic instruments is the existence of barriers and exclusive clauses constraining the derivative product. Breaking such barriers usually results in steep changes in the payoff function, which are most difficult to foretell.

Pricing is a key challenge with an exotic, particularly so as the instrument's complexity increases and at the same time the number of transactions breaks previous records. The growth in the volume of exotic options traded over the last couple of years has been unprecedented, although so far many companies have not enjoyed the benefits offered by the more innovative products because of

- Lack of knowledge and understanding
- Lagging risk control procedures
- The scarcity of required analytical skills

The interest that market players express in complex derivatives and synthetics (see the following section, "Synthetic Financial Instruments") rests on the fact that through them it is possible to build personalized instruments that, bankers suggest, can meet any financial need at the investor's side. However, both institutional investors and corporate treasurers are attracted by them often with little understanding of

- What they involve
- The amount of exposure that is assumed in case worst comes to worst

There exist plenty of unknowns behind the exotic products being designed and traded today, including airbags, options on options, memory-independent options, options on many underlyings, and much more. Volatility changes and correlation effects require the establishment of an experimental option pricing policy, whose assumptions, simplifications, and shortcomings must be clearly stated and explained—a knowledge not within everybody's reach.

The interest corporate treasurers express in derivatives first started in the early to mid-1990s. "It has not yet reached epidemic proportions, but it is a growing problem," said, at the time, Robert Studer, then president of the Union Bank of Switzerland.[4] His reference was to the tendency for banks' corporate customers to run their treasury for profits rather than for cash management and pure risk control.

Good management practice requires that prior to making bets on exotic derivatives, it is necessary to develop not only good understanding but also reliable price monitoring and measurement techniques. Without them, one should never invest in the multitude of exotics offered in the market. Among the "musts" is the definition of the payout function on a life-cycle basis, as well as its relation to hedging liquidity and market volatility. A similar policy should be followed with synthetic and structured derivative instruments (as discussed in the following sections).

In conclusion, short of adequate preparation, proper staffing, and full understanding of risk and return, the most likely outcome will be a torrent of red ink. As exotics are becoming the instrument of choice in financial engineering, losses suffered by many corporate treasurers, pension fund managers, bankers, and investors have been recently hitting the headlines. If the reader wishes to retain a valuable message from this section, it would be that he or she needs to really appreciate that custom-made and exotic derivatives are bringing with them a host of new learning requirements and associated exposures. Without the ability to make these instruments reveal their risks, and to do so before commitment, exotics can be deadly because the doors of risk and return are adjacent and indistinguishable.

SYNTHETIC FINANCIAL INSTRUMENTS

Some experts consider synthetic and structured (structured financial instruments are discussed in the following section) financial instruments as not too different from one another. This, however, is not the majority opinion. According to the international financial reporting standards (IFRS), a synthetic instrument is a financial product designed, acquired, and held to emulate the characteristics

---

[4] *Economist*, London, June 4, 1994.

of another instrument. Such is the case of a floating-rate long-term debt combined with an interest rate swap. This involves

- Receiving floating payments
- Making fixed payments, thereby synthesizing a fixed-rate long-term debt

Another example of a synthetic is the output of an option strategy followed by dealers who are selling synthetic futures for a commodity that they hold by using a combination of put and call options. By simultaneously buying a put option in a given commodity, say, gold, and selling the corresponding call option, a trader can construct a position analogous to a short sale in the commodity's futures market.

Because the synthetic short sale seeks to take advantage of price disparities between call and put options, it tends to be more profitable when call premiums are greater than comparable put premiums. The holder of a synthetic short future will profit if gold prices decrease and incur losses if gold prices increase.

By analogy, a long position in a given commodity's call option combined with a short sale of the same commodity's futures creates price protection that is similar to that gained through purchasing put options. A synthetic put seeks to capitalize on disparities between call and put premiums.

Basically, synthetic products are covered options and certificates characterized by identical or similar profit and loss structures when compared with traditional financial instruments, such as equities or bonds (synthetic options are discussed in Chapter 9, and synthetic futures in Chapter 12). Basket certificates in equities are based on a specific number of selected stocks.

A covered option involves the purchase of an underlying asset, such as equity, bond, currency, or other commodity, and the writing of a call option on that same asset. The writer is paid a premium, which limits his or her loss in the event of a fall in the market value of the underlying. However, his or her potential return from any increase in the asset's market value is conditioned by gains limited by the option's strike price.

The concept underpinning synthetic covered options is that of duplicating traditional covered options, which can be achieved by both purchase of the underlying asset and writing of the call option.

The purchase price of such a product is that of the underlying, less the premium received for the sale of the call option.

Moreover, synthetic covered options do not contain a hedge against losses in market value of the underlying. A hedge might be emulated by writing a call option or by calculating the return from the sale of a call option into the product price. The option premium, however, tends to limit possible losses in the market value of the underlying.

Alternatively, a synthetic financial instrument is done through a certificate that accords a right based on either a number of underlyings or on having a value derived from several indicators (more on this in "Structured Financial Instruments"). This presents a sense of diversification over a range of risk factors. The main types are

- Index certificates
- Region certificates
- Basket certificates

By being based on an official index, index certificates reflect a given market's behavior. Region certificates are derived from a number of indexes or companies from a given region, usually involving developing countries. Basket certificates are derived from a selection of companies active in a certain industry sector.

An investment in index, region, or basket certificates fundamentally involves the same level of potential loss as a direct investment in the corresponding assets themselves. Their relative advantage is diversification within a given specified range; but risk is not eliminated. Moreover, certificates also carry credit risk associated to the issuer.

Also available in the market are compound financial instruments, a frequently encountered form being that of a debt product with an embedded conversion option. An example of a compound financial instrument is a bond that is convertible into ordinary shares of the issuer. As an accounting standard, the IFRS requires the issuer of such a financial instrument to present separately on the balance sheet the

- Equity component
- Liability component

On initial recognition, the fair value of the liability component is the present value of the contractually determined stream of future cash flows, discounted at the rate of interest applied at that time by the market to substantially similar cash flows. These should be characterized by practically the same terms, albeit without a conversion option. The fair value of the option comprises its

- Time value
- Intrinsic value (if any)

The IFRS requires that on conversion of a convertible instrument at maturity, the reporting company derecognizes the liability component and recognizes it as equity. Embedded derivatives are an interesting issue inasmuch as some contracts that themselves are not financial instruments may have financial instruments embedded in them. This is the case of a contract to purchase a commodity at a fixed price for delivery at a future date.

Contracts of this type have embedded in them a derivative that is indexed to the price of the commodity, which is essentially a derivative feature within a contract that is not a financial derivative. International Accounting Standard 39 (IAS 39) of the IFRS requires that under certain conditions an embedded derivative is separated from its host contract and treated as a derivative instrument.

As it is to be expected, both the U.S. generally accepted accounting principles (GAAP) and the IFRS include clauses that aim to standardize accounting for synthetics. For instance, the IFRS specifies that each of the individual derivative instruments that together constitute a synthetic financial product represents a contractual right or obligation with its own terms and conditions. Under this perspective,

- Each may be transferred or settled separately.
- Each is exposed to risks that may differ from the risks to which other financial products are exposed.

Therefore, when one financial product in a synthetic instrument is an asset and another is a liability, these two do not offset each other. Consequently, they should be presented on an entity's balance sheet on a net basis, unless they meet specific criteria outlined by the aforementioned accounting standards.

STRUCTURED FINANCIAL INSTRUMENTS

Like synthetics, structured financial products are derivatives. Many are custom-designed bonds, some of which (over the years) have presented a number of problems to their buyers and holders. This is particularly true for those investors who are not so versatile in modern complex instruments and their further-out impact.

Typically, instead of receiving a fixed coupon or principal, a person or company holding a structured note will receive an amount adjusted according to a fairly sophisticated formula. Structured instruments lack transparency; the market, however, seems to like them, the proof being that the amount of money invested in structured notes continues to increase, and, according to some estimates, it currently exceeds $1 trillion.

One of many examples of structured products is the *principal exchange-rate-linked security* (PERLS). These derivative instruments target changes in currency rates. They are disguised to look like bonds, by structuring them as if they were debt instruments, making it feasible for investors who are not permitted to play in currencies to place bets on the direction of exchange rates.

For instance, instead of just repaying principal, a PERLS may multiply such principal by the change in the value of the dollar against the euro; or twice the change in the value of the dollar against the Swiss franc or the British pound. The fact that this repayment is linked to the foreign exchange rate of different currencies sees to it that the investor might be receiving a lot more than an interest rate on the principal alone—but also a lot less, all the way to capital attrition. (Even capital protection notes involve capital attrition since, in certain cases, no interest is paid over their, say, five-year life cycle.)

Structured note trading is a concept that has been subject to several interpretations, depending on the time frame within which the product has been brought to the market. Many traders tend to distinguish between three different generations of structured notes. The elder, or first generation, usually consists of structured instruments based on just one index, including

- Bull market vehicles, such as inverse floaters and cap floaters
- Bear market instruments, which are characteristically more leveraged, an example being the superfloaters

Bear market products became popular in 1993 and 1994. A typical superfloater might pay twice the London Interbank Offered Rate (LIBOR) minus 7 percent for two years. At currently prevailing rates, this means that the superfloater has a small coupon at the beginning that improves only if the LIBOR rises. Theoretically, a coupon that is below current market levels until the LIBOR goes higher is much harder to sell than a big coupon that gets bigger every time rates drop. Still, bear plays find customers.

Second-generation structured notes are different types of exotic options; or, more precisely, they are yet more exotic than superfloaters, which are exotic enough in themselves. There exist serious risks embedded in these instruments, as such risks have never been fully appreciated. Second-generation examples are

- Range notes, with embedded binary or digital options
- Quanto notes, which allow investors to take a bet on, say, sterling London Interbank Offered Rates, but get paid in dollars

There are different versions of such instruments, like you-choose range notes for a bear market. Every quarter the investor has to choose the "range," a job that requires considerable market knowledge and skill. For instance, if the range width is set to 100 basis points, the investor has to determine at the start of the period the high and low limits within that range, which is far from being a straight job.

Surprisingly enough, there are investors who like this because sometimes they are given an option to change their mind; and they also figure their risk period is really only one quarter. In this, they are badly mistaken. In reality even for banks you-choose notes are much more difficult to hedge than regular range notes because, as very few people appreciate, the hedges are both

- Dynamic
- Imperfect

There are as well third-generation notes offering investors exposure to commodity or equity prices in a cross-category sense. Such notes usually appeal to a different class than fixed-income investors. For instance, third-generation notes are sometimes purchased by fund managers who are in the fixed-income market but want to diversify their exposure. The heavy hammer that in

December 1994 hit the Orange County Fund and brought it to bankruptcy speaks volumes of the exposure taken by the buyers of these
instruments.

In spite of the fact that the increasing sophistication and lack of
transparency of structured financial instruments sees to it that they
are too often misunderstood, and they are highly risky, a horde of
equity-linked and commodity-linked notes are being structured
and sold to investors. Examples are LIBOR floaters designed so that
the coupon is "LIBOR plus":

> Counting in basis points every day that the spread between,
> say, the two-year Treasury bill and six-month LIBOR is less
> than a specified number of basis points, but having zero
> return when it is out of that range, which could happen quite
> frequently.

An irony associated to this structured product is that when
buying it, the average investor has no clear idea that he or she bets
against a set of forward yield curves, which tend to slope upward
but may be flat or trend downward (see Chapter 14). Yield curves
behave in a way that is absolutely out of the investor's control.

The pros say that flexibly structured options can be useful to
sophisticated investors seeking to manage particular portfolio and
trading risks. However, as a result of exposure being assumed, and
also because of the likelihood that there is no secondary market,
transactions in flexibly structured options are not suitable for
investors who are not

- In a position to understand the behavior of their intrinsic
  value
- Financially able to bear the risks embedded in them when
  worst comes to worst

The message the reader should retain from the preceding two
sections of this chapter is that the price of novelty, customization,
and flexibility offered by synthetic and structured financial instruments can be expressed in one four-letter word: *risk*. Risk taking is
welcome when we know how to manage our exposure, but it can be
a disaster when we don't—hence, the *wisdom* of learning ahead of
investing the challenges posed by derivatives and how to be in
charge of risk control.

CHAPTER 3

Strategic Use of Derivatives

CAPITALIZING ON CREATIVITY

Prior to establishing a course of action, bankers, traders, and investors should be keen to examine the alternatives and establish a plan. Strategy is a master plan against an opponent, and financial strategy is no exception to this rule. As such, it is intended to position a company (or an investor) against the market. Thoroughly done, strategic evaluations serve a triple purpose:

- They demonstrate the alternatives that exist, as well as their risks and opportunities.
- They assist in achieving a higher level of familiarity with the way the market works.
- They help in optimizing one's approach by providing a reference guide to implementation of the chosen course, including specific choices.

For instance, an investor who has confidence in an emerging market but not on the local currency can obtain exposure to this market's equities while hedging away the currency risk by using foreign exchange derivatives. As another example, because of cost differences between cash and futures markets, an asset allocation program might be more cost-effective by using derivatives, provided that exposure is kept under lock and key.

- In fixed-income markets, derivatives are often used for customizing reasons.

- On the equity side, derivatives are employed to increase liquidity, act as proxies, or help in price discovery.

The rich array of even the most basic derivative financial instruments briefly reviewed in Chapter 2 helps in documenting that the derivatives business is not merely a middleman operation. With the exception of exchange-traded products that are standardized, rarely will traders resell exactly what they bought. Financial analysts as well as engineers, physicists, and mathematicians working as *rocket scientists* reconfigure the original derivative instruments by changing

- The option strike price
- The currency being used
- The interest rate terms, or some other variable

Sometimes this reconfiguration is done to create a new instrument and in other cases to offset the initial trade. Freedoms taken in product redesign is one of the reasons why derivatives have been revolutionizing corporate finance and banking. They are impacting in a fundamental way on the risk appetite of companies and investors (see the section "Risk Appetite and Risk Aversion" later in this chapter) by altering traditional risk and reward parameters:

- With a bond or a stock, an investor's chief concern is whether the price will go up or down.
- Derivatives introduce a whole new class of variables focusing on volatility and therefore on *how fast* a security's price goes up or down.

The introduction of new variables in product design has changed the rules of the game. In the late 1980s and early 1990s, as the derivatives market took off, experiments with new financial instruments became the sign of distinction of top-tier banks. Though the sophistication of financial experiments has not reached that of similar activities in engineering and physics, analysis and experimentation—therefore *creativity*—has opened up new perspectives in service science.

Instrument novelty and design flexibility interest the bank's clients. For instance, the financial institution may provide an oil-exploration outfit with a floor on the price of oil by selling it as a commodity put. This allows a wildcatter to finance a drilling deal with greater leverage and less upfront capital because he or she is taking on only limited commodity risk.

As this example suggests, the key to using derivatives in a successful way is to match an appropriate financial strategy to a particular objective, within a given time horizon. No bank and no investor, however, is likely to ever employ all possible options strategies for the simple reason that most such strategies are

- Too obscure in terms of risk and return or,
- Simply irrelevant to the goal(s) the investor is trying to reach at any given moment.

Computer simulation helps to unearth a new instrument's secrets. In part because of simulation and in part because of new insight provided through mathematical analysis, rocket scientists realize that a lot of creative design can be done with financial instruments. At the same time, the most brilliant among them have also found out that a torrent of innovation may be dangerous without a concomitant development of rigorous risk management methods.

Suppose a bank sells a call option on a security and that security shoots up in price. The buyer wins, but the bank *might* also win if it has hedged out the price risk. The opposite is also true; even with hedging (Chapter 4), the bank may lose because

- The price change in the derivative product and its underlying may well be asymmetric, and
- *Asymmetry* in prices of financial instruments upsets even the most carefully laid out plan.

Not just with derivatives, but in every walk of life, a sound policy requires looking for asymmetries well before making a decision. Nowhere is this advice more important than in *pricing*. For example, there is no easy rule-of-thumb approach in choosing the option's strike price. The writer's and investor's decisions may be influenced by considerations like:

- Are my own price expectations bearish or bullish?
- How much risk am I willing to take on order to realize a potentially larger reward?
- What is likely to happen to the price of the underlying? How will this impact on the derivative product's price?

Critical questions connected to pricing are also part of the creativity equation because they are vital from a risk and reward perspective. And as Chapter 2 brought to the reader's attention, the relation between a derivative product's price and that of its underlying is not linear—and it may be chaotic. Many unknowns are associated with the strategic use of derivatives, and nothing short of a thorough analysis and experimentation can provide a measure of assurance regarding end results.

THE CUSTOMIZATION OF FINANCIAL PRODUCTS

One of the strategic advantages provided by derivatives is that they can be customized. Experts suggest that, in the years to come, the trend to customization will gain momentum as the investor population increases and its focus shifts from acquiring a stock of goods to that of maintaining its financial well-being.

An opinion frequently heard in the course of the research that led to this book is that the shift toward the personalization of financial instruments, as contrasted to the sale of products off the racks, has not yet been properly appreciated by most bankers. Yet this switch has many surprises in store, not only for the financial community, but also for governments, industry at large, and the general public.

The right strategy in customization of derivative financial products is first to identify and then address the end user's requirements accounting for the risks but without swamping creativity. Experimentation is at a premium because product design must be

- Flexible
- Resilient

Governments, said a British banker during our meeting, try to resolve this dilemma of customized instruments offered to retail customers with regulation; but this has not always worked well. Effective supervision poses great technical demands on the regulators themselves, and many central bankers are simply not up to it. Furthermore, there is always the danger that poorly studied regulatory rules will

- Prevent innovation
- Swamp competition

According to this banker's opinion, before considering technical details, one should set up the framework of *how to think* of customized derivative products. Philosophically, we may compare
their importance to that of the paper money introduced in France in
the 1710s, which lost its worth with the Mississippi Bubble and
bankruptcy of the Royal Bank. Or we can look at customization as
a generic development that is here to stay.

Regarding this second option, a good example at the corporate
level is provided by Cisco Systems. Quoting from its annual statement: "The Company uses derivative instruments to manage exposures to foreign currency. The Company's objective in holding
derivatives is to minimize the volatility of earnings and cash flows
associated with changes in foreign currency." This *is* hedging
(Chapter 4), and the solution Cisco seeks is one customized to its
requirements.

All companies conducting business on a global basis and having investments in several countries are exposed to adverse movements in foreign currency exchange rates. To protect themselves,
they enter into foreign exchange forward contracts, which help to
minimize the short-term impact of foreign currency fluctuations on
payables, receivables, and investments. Notice, however, that as it
states in its annual report, Cisco does not enter into foreign
exchange forward contracts for trading purposes—and therefore
"for profits." Moreover,

- Its foreign exchange forward contracts are related to
  current assets and liabilities.
- In the general case, its exchange contracts connected to
  investments have maturities of less than one year.

This example demonstrates in a practical way what is meant
by "customizing derivative contracts" to the end user's policies and
needs. This is a sound way of looking at risk and return with exposure control as the main target. Correctly, Cisco's senior management has also put time limits on

- Interest rate swaps (less than two years)
- Currency swaps (less than one year)

There are, as well, operational restrictions that impact on the
choice of derivative instruments' customization. For instance, interest

rate or currency swaps must be linked to a bank loan or debt issue, commodity futures and commodity swaps must be connected to ongoing business, and so on. Moreover, in a well-managed firm, the board's guidelines correlate with the rules established by regulators.

Here is an example: According to GAAP, as well as the IFRS, *management intent* is an important element in the classification of derivative products as marked-to-market for financial reporting purposes, or carried at the original contractual price. The former is the case of instruments intended for trading; the latter of those held to maturity.

One of the issues discussed in meetings on customization of derivative financial products has been the impact of regulation. Opinions were divided. Some bankers welcomed regulation as long as it does not stifle competition and innovation (more on this in the following section). In the opinion of other bankers, however, regulatory controls and restrictions carry with them the danger of swamping economic growth, and if regulators overdo their prudential supervision, they might strangle risk taking.

In the course of these same research meetings, there has been a convergence of opinions regarding the fact that in the last 40 years, no other financial product has puzzled regulators as much as the explosion of futures, options, and swaps in currencies, equities, interest rates, and commodities. Several commercial and investment bankers said that this is understandable because instruments whose value is determined by the underlying cash markets has been a concept with which there has existed precious little experience, yet it requires

- Devising customized, over-the-counter contracts to meet customer requirements
- Developing plans that permit the swapping of practically anything into anything else
- Working out risk adjustments through new instruments and financial procedures

These are processes still in their beginning, while synergy has given derivatives a market of their own with aggressive players seizing opportunities to enhance yields by exploiting inefficiencies within and between markets. Additionally, this has increased the risk appetite of market players.

Consider as an example the case of Long Term Capital Management (LTCM), which was billed at its time as the Rolls-Royce of hedge funds. One of its many plays was tax optimization. If the LTCM partners had borrowed $800 million and had invested it in their firm, this would have meant

- Increasing the spot price of the stock
- Paying a high interest cost
- Paying 39.6 percent in taxes, and
- In a downside, possibly losing all of the $800 million

As it were, through a custom-made derivatives product, they got that money from a major commercial bank—which, with the crash of LTCM, lost all of the $800 million as well as the $266 million in options fees it had received from the LTCM partners and reinvested in the firm. Ironically, as part of this torrent of red ink, the bank with the custom-made derivative also had to pour another $300 million into LTCM, under pressure by the New York Fed.

OVER-THE-COUNTER DERIVATIVES TRANSACTIONS

Over the counter (OTC) *financial transactions*, also known as *off-exchange transactions* (see also Chapter 1), offer a great many opportunities to sell and buy customized derivative products. But they also involve greater risk than dealing in *exchange-traded* financial instruments because there is no open market through which to

- Assess the value of the asset
- Estimate the exposure being assumed
- Quickly liquidate an investment position

Because OTC derivative financial instruments are usually custom-made, they rarely have a secondary market. The liquidation of a position in a portfolio position contracted over the counter is usually a rather complex affair. Sometimes the investor is liquidating the position in distress as in a fire sale, while in other cases a still liquid big player buys out the whole portfolio or a big chunk of it.

In contrast to OTC deals, in the exchanges, fair value estimates are done through bid and ask. Bid and ask prices need not be quoted over the counter. However, if and when they are, they will be established by dealers in these instruments with personal considerations in mind. Consequently, it may be difficult to estimate what a fair price is.

In turn, opaque pricing leads to difficulties in estimating exposure. This is an equally important constraint because typically OTC derivatives involve greater risk than investing in standardized on-exchange derivative instruments. On the other hand, as we have seen in the preceding section, major advantages of OTC transactions are their flexibility and customization.

The fact that there is no exchange market on which to close out an open position is a risk factor. For instance, it may be difficult, or outright impossible, to decide on whether or not to liquidate an existing position because it is not feasible to assess the value of that position; or to test one's exposure given that bid and offer prices need not be quoted. Yet, in spite of that, the number of types and volume of derivatives traded over the counter has increased considerably in the past few years.

Prior to the introduction of credit derivatives, currency products dominated OTC, while interest rate instruments were by far the most traded in exchanges. Tables 3.1 and 3.2 present real-life percentages at a major money center bank, with gross volume of buy and sell contracts combined in these statistics.

T A B L E 3.1

Notional Principal in Derivatives: OTC versus Exchange Traded

OTC	77.1%
Currency Products	41.0%
Interest Rate Products	30.0%
Equity Derivatives	5.0%
Precious Metals and Other Commodities	1.1%
Exchange Traded	**22.9%**
Currency Products	1.0%
Interest Rate Products	21.0%
Equity Derivatives	0.5%
Precious Metals and Other Commodities	0.4%

TABLE 3.2

Notional Principal Amounts by Taxonomy of Derivative Instruments

Currency Products	42.0%
Over the Counter (OTC)	41.0%
Exchange-Traded	1.0%
Interest Rate Products	**51.0%**
OTC	30.0%
Exchange-Traded	21.0%
Equity Derivatives	**5.5%**
OTC	5.0%
Exchange-Traded	0.5%
Precious Metals and Other Commodities	**1.5%**
OTC	1.1%
Exchange-Traded	0.4%

Credit derivatives and structured credit products, especially collateralized debt obligations (CDOs), further changed the trading pattern in favor of OTC transactions. They have also introduced a great amount of credit risk, over and above the market risk of past deals, with the subordinated tranches of CDOs being very sensitive to changes in creditworthiness. As Figure 3.1 demonstrates, even AAA credit ratings have a probability of default over a 10-year time frame.

In practically all types of over-the-counter transactions, counterparty risk is highly important since there is no exchange to effect delivery versus payment (DVP). Additionally, regulators have repeatedly voiced concerns that in the face of stiff competition for prime broker mandates for hedge funds, banks are lowering their risk standards including making concessions to counterparties regarding required transparency of

- Collateral posted
- Business relationships at large

Another source of regulatory worries about OTC counterparty risk is the high concentration of market makers and big banks. This is particularly visible in the market for credit instruments, and for

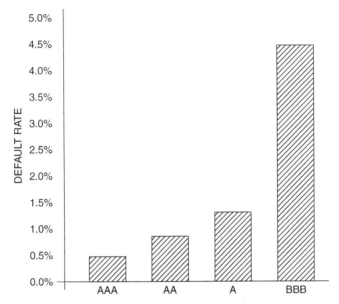

Figure 3.1 Probability of default of AAA, AA, A, and BBB corporate bonds over a 10-year time frame

U.S. dollar interest rate options. In case of financial turbulence, this highly concentrated intermediary function can turn into a highly unsettling factor.

While concentration on a small group of financial institutions with plenty of capital and significant expertise probably tends to reduce the likelihood of a disruption in financial markets, in case some other reason creates a market disruption, it increases the potential for systemic risk. For instance, a disruption, precipitated by a voluntary or forced withdrawal of a big intermediary can lead to

- Big bank counterparty risk
- Market risk in the aftermath of megafailure
- Liquidity risk, which can spread globally

Experts look at this multiple type of exposure as the downside of credit risk transfer practices and instruments. They also point out that though risks faced by banks in their interbank positions are different for assets and liabilities, in the general case shocks can be quickly transmitted within the banking system through the interbank market.

This likelihood is making mandatory the regular monitoring of interbank linkages, as well as of business relations between banks and hedge funds. At the same time, simply mapping of prevailing interbank relationships is not sufficient to measure contagion risk in the whole interbank market. The proper measurement of contagion

- Calls for detailed consolidated data on each bank's interbank exposures
- Requires taking into account the different risk mitigation techniques such as collateralization, netting, and hedging

Critics say that major, opaque OTC transactions add to interbank positions, creating a channel for contagion through credit risk, while interbank liability positions expose institutions to funding risk. Ready access to a large pool of interbank lenders reduces the risk of a loss of liquidity for financially sound institutions in the case of the withdrawal of any specific creditor bank. On the other hand, cross-border interbank credit risk implies an increase in cross-border creditor exposure.

Moreover, from a strategic viewpoint, counterparty risk and market liquidity risk are closely interlinked, with the latter particularly associated with the simultaneous unwinding of similar trading positions because of so-called crowded trades. This usually happens in the event of an abrupt change in expectations leading to

- Sharp swings in market prices
- Impact on the market values of the OTC derivatives contracts

When such an event takes place, it causes risk exposures to counterparties to increase, leading to margin calls for additional collateral. In turn, this might exacerbate tensions that could spill over to other markets, with rise in risk premiums and market liquidity tensions in the credit markets as well as a significant change in risk appetite.

RISK APPETITE AND RISK AVERSION

One of the biggest challenges facing bankers, traders, and investors, as well as the financial industry at large, is that risks are less known, more frequent, and larger than they have been prior to the advent of derivative financial products. This creates the threat that, undetected, a small mistake can create unexpected headwinds.

A rapidly growing *risk appetite* finds itself behind a lot of unexpected financial consequences. Its notion relates to the willingness of investors, speculators, and other market participants to take more and more risks when volatility is low and creditworthiness high without necessarily calculating what will happen if there is a major reverse.

Risk appetite can be measured through the exposure assumed by people and companies, as well as by the financial market as a whole. The innovative ability of new financial instruments promotes risk appetite. For instance, in 2002 Goldman Sachs and Deutsche Bank developed a species of economic derivatives that gave holders a chance to take bets on the direction of macroeconomic variables like

- Inflation
- Unemployment

This product became available to the wider market; it is not marketed only to people and companies who more or less know how to administer stiff tests on exposure. For instance, labor unions can buy an *unemployment derivative* that allows them to bet on the outcome of a strike or the effects of inflation on wages. By doing so, they commit funds without the hindsight that comes by knowing how to analyze in advance risk and return.

It needs no explaining that as the types of instruments expand, so does the market. If people with risk appetite can buy disability insurance to protect themselves in case illness prevents them from working, why should one be unable to buy a *livelihood* derivative that compensates its holder if his or her chosen career does not flourish? Or a *value* derivative that pays out if the market value of one's house falls?

Sounds impossible? It is not so. Who would have thoughts 20 years ago about derivatives that permit the investor to sell and buy credit risk? Since the mid-1990s, as the preceding section has briefly explained, credit derivatives enable the bank to sell the credit risk in its loans portfolio and allow a buyer to diversify the exposure embedded in his or her securities holdings by mixing credit risk and market risk.

A growing risk appetite sees to it that some institutional investors like that mix. Indeed, many analysts consider credit derivatives as default mitigating instruments whose time has come. Others, however, believe that investors should be more careful because these are products banks must aggressively sell to prune their portfolio from bad loans. Investors' feelings are mixed.

- In the mid-1990s insurers, mutual funds, pension funds, and smaller banks expressed increasing interest for credit derivatives.
- Ten years later, however, many institutional investors have been accusing big banks for predistributing loans losses, a practice they consider to be unfair.

For instance, in 2002 Calpers, California's huge pension fund, joined with several other pension funds to sue JPMorgan Chase and Citigroup, the underwriters of WorldCom's $11 billion last issue, for alleged lack of due diligence. As Figure 3.2 shows, the years 1999 to 2001 were those of the big take-off of credit derivatives, both in the United States and in the global market, but a number of bankruptcies led to a resurgence of risk aversion.

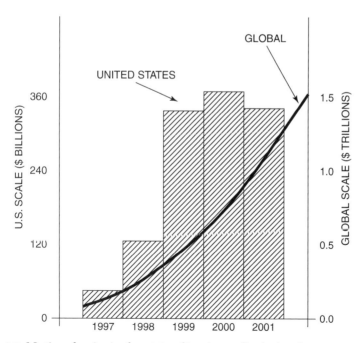

Figure 3.2 Notional principal outstanding in credit derivatives

Source: Bank for International Settlements (BIS), 72nd Annual Report, Basel, Switzerland, 2002.

It does not need explaining that, like volatility, risk appetite changes over time, because it is subject to market sentiment that itself exhibits cyclical fluctuations. By contrast, some economists look at *risk aversion* as a relatively time-invariable degree of caution toward uncertainty, at least among certain investors. These economists add that the reason for lack of complementarity lies in the fact that

> Risk aversion reflects the underlying attitude to all types of financial exposure rather than only describing risk reception within a specific financial market environment.

In the opinion of some experts, prudential regulation and supervision see to it that risk appetite and risk aversion are not a zero sum game. Therefore, even if risk aversion is the more general market sentiment, central bankers are concerned by spikes in risk appetite that could create systemic risk. The February 2007 Monthly Bulletin by the European Central Bank provides a crisp definition of the deeper meaning of each term:

- *Financial regulation* outlines the prudential rules to which credit institutions and other financial entities have to comply to assure compliance to rules and an effective risk management.
- *Financial supervision* aims at assuring that credit institutions, and other supervised entities, monitor and manage all relevant risks in an able manner.
- *Systemic risk*, and therefore financial stability monitoring, measuring, and assessment, identifies sources of vulnerability and exposures for the financial system as a whole.

Given the spikes in risk appetite, as well as the fact that financial innovation leads to an increased risk appetite, these three bulleted points constitute a basic risk control framework that permits regulatory authorities to intervene in order to facilitate, if necessary, an orderly winding up of the institution—as well as to mitigate generally adverse effects on financial stability (see "Learning a Lesson from Henry Kaufman" later in this chapter).

The same ECB documents point out that cross-border trading and diversification of financial instruments helped to make markets more liquid and to increase the shock-absorbing capacity of the financial sector. However, this increased integration also involves unknowns and requires effectively addressing financial disturbances and their systemic implications. For this purpose, simulation exercises on factors affecting financial crisis can provide regulators with a fruitful insight.[1] A similar statement is valid for commercial bankers, traders, and investors.

LEARNING A LESSON FROM GEORGE SOROS

In his testimony to the U.S. House of Representatives Committee on Banking, Finance, and Urban Affairs, on April 13, 1994, George Soros said: "We use derivative instruments to much lesser extent than generally believed, very largely because we don't really understand how they work." If one of the smartest financial operators admits that this is the case, think about the myriad bankers, treasurers, and investors who

> Don't even understand the fundamentals of derivatives, yet they engage in trades where risk can easily escape management control.

The message delivered in this testimony is that few people really appreciate the tricks of the trade connected to derivatives. One of them is the ability to rapidly generate imaginary profits or virtual losses, which, however, have aspects of legality and can be shown in the income statement (profit and loss, P&L) as the real thing. Similarly, derivatives can be used as a way to hide investment losses, even big ones.

What about staying at the safe side by forecasting future events in the financial markets? "The financial markets cannot possibly count the future directly because they don't merely discount the future. They help to shape it," Soros advised, adding that a boom-bust sequence can develop if the market is dominated by a trend-following behavior where traders and investors are

> Selling because prices fail and buying in response to a rise in prices.

---

[1] European Central Bank (ECB), *Monthly Bulletin*, Frankfurt, February 2007.

This is a self-reinforcing behavior that can produce a market crash. Mutual funds, pension funds, hedge funds, and insurance companies, among other entities, enter into it because their performance is measured relative to their peer group, not by an absolute yardstick of earnings.

In his book *F.I.A.S.C.O.*, Frank Partnoy, a former investment banker who is now professor of finance, makes reference to a Japanese firm whose management, after experiencing significant losses, asked Morgan Stanley how it might be able to generate some quick profits to hide the red ink. Could this be done using derivatives and perhaps some creative accounting? Partnoy makes the point:

> In the United States fraudulent financial accounting is subject to liability, sometimes criminal. But in Japan, accounting standards are lax, and Japanese securities firms are ahead of U.S. companies in engaging in financial fraud with great success.[2]

The whole deal had to be structured in a way that it would maintain a realistic semblance of reality, betting that it might not be discovered for many years, and even if it were, authorities would likely look the other way. What the company in reference needed was "reasonable credibility," a sort of a safe way of handling an anomalous deal that generated false profits.

Part of the calculation entering into such trades, whose aim is to sugarcoat the balance sheet, is that regulators have a tough time policing creative accounting and other financial misdeeds. In fact, this might become an impossible task *if* traders are careful to design and execute increasingly more complex schemes.

Precisely for this reason, several experts suggest that the heydays of the offshores are now past. This has happened not so much because of government restrictions as for the fact that financial institutions have found out that the use of derivatives is more effective than offshoring. It can waive certain tax provisions, particularly those that might have a major tax impact, through the appropriate investment formula.

Additionally, some of these trades are so secretive that only a handful of people at the financial institution are aware of what

---

[2] Frank Partnoy, *F.I.A.S.C.O.: The Truth about High Finance*, Profile Books, London, 1997.

takes place, and sometimes they are sworn to secrecy. Secrecy is a "must," particularly in the case of creative accounting involving liabilities, a very lucrative domain.

Secrecy is as well at a premium because many derivative deals are the product of research and development; therefore, the benefit derived from them is akin to that of patents. (There are no patents in the banking industry.) The optimization of taxation provides an example. Taxation of derivatives transactions depends on their particular legal form and on their underlying:

- A withholding tax obligation is triggered upon the payment of interest,
- But swap payments escape this tax clause, thereby opening a floodgate of tax avoidance.

Profits from deals with payments made under swap agreements are typically computed by reference to a notional principal amount (Chapter 13). As such, for tax purposes they are not regarded as interest because no underlying loan exists between the counterparties. Even though certain swap payments may have characteristics of annual receipts, authorities do not necessarily look at them in that way.

A similar argument is valid about swap receipts and payments that relate to interest on trade borrowings. In computing trading profits, the interest on trade borrowing is tax deductible. Other derivative instruments, too, fall into this class of tax characteristics laying in a twilight zone between what "is" and "is not" taxable.

For example, for tax purposes profits derived from the use of financial derivatives in the ordinary course of banking tend to be regarded as being part of trading profits. Different jurisdictions, however, have heterogeneous approaches to this issue, and permitted freedoms in accounting treatment play an important role in determining whether a transaction is subject to profits recognition.

LEARNING A LESSON FROM HENRY KAUFMAN

In year 2000, because of concerns about repercussions of disorderly failure of a very *large and complex financial institution* (LCFI), including its effect on stability of the international financial system, the Group of 10 (G-10) finance ministers and central bank governors, the Basel Committee, and the Financial Stability Forum (FSF) of the Bank for International Settlements (BIS) formed a joint task force to review the main issues likely to be faced in winding down an LCFI. In the aftermath:

- A number of preparatory measures have been identified.
- Regulatory responses have been examined in conjunction with national contingency procedures.

A great deal of concern sprang from the fact that about 90 percent of the world's 500 biggest companies, and a great deal of smaller ones, use derivatives in a rather intensive way. Many of the worries over derivatives exposure don't stem from any inherent evil but from the fact that there has been an alarming increase in the number of things bankers, investors, and regulators know nothing about. The downside of such thin experience in handling new and complex instruments has four aspects:

- Failure to comprehend what different portfolio positions mean in terms of exposure
- Improper or outright false evaluations of risk and reward, in a massive derivatives portfolio
- Likelihood that the instruments' power disguises the intentions of their users
- Existence of a widespread lack of rigorous risk management policies and tools, including misuse of models and absence of internal control

Investment companies, too, have these concerns. Bill Gross, the manager of PIMCO, a multi-billion-dollar bond fund, was quoted having suggested derivatives contracts contain dormant losses that will come to haunt their owners, typically insurance companies and banks. They also enable corporate treasurers to gamble with shareholders' money.[3] Moreover, the use of derivatives by governments carries risks that have received too little attention, says Benn Steil of America's Council on Foreign Relations:

- Governments have employed derivative financial instruments mainly to tap cheap capital,

---

[3] *Economist*, January 24, 2004.

- But there is a widespread belief in the financial industry that governments do not know what they are doing when they use derivatives to create liquidity.

Mid-March 2007 Dr. Henry Kaufman gave a speech on Wall Street distinguished by a clear diagnosis. The current economic and market challenges, Kaufman pointed out, have their origin in the changing definition of liquidity. Classically, liquidity has been an *asset-based* concept. Companies were liquid if they had cash on hand and easy marketable other assets.

This has changed, Kaufman said. Today, firms and households alike often blur the distinction between liquidity and credit availability; and at the same time securitization and new technology have stimulated risk appetites. They also fostered the attitude that credit usually is available at a reasonable price. This is not always true because

> Credit matters, and with overleveraging, credit can quickly unravel, as it has happened in early 2007 in the United States, with subprime credit.

Moreover, many risk management models are defective because they assume constancy in market fundamentals and do not account for the market's changing structure (see also the following section in this chapter). But as Henry Kaufman aptly suggested in his mid-March 2007 conference, risk modeling is so profitable that it becomes in a way *riskier*:

> Aggressive models make the most money, and reliance on judgment and reason tend to be pushed aside.

In late February 2007, a sudden rise in risk aversion unnerved equity markets. Complacency had taken hold because the equities' and commodities' long rally was underpinned by the wrong belief that global liquidity had made it safer to invest in riskier assets. The rise in subprime debt spreads shattered this conception, and there were as well other negative events.

But not everything was downbeat in late February and early March 2007. Junk-bond credit was especially strong, with spreads falling to record lows—which is the very notion of easy credit. Contrary to all investment logic, investors were piling low-yielding debt from companies with poor credit ratings and shrinking profit margins. Still, according to a growing body of opinion, the era of cheap credit was ending, with the only question still to be settled being when the cheap credit bubble will burst.

HIGH TECHNOLOGY FOR PROCESSES
AND PRODUCTS

In Chapter 1, the section "The Technology Side of Service Science" brought the reader's attention to this subject. Over the last half dozen years, the automation of over-the-counter derivatives transactions has accelerated. By 2007 more than one-third of credit derivatives deals have been confirmed online compared with only 6 percent in 2004. But the technology being used in these transactions is not state of the art, and regulators are uneasy.

Back in February 2005, in the United Kingdom, the Financial Services Authority (FSA) said that it was concerned at the large number of credit derivatives deals in which there were delays in the two sides' confirming the transaction. The FSA warned banks and other financial services companies about the level of technology of their systems. In response, the banks blamed other factors for their failure to keep up with confirmations. For instance,

- The complexity of deals being made
- The rapid growth of the credit derivatives market

The rapid growth in credit derivatives has led to capacity bottlenecks in settlement, banks said—forgetting they were the agents of such growth. They also added that if this continues, it can lead to problems in determining the exposure that has actually been incurred, impairing risk management in the event of market strains.

It does not need to be explained that the sophistication of financial instruments, risk management, and high technology closely correlate—a fact that has not yet been widely appreciated in boardrooms. New technology challenges are caused by the evaluation of risk and return connected to complex instruments for which there are no publicly quoted market prices (see the section "Over-the-Counter Derivatives Transactions" earlier in this chapter). Therefore, their analysis is based on models of which many

- Are designed with insufficient data
- Utilize rather elementary algorithms

Sophisticated technological solutions are also necessary to guarantee proper functioning of the risk transfer mechanism that pushes assumed credit and market exposure to the retail sector, outside the circle of the financial system's main players. This is aggravated by the fact that most institutional and practically all private investors are unable to adequately assess the risks parameters with which they are now confronted.

High tech is as well needed for the study of covariance in market factors. Many studies on globalization superficially suggest that the world's financial markets act more or less in unison. This is not true. To the contrary, money is made by exploiting distortions and anomalies, like undervalued stocks or other commodities, prevailing in "this" or "that" market.

Attentive portfolio managers know that they must be dealing with currency, interest rate, credit, and other risks in their portfolio and that to do so effectively, they must understand comovement of factors influencing the markets. Statistical evidence must be tortured to reveal its secrets and lead to prognostication of possible, but not sure, oncoming risk events. While a few financial institutions are up to the task, the majority is way behind. It is indeed curious but true that

> The greater is the amount of money spent on information technology, the lower is the share of modernity in its development and usage because obsolete approaches known as "legacy solutions" still have the upper hand.

Sophisticated knowledge-enriched information systems are not Cobol-based procedures that grew over time by outpacing their original technical requirements. Intelligent systems have their own design requirements, and these must be fulfilled in the most dependable manner to perform their mission without failure. This requires

- Clear strategic objectives
- A metaphysical view of the nature of complexity
- End-to-end system reliability at 99.9 percent level, as a minimum (see Chapter 6)
- A new management culture that knows that it has to be in charge at any time, in any place, for any instrument

A practical reference on management control the way it has been exercised at Boeing explains the meaning of this last bulleted point. To turn around Boeing's civilian aircraft division, Alan Mulally had set up weekly meetings, which were run from a video-conference office. It was like a war room, with all the division's main operating data projected onto screens:

> Every Thursday Mulally painstakingly took his executives through every line of figures, and he maintained this ritual throughout his tenure, so that he always knew exactly what was going on.

This hands-on approach is one of the pillars of service science. A policy of direct control allows top management to base decisions on *hard data* rather than vague hunches and hearsay. The leaders of the banking industry, however, appreciate that results can be obtained from interactive computational finance only when the latter benefits from high-technology support.

The same principle applies in all fields of economics. One of the hypotheses in need of steady testing is whether continued firmness in financial assets lends support to a currency, at least over the near term. The assumption underlying this premise is that currencies trade as a function of *asset prices* rather than interest rates.

In conclusion, behind the statement that technological development must match those of inventive financial products lies the fact that strong growth in complex financial instruments has been accompanied by a rise in operational risk, and this adds to the risk control challenge. The problem is that while in many institutions galloping competition creates a pressure to develop new financial products to stay ahead of the curve, not enough attention is paid to the steady updating of control systems, and this lag can have very severe consequences.

Hedging

THE SEARCH FOR EFFECTIVE HEDGES

The *Oxford Popular Dictionary and Thesaurus* defines a *hedge* as a fence of bushes or shrubs; and, alternatively, as avoiding giving a direct answer or making a commitment. Neither definition is directly applicable to financial hedging, but ironically, both have a bit of truth in them, particularly in connection to *hedges for profits*, which is a hedging activity only in name (more on this later).

In banking, finance, and treasury operations, the objective of *true hedging* is the reduction of risk that has been assumed through trading and investment. Hedges are made, for instance, for physical commodities using futures and options. But while a hedge may reduce the *price risk* in the physical commodity market, it also becomes subject to *basis risk* and other exposures. *Basis risk* is the difference between

- The spot price of the commodity being hedged,
- And the futures price provided by the hedge.

The magnitude of basis risk should decline toward zero as the futures delivery day approaches, given that futures prices and spot prices tend to converge. There exist, however, anomalies in the market, while in bilateral agreements basis risk is influenced by the type of deal being made by the counterparties.

Both with futures and with forwards, in the background of basis risk is the possibility of loss from imperfectly matched positions in two related market segments or instruments. Examples would be an exposure to a loss from a maturity mismatch resulting from a change in the shape of the yield curve or the variability of returns stemming from possible changes in the pricing basis or spread between two rates or indexes—which practically means that there are no perfect hedges.

In theory, but only in theory, hedging aims to reduce the risk on a *hedged* instrument by combining it with a *hedging* instrument. The latter may be an option, forward, future, or swap. Also theoretically, value changes in one instrument are offset by value changes in the other instrument. Practically, this is never the case because the price behavior of the hedged and hedging instruments are, most often, asymmetric.

Futures contracts can be flat as opposed to current market prices for the same commodity, a reason why hedging can give asymmetric results. Additionally, the hedging strategy being chosen and particular conditions existing at the time of initiating a hedge will be chief determinants of both the hedge instrument and the scenario to be followed over the hedging period. For instance, a given strategy may exploit seasonal and intercommodity price patterns in two ways:

- As a guide to selecting the hedge vehicle
- As a way of evaluating a chosen hedge program

However, the reader should notice that the historical pattern of direction of a commodity's price volatility, or the extrapolation of futures price trends from current spot prices, is not a reliable guide to the pattern that spot prices will actually take. This is true even if the underlying seasonal variation in prices is the market perception of the general direction of the prices in one or more commodities.

In principle, *sound hedging* requires a global market viewpoint as well as consideration of trends in prices of different commodities and industry sectors. Moreover, a great deal depends on the intended use of the hedge. No matter which is the management's intent (see the section "Management Intent" later in the chapter), hedging is a focused process, and therefore it cannot be "generally effective."

A given hedge tends to be regarded as *effective* if, at inception and throughout its life, the holder entity or investor can expect that the changes in the fair value or cash flows of a hedged item will be

almost fully offset by changes in the fair value or cash flows of a
hedging instrument. This is very rarely, if ever, the case. As a result,
banks tend to regard a hedge as "more or less effective" if the actual
outcomes are within a range of 80 to 125 percent from targeted fair
value or cash flow.

There exist different types of hedges. *Cash flow hedges* are interest rate swaps designed to protect against changes in cash flows of
certain variable-rate debt issues. By contrast, *fair value hedges* primarily consist of interest rate swaps used to protect against changes
in the fair value of fixed-rate medium- to longer-term debt, due to
changes in market interest rates. Foreign currency interest rate
swaps are also used as hedging instruments. A key factor in measuring hedge effectiveness is coverage of the interest rate risk exposure of the underlying hedged debt instruments.

Hedging the risk associated with credit derivatives provides
another example on the importance of a strategically sound and
consistent hedging program, Standard & Poor's looks for policies
that would limit the amount of single-name exposure. For instance,
this type of policy would be one that could be transferred by means
of a single credit derivative transaction with a single counterparty.
Because of legal risk and for other idiosyncratic reasons, a counterparty providing credit protection may balk when its obligation
reaches a large amount like half a billion dollars.

Even *if* there is no basis risk, many credit derivatives involve
the risk that a protection seller will not be able or willing to make
contractual payments. This is particularly true when the creditworthiness of a counterparty is highly correlated with that of the reference entity. Thus an effective hedging strategy would not permit
protection to be purchased from correlated parties. This is a sound
principle, but it is not generally observed.

Furthermore, *legal risk* is a significant consideration in all
credit hedging strategies. With credit derivatives, legal cases can
arise over the definition of a credit event or the validity of a price
discovery process. There may as well be claims of misrepresenta-
tions or of unfair sales practices. Here again, the likelihood of legal
risk zooms when the amounts due become large, as they do from
time to time.

An interesting example of the amount of assumed exposure by
protection writers—because of market value changes and potential

changes—is provided by credit default swaps (CDSs). It is indeed possible for a protection seller (or buyer) to lose (or gain) the entire notional value of a CDS

If the reference entity defaults and

There is *no recovery* value to its obligations.

Like a loan equivalent amount, the notional principal amount (Chapter 2) becomes a useful yardstick of potential losses. By contrast, with other derivatives the amount of the loss is only the amount of the price move and it will likely represent only a portion of the notional amount. Therefore, experts consider as effective hedges those that do not evidence significant

- Basis risk
- Legal risk
- Other types of counterparty risk

Contracts *might* avoid basis risk if they have the same or longer maturity date, if they have the same reference obligation as the hedged obligation, and if they are denominated in the same currency as the hedged obligation. Also, contracts might avoid risk, most evidently, if the credit event is one relevant for offsetting losses that could be suffered on the hedged instrument— always keeping in mind that even in the case of carefully constructed hedges, at the end of the day the results may be asymmetric.

HEDGING PRACTICES

In principle, to the extent that bankers, treasurers, and investors are hedged, they should be seen mainly as intermediaries in a chain of risk transfer. This description makes sense because what they essentially do through hedging is swap risks with each other. Under this condition, it is possible that a hedging trade initiated by one party could trigger a chain of trades between other parties in a chain of positions open to profit and loss.

In reality, this chain reaction is more complex because nearly every financial instrument has special requirements for hedging. For instance, to receive credit from Standard & Poor's for entirely removing credit risk—and therefore no longer requiring capital support—tranched securitizations must assure that a substantial amount of potential credit risk inherent in a pool of assets will be born by investors in subordinated tranches. This requires

- The observance of criteria making evident that all tranches (rated and unrated) are sold
- Assurance there is no early amortization feature protecting investors when the asset performance deteriorates by requiring the buildup of cash reserves on the originator's side

This and similar examples help in demonstrating that effective hedging is a proactive practice, designed to minimize losses that may occur today and in the future. Instruments available in the financial and commodity markets enable the hedge to shift the risk with the goal to protect one's position. But as the preceding section demonstrated, hedging is achieved only up to a point.

The way the technical literature has it, counterparties enter into hedging transactions in order to protect a particular asset, liability, or cash flow from movements in a given market or markets. In that sense, from a risk management standpoint transactions made for hedging purposes have been generally thought to be benign.

In its most genuine practice, a hedge involves establishing a position, say, in the futures market, that is equal and opposite to a position in the actual commodity. For example, a silver producer long 100,000 ounces of physical metal may hedge by going short in futures contracts by establishing an equal and opposite position.

In this manner, the hedger can fix a futures price for his or her commodity in today's market by using derivative instruments, using the concept that a loss in one position should be offset by a gain in the other. The downside is that this process of hedging works well only when cash prices and futures prices tend to move in tandem—and while the risk of an adverse change in this relationship is considered to be generally less than the risk of going unhedged, this is not always true.

An example is provided by hedges made for tracking reasons. These contrast to the strategy of the pure hedger who seeks to avoid risk in that the traders making them willingly assume risk while trying to predict price movements before they occur. Essentially, they aim to profit from market volatility. *Hedges for profits* capitalize on the highly leveraged nature of derivatives contracts, which permits hedgers to turn into speculators.

A simple way to distinguish investors from speculators is that the former risk their own capital with the hope of making profits from volatility in market prices. By hedging, they seek to offset some potential losses. By contrast, speculators typically use the capital of others—often borrowed or trusted money—and assume the risk that investors seek to avoid.

Etymologically, the term *speculator* is not necessarily diminutive. Originally, it has been derived from the Latin *speculari*, which means to watch and observe, which is precisely what wise investors are doing. In a nutshell, they

- Watch price movements.
- Observe market trends.
- Take notice of supply and demand.
- Monitor commercial deals.
- Evaluate factors affecting prices.
- Make their buy or sell decisions.

Like investors, speculators don't want to lose their capital, but in the search for higher and higher profits, this is one of the risks. In fact, both investors and speculators do everything possible to minimize risk and maximize returns, trying to enter the market at the right time and at the right price, but because they are using their own money, investors are more cautious. They act on their caution through

- Scenario analysis
- Simulation
- Stress testing

All this is written in the understanding that, as its name implies, a hedge is done for pure hedging reasons. *If* hedging is done for damage control purposes, *then* it is proper to study the motivations behind it and most specifically whether it corresponds to a transaction that exposes one's portfolio (or his or her company) to risks. For instance, the treasurer may try to obtain a form of price insurance that permits him or her to

- Take the guesswork out of projecting future costs, or
- Hold onto a cash flow without sustaining losses as a result of foreign exchange volatility.

Many bankers *prehedge* by taking positions on the basis of orders and inquiries by clients, before executing the client's trade. Prehedging procedures, however, are not written in stone. In April 2004, after the Deutsche Bank was fined £190,000 ($391,400) by the Financial Services Authority (FSA) for failing to notify a client it had prehedged a trade, four of the largest investment banks wrote to their European fund managers outlining their policies on prehedging.

The FSA said that prehedging was allowed only as long as clients were informed in advance. In the general case, however, there is lack of consensus between buysides and sellsides on a standard for prehedging practices, and the banks themselves are divided over whether prehedging benefits or damages clients:

- UBS has declared itself against prehedging. Merrill Lynch has also shown concerns about the practice.
- Deutsche Bank and Goldman Sachs have taken the opposite view, believing prehedging is acceptable as long as it is disclosed.

Merrill Lynch said in a letter to clients that it would not prehedge as a matter of course, but it does not rule out doing so at clients' request. By contrast, Goldman Sachs stated it would prehedge unless instructed not to by clients.[1]

In principle, but only in principle, prehedging decreases the bank's risk when taking on fund management portfolios, and it also allows it to offer a lower execution fee. On the other hand, it can result in a worse execution price for clients. The reason lies in the fact that banks often anticipate the details of risk trades:

If brokers guess correctly,

Then, and only then, they can take a position ahead of the trade and make a profit.

Precisely because many guesses turn out to be wrong, not everybody agrees with the notion that hedging provides protection.

---

[1] News item, *Financial Times*, September 6, 2004.

In the 2003 Annual Report by Kinross Gold Corporation, its president and CEO Robert M. Buchan writes: "During 2003, we continued to deliver into our depleting gold hedge book, reducing it by over half to 225,000 ounces. By the first quarter of 2005 we will have extinguished the remainder, and *be completely unhedged*." (Emphasis added.)

Buchan explains that Kinross Gold reduced its gold hedging exposure consistently as the financial leverage of its balance sheet declined. Management decided to put the company in a position to react, if or when opportunities arose, by means of acquisitions rather than hedges.

TYPES OF HEDGING INSTRUMENTS

Futures and options are generally traded by investors who aim for a reasonable profit and use derivatives to manage price risk. Any producer can be an investor. The producer of a commodity such as corn can reduce the risk of falling corn prices by selling a futures contract, but as "Hedging Practices" has shown, guessing the direction of market shifts is far from being an exact science.

Price discovery through hedging is made possible by the fact that futures and options markets provide a competitive price setting mechanism for financial instruments and commodities. The market absorbs information allowing prices to be derived, and this sees to it that the buyer and seller are exposed not only to market forces but also to market values. Moreover, through derivatives, market players add liquidity to the market, and this sometimes results in price shifting.

In their way, properly functioning futures and options deals increase the competitiveness of cash by contributing to price-oriented information flows, as well as by activating the forces of supply and demand determining the price. But every financial instrument and every commodity has its own characteristic ways in which products are timed, valued, inventoried, and traded:

- The lifespan of futures and options contracts is relatively short.
- Unlike stocks or bonds, it is not possible to buy a commodity futures contract and put it away for years.

While traders and investors have a choice of several contract months near and distant from which to choose, the life of a futures contract is generally less than 24 months. It takes skill and a considerable amount of know-how to keep abreast of factors affecting market fluctuations and to analyze one's own position comparing it to the market's trend(s).

Part of the challenge is the choice of the derivative instrument to best fit a given situation. Caps, collars, floors, basis swaps, and leveraged swaps are interest rate swap agreements. As we will see through practical examples in Chapter 14, interest rate caps and floors provide the buyer with protection against rising and falling interest rates, respectively. Interest rate collars combine a cap and a floor, limiting volatility within a predetermined interest rate range.

Basis swaps are a variety of interest rate swap agreements by which variable rates are received and paid, but they are based on different index rates. *Leveraged swaps* are another type of interest rate instrument whereby changes in the variable interest rate are multiplied by a contractual leverage factor, such as four times the three-month London Interbank Offered Rate (LIBOR).

Also used for hedging purposes, other derivative instruments address fluctuations in foreign exchange rates that impact the value of outstanding contracts. *Currency forwards* and options are commonly employed to manage currency risk. *Currency swaps* are often preferred in situations in which

- A long-dated forward market is not available, or
- The client needs a customized instrument to hedge a foreign currency cash flow stream.

Typically, parties to a currency swap initially exchange principal amounts in two currencies, agreeing to exchange interest payments and to reexchange the currencies at a future date and exchange rate. With OTC transactions, the contract fills in the details.

Equity price risk can be hedged through *equity options*, warrants, and other equity securities. Equity options may require the writer to purchase or sell a specified stock or to make a cash payment based on changes in the market price of that stock, basket of stocks, or stock index.

Credit spread risk (Chapter 11) arises from the possibility that changes in credit spreads will affect the value of a financial instrument.

Credit spreads represent the credit risk premiums required by market participants for a given credit quality—that is, the additional yield that a debt instrument issued by an entity rated AA or less must produce over a risk-free alternative such as U.S. Treasury instruments.

Swaps and options can be designed to mitigate losses due to changes in credit spreads, as well as a credit downgrade or default of the issuer. With derivatives, *default risk* stands at the level of the current cost of replacing derivative contracts in a gain position. Default risk exposure varies by type of derivative instrument, depending on whether these products are over the counter or exchange traded, as well as some other criteria. Typically,

- Futures contracts are exchange traded, and usually require daily cash settlement.
- Swap agreements and forward contracts are OTC transacted, hence exposed to default risks to the extent of their replacement cost.

To reduce default risk, companies require collateral, principally securities of the U.S. government and its agencies or other gilts.[2] From an economic standpoint, they evaluate default risk exposure net of related collateral. Master netting agreements could provide protection in bankruptcy, in certain circumstances. In some cases, they may also enable receivables and payables with the same counterparty to be offset on the consolidated balance sheet.

RIGHT AND WRONG HEDGES

In America, the Financial Accounting Standards Board (FASB) has established a rule requiring companies to show whether they are using derivatives to hedge risks connected to their business or if they are just taking a risky bet in the hope of making extra profits. In the background of this rule lies the fact that true hedging, such as buying forward against a rise in the exchange rate of the euro, pound, yen, or any other currency directly connected to current commitments, is one thing; speculative hedging is another.

---

[2] Gilts is a British term for Treasuries.

A fundamental principle of a time hedge is that through the use of analytics, the bank can limit its risk even when confronted with large positions. This, however, requires a well-thought-out policy (see the following section), the skill of rocket scientists, and sophisticated computer support (Chapter 3). In its heydays, Bankers Trust had in place a real-time interactive system that assisted in calculating exposure both quantitatively and qualitatively—the latter on the basis of adverse news.

A practical example helps in appreciating how much attention must be paid to potential exposure as a prerequisite to the right hedge. Bankers Trust had calculated its potential exposure to Digital Equipment Corporation (DEC) not only in terms of loans but also in terms of the batteries of Vaxes[3] the bank employed and their software. The information technology department estimated that exposure to DEC stood at

- Some $300 million in loans
- Roughly $1 billion in software
- About $300 million in worth of equipment

At a cost of 1 percent per year, the bank bought insurance on DEC as a counterparty for 50 percent of the sum of its loans, hardware, and software exposure. This may seem farfetched at first sight, but there is considerable similitude between taking insurance on software and hardware in case of vendor failure and hedging financial positions.

For instance, in the case of DEC's bankruptcy, Bankers Trust would have been exposed to the whole of $1.6 billion identified in the above bulleted points. With the insurance coverage it would have benefited from a windfall of $800 million, allowing management to put its hands around the IT conversion problem without a spike in costs and risks.

Not all institutions are that prudent. Many banks have an extremely large exposure with their preferred computer vendor and its wares, but they have no plan for what to do in case of adversity. *If this vendor goes under, then* the bank may as well call it quits because

---

[3] Vax, a DEC product, has been the wonder computer of the late 1970s and 1980s, which practically killed—in terms of cost effectiveness—the mainframes.

no financial institution can today operate without computer support. Besides indispensable computational assistance, practically all client relationships and all accounts are locked into the database.

Hedging computer vendor risk is not different from similar hedging plans applied to interest rates, currency rates, equities, energy, commodities, real estate, and more domains. The principle is to protect the portfolio by buying a premium and, having done so, to keep analyzing the changing pattern of IT risk as new investments are made and new programs are written.

The concept is not different from that applied to financial positions in which, for risk-offsetting purposes, banks use *delta hedging*—by taking positions that match the market response of the underlying positions over a narrow range of price or rate changes. In the domain of operational risk too, hedging is a balancing act that must be steadily fine-tuned.

Practical examples document that hedgers must do plenty of homework when they study their moves, as well as during the contract's life cycle. The experience of Japan Airlines (JAL) at the end of 1995 shows that when they are deprived of appropriate analysis, hedging instruments can negatively affect the treasury and P&L of companies. Beginning in the mid-1980s, JAL took out forward currency contracts to buy dollars for yen, to hedge the future purchase of aircraft. However,

- Contrary to the airline's projections, the dollar weakened against the yen, resulting in a loss of ¥176.3 billion ($1.7 billion) at end of 1994.
- These losses were being ignored until the aircraft were purchased, at which time (most irrationally) the extra cost was spread over the life of the assets through higher depreciation.

Nobody at JAL was ready to admit that so much money was lost as a result of wrong hedging until an accounting change brought the torrent of red ink to light. With it, JAL added its name to the lot of Orange County, Metallgesellschaft, Procter & Gamble, Sumitomo Corporation, and many others who lost big money through mismanaged derivatives deals.

In other cases, senior management has come forward with a frank admission of misjudgment. Said Hirokazu Nakamura, then chairman of Mitsubishi Motors: "Mitsubishi has been long and wrong on the direction of the yen. While the yen passed the 100 bar to the dollar, Mitsubishi had hedged at 90 yen to the dollar, till March 31, 1996. Hence, the dollar appreciation would *not* show in the bottom line for another 7 months."[4]

When steady vigilance indicates that hedges have taken a negative turn, *dehedging* may be the solution. An example is the situation that developed in early 2003 in the Middle East, which pushed north the prices of both crude oil and gold. Experts said that another key element to the rise in gold price had been a turnaround in hedging behavior by the gold mines and bullion banks. Historically,

- Gold mines have sold production forward.
- Banks have borrowed gold, sold it, and invested the proceeds.

Under certain conditions, forward sales can protect the mines against falls in gold prices and at the same time provide an income. In 1999, for example, producers added 500 tons of gold to supply through hedging. But by 2003, the miners were reversing these positions. According to some estimates, from the second quarter of 2002 to the end of the first quarter 2003, gold mines took some 500 tons of gold *out* of the market through what became known as *dehedging*.

One reason for this particular dehedging policy was falling dollar interest rates, which made it less profitable for miners to sell gold forward or for speculators to sell the metal short. With very low interest rates the opportunity cost of holding gold became very low. It does not pay enough dividends to sell forward and reinvest the proceeds or to borrow gold.

To be attractive, the cost of borrowing gold must be less than the cost of borrowing money. For instance, in the mid-1990s, investors could have borrowed gold at less than 1 percent, then sold it and invested the proceeds at around 7 percent. But by 2002 to 2003 this gap narrowed tremendously, while investors ran for cover when they heard worse-than-expected news on the dollar. To the contrary, speculators started being very active in the *carry trade*—borrowing yen and investing in dollars and commodities.

---

[4] News item, *Asian Wall Street Journal*, September 12, 1995.

MANAGEMENT INTENT

According to accounting rules that were first established in the United States in the late 1990s with the adoption of the *generally accepted accounting principles* (GAAP), and eight years later in Europe with the adoption of the *international financial reporting standards* (IFRS), in its financial reporting to supervisory authorities, shareholders, and the market, a quoted company should recognize and categorize derivatives financial instruments as either

- *Trading transactions*, including all customer and proprietary deals whether for profits or hedging, and/or
- *Nontrading transactions*, held for *strictly hedging* purposes as part of the bank's risk management policy against assets, liabilities, or cash flows.

In the aftermath of the FASB's Statement of Financial Accounting Standards 119, "Accounting for Derivative Instruments and Hedging Activities," American banks have classified their derivative transactions into three types: fair market hedges, cash flow hedges, and hedges of net investment in a foreign entity. An immediate effect of such classification is that of predefining *management intent*, a pivotal point in clarifying the type of risk the credit institution is taking in its derivatives transactions.

Another effect of the aforementioned classification of derivatives instruments is the increased attention to cash flow by commercial banks, which has much to do with financial reporting systems and the fact that the latter has become more precise. "We feel the more disclosure we have, the better it is for the financial system," said an executive of the Federal Reserve of San Francisco, in the course of our meeting.

Accurate and timely disclosure measures help to bring systemic risk under control. This, however, is not everybody's opinion. Contrarians say that many quantitative milestones have yet to be crossed for there to be full understanding, in a factual and documented manner, of how an expanding financial market really works. Part of the puzzle is the metrics and measures necessary to reflect the correlation among factors affecting volatility in the markets. The way an expert at the Bank of America put it:

> Due to a 50-basis-point difference in interest rates, there is a 10 percent increase in volatility, but nobody really has the

measurement procedures needed to prove or disprove such statement.

Indirectly, the implication has been that changes in volatility have an impact on management intent. Other commercial bankers have commented that while the management intent distinction is important, it is not easy to implement it because, as a notion, it is a qualifier.

In the opinion of other experts, derivatives are trading transactions unless it can be demonstrated that they constitute *nontrading* transactions. A derivatives transaction could qualify as nontrading if it matches or eliminates the risk from potential movements in interest rates, exchange rates, commodity prices, and other market value issues inherent in assets, liabilities, and inventoried positions—but as the previous sections demonstrated, there are no perfect hedges.

A way to go around this reference is to define the limits of a hedge and its confidence intervals. The problem associated with doing so is that a hedge may relate to only a portion of a larger asset or liability—and it may involve only a predetermined portion of risks. Or it may cover only a given period of the exposure.

This is further complicated by the fact that hedged positions may result from grouped transactions, or they can include embedded off-balance-sheet instruments and their exposures. They may also relate to specific anticipated transactions expected with reasonable certainty to arise in the normal course of banking or treasury business but without assurance this will happen.

Experts participating in the research that led to this book also suggested that in most cases nontrading transactions are fairly complex, requiring very careful analysis as, for instance, in the separation of a legal title to an item from rights or some other type of access to the principal future economic benefits associated with it. Exposure to the principal risks inherent in projected benefits must also be accounted for.

According to other opinions, complex transactions frequently involve the inclusion of options, covenants, or conditions on terms in which management intent may play a key role. Moreover, in some cases it is important to link a nontrading derivatives transaction with others in such a way that the commercial effect can be understood.

What these references basically mean is that while nontrading derivatives transactions should be clearly identified and properly documented in advance, their execution might change some of their characteristics. Hence, there should be an ongoing assessment of them to confirm that nontrading transactions remain closely related to risk control.

Certified public accountants (CPAs), too, expressed concerns about the fact that financial disclosures require the classification of a derivative as a hedge according to management intent. Some commented that a lot of ambiguity can be derived from basing accounting distinctions on what management *might* want to do at a given time. Others admitted that the idea of asking a company to explain its own objectives and policies in regard to derivative instruments is not without merit.

Greater detail could be included, for example, about how the company approaches mismatch risk or the extent to which foreign currency debtors and creditors are hedged to the local currency of operations. A similar statement was made about hedging of futures transactions, which might provide a quantifiable measure of intent.

Some CPAs suggested that quantitative disclosures would cover more or less adequately the indicators of risk if it were not for the fact that derivatives quickly transform the risk profile. A minority opinion has been that new disclosure rules must appreciate the extent of leverage; and, in its way, this helps in quantification of intention.

It is appropriate to point out that management intent also exists with nonderivative instruments. An example is leveraged buyouts; another is refinancing agreements. In all these cases, management intent varies from one firm to the other and over time. It is frequently based on internal considerations that are subjective, rather than on external economic factors; and it involves commitments that might lead to losses being reported as assets and gains as liabilities, as it happens when a realized loss on a hedge is deferred.

Aware of these possibilities, accounting standards boards and regulators have advanced rules that significantly limit cherry picking. This is particularly crucial as not only do derivatives enable investors to assume a wide variety of risks but also several of these transactions mitigate existing risks that might have been wrongly judged in the first place.

For this reason, as the following section demonstrates, a better definition of disclosure requirements associated with hedges helps in assessing real exposure—and this is good for the bank, its shareholders, and the regulators. At the same time, in order to correctly interpret management intent, certified public accountants and supervisors have to understand the policy of the board and the CEO, as well as that of the company treasurer. Without this understanding, it is not possible to say how risk prone or risk averse a company is.

HEDGE ACCOUNTING

Theoretically, through hedging, changes in one instrument's value are offset by value changes in the other instrument. But as discussed in the previous paragraphs, this is practically never the case because the behaviors of the hedged and hedging instruments are most often asymmetric. Still, the resulting differences must be recorded in an accurate manner for financial reporting purposes.

If different accounting valuation methods are used for the different instruments, such as historical cost and accruals for the hedged item and marking-to-market for the hedging, this will result in profit and loss account volatility. Hence accounting standards bodies have developed a specific accounting treatment, known as *hedge accounting*—a process subject to well-established rules.

The principle is simple. While an effective hedging relationship is one in which the entity achieves offsetting changes in fair value or cash flows for the risk being hedged, the hedge's effectiveness or ineffectiveness must be recorded in accounting terms that are the same for all parties. For financial reporting purposes,

- The gain or loss on hedge transactions must be included in the profit and loss account, and
- Whether an asset or liability, the offsetting loss or gain on a firm hedge contract must be recognized and included in earnings.

With the IFRS, *hedge accounting* works in two ways. It either defers the recognition of losses or it brings forward the recognition of gains in the profit and loss statement. In this manner, gain or loss from the hedged instrument is recognized at the same time as the offsetting gain or loss from the hedging instrument.

For a derivative instrument designated as a *fair value hedge*, the gain or loss is recognized in earnings in the period of change together with the offsetting loss or gain on the hedged item attributed to the risk being hedged. For a derivative designated as a *cash flow hedge*, the effective portion of the derivative's gain or loss is recognized in earnings when the hedged exposure affects earnings. The ineffective portion of gain or loss is also recognized in earnings.

Full-fair-value accounting does away with the hedge accounting practice. To avoid situations in which hedging relationships are identified ex post to deliberately massage profits and losses, the International Accounting Standards Board (IASB) laid down a number of specific requirements to qualify for hedge accounting. The most important are the following:

- Hedging relationship must be clearly identified and documented at inception.
- Such relationships must be effective in their deliverables.
- *If* this was a forecasted transaction, *then* the hedge's aftermath must be highly probable.

The message conveyed by these three requirements is that a hedge can qualify for hedge accounting only if it passes an *effectiveness test*. For instance, changes in the value of the hedged item and the hedging instrument should *almost* fully offset each other at designation. In addition, actual results realized over the life of the hedge must remain within a narrow margin in order for it to continue to be considered effective, which is a precondition for hedge accounting.

The International Accounting Standard 39 (IAS 39) of the IFRS permits a company to apply hedge accounting if it is fully compliant with specified hedge criteria. A basic principle is that over the entire life of an effective hedging instrument, change(s) in fair value or cash flows of the hedged item can be expected to be almost fully offset by changes in the fair value or cash flows of the hedging instrument. When this is the case, the net impact on profit and loss over time is relatively small. As already noted, however, this is an ideal case.

Moreover, it can happen that the hedged item is one that would normally not be recorded at fair value because the accounting rules allow that it be held at cost less impairment. In contrast, the hedging instrument would normally be accounted for at fair value. When this happens,

- During specific accounting periods, there can be substantial differences in the profit and loss effect for the two items.
- Such differences and discrepancies will affect the P&L even if, over the whole life of the instrument, they could be expected to balance out.

Keeping these references in mind, we come to the conclusion that applying hedge accounting under the international financial reporting standards means that changes in fair values of designated hedging instruments do affect reported profit and loss in a given period. This can happen not only to the extent that a hedge is ineffective but as well because of the outlined reasons.

The case under the U.S. GAAP is somewhat different. In June 2000, in response to comments made by industry players on the Statement of Financial Accounting Standards (SFAS) 133, the FASB released SFAS 138, an amendment to SFAS 133, primarily addressing issues relating to the implementation of the earlier statement. Among other changes, SFAS 138

- Makes changes in the way the effectiveness of certain interest rate hedges is determined.
- Reduces the number of categories of transactions that are subject to treatment as derivative transactions under SFAS 133.
- Alters the treatment of hedges related to certain foreign currency denominated assets or liabilities.
- Modifies the treatment of certain intercompany derivatives that have been offset on a net basis by contracts with unrelated third parties.

Subsequently, in April 2003 the FASB issued SFAS 149, an amendment of SFAS 138 that further clarifies accounting for derivative instruments, including certain derivatives embedded in other contracts. It also addresses hedging activities focusing on circumstances under which

- A contract with an initial net investment meets the characteristics of a derivative.
- A derivative contains a financing component that warrants special reporting in the consolidated statement of cash flows.

For instance, after SFAS 149, if an entity determined that certain derivative instruments contained a financing element at inception and the entity was deemed the borrower, these would be included as a separate component with "Cash flows from financing activities." Prior to SFAS 149, these derivative instruments were included within "Cash flows from operating activities." Further improvements in financial reporting have been provided by SFAS 157, released in late 2007 and targeting the calculation of fair value.

While in the general case the adoption of newer reporting standards did not have a significant material impact on the financial position of reporting companies, in terms of results of operations or cash flows, this is a good example of how dynamic accounting standards must be in order to confront the developing financial environment. Steady vigilance by standards setters is also necessary to close loopholes that invariably develop, as companies learn from a statement's fine print that there is a gray area between what "should" and "should not" be done.

PART TWO

Beware of Assumed Exposure
and Illiquidity

CHAPTER 5

Liquidity, Solvency, and Derivatives Exposure

LIQUIDITY AND SOLVENCY

Liquidity refers to an entity's ability to meet in the most timely manner its current financial obligations. Therefore, liquidity is a relative concept having to do with the size and frequency of liabilities due in connection to current assets and liabilities (A&L) management, as well as the resources one intends to use in order to provide the funds necessary to meet contractual requirements.

In contrast, *solvency* refers to an entity's ability to meet interest cost, repayment schedules, and other financial obligations in the longer term. Failure to do so will damage the bank's, or any other entity's, relation to its counterparties and eventually lead it to its bankruptcy. The most important elements in judging a company's solvency are

- Debt capital
- Equity capital

Debt capital is a different name for liabilities, particularly those of medium to longer term. Failure to meet debt capital requirements usually obliges creditors to take legal action, which may force the entity to deposit its balance sheet. *Equity capital* is much less risky to the firm because shareholders receive dividends only at the discretion of the board. Equity capital is first on the line in satisfying the entity's solvency requirements.

While according to the foregoing definitions *liquidity* and *solvency* are two different concepts, under conditions of market stress, such as panics or huge drops in stock market values, they tend to merge. As Gerard Corrigan pointed out to Alan Greenspan in October 1987 when the New York stock market descended to the abyss (a 14.5 standard deviation event), illiquidity could morph into insolvency—hence the decision by the New York Fed to lend to banks that faced immediate illiquidity problems.

Liquidity, therefore, should be watched as carefully as solvency, and this must happen at all times. Watching over liquidity should be relatively simple if only factors with a considerable level of certainty enter into the debt capital–equity capital equation. This is not the case for three basic reasons:

- There is speculative demand for money.
- Extreme or unexpected events create spikes in liquidity requirements.
- Market players have a choice between holding money and holding other assets that are not liquid.

Economic theory teaches that this choice is governed by an assessment of the consequences of today's decisions on further-out liquidity, as well as on the risk and return characteristics of inventoried positions in the portfolio. Another critical factor is the likelihood of increased uncertainty surrounding asset returns, which affects money demand.

The need for accumulating liquidity in response to rising market uncertainty is captured at the microeconomic level by the so-called buffer stock theory of money demand. According to this theory,

- Economic agents react to unexpected changes in their cash flows by increasing money holdings, and
- This accumulation of liquidity can then act as a buffer to smooth out irregular demands for cash.

Capital adequacy specified by the Basel Committee on Banking Supervision under Basel I, Basel IA, and Basel II[1] provides credit institutions with a liquidity buffer stock, even if this is essentially a

---

[1] Dimitris N. Chorafas, *Economic Capital Allocation with Basel II, Cost and Benefit Analysis*, Butterworth-Heinemann, London and Boston, 2004.

solvency regulation specifically targeting credit risk (more on capital adequacy in Chapter 6). Basel II also addresses operational risk, while the focal point of the 1996 market risk amendment is the assurance of a credit institution's solvency in connection to market risk.

National regulators such as the Basel Committee on Banking Supervision have projected a standardized procedure for calculating a bank's capital adequacy for credit risk positions. By being more sophisticated than Basel I, Basel II pays attention to individual borrowers' probabilities of default, with credit risk weighting linked to internal or external credit assessments—the latter provided by independent rating companies such as Standard & Poor's, Moody's Investors Service, and Fitch Ratings.

Regulation requirements do not address liquidity assessments of derivatives positions. Good business sense, however, suggests that these must be transparent in the sense that they are comprehensible, verifiable, and available at least to all parties who have a legitimate interest in risk evaluation and risk control. The following requirements should guide the treasurer's and the risk manager's hand when they evaluate the entity's liquidity position:

- Evaluations should be *objective* and should include a systematic approach to the analysis of cause and effect.
- Evaluations should be based on a general *methodology* that promotes transparency of results from marking-to-market or marking-to-model positions.
- The assessments must be credible, reliable, and subject to at least a monthly review, as well as to ad hoc tests.

Models can make significant contributions to liquidity assessment, provided appropriate standards are established, including level of confidence being chosen (Chapter 6) and accuracy of estimation. Higher accuracy (rather than greater precision) can be instrumental in identifying a potential financially distressed institution.

Under Pillar 2 of Basel II, which covers the supervisory action undertaken by national regulators, some jurisdictions advance new liquidity rules aimed to modernize existing quantitative liquidity approaches by creating a prudential supervisory regime that is

- Principles based and
- Risk oriented.

For instance, from 2007 in Germany credit institutions have been given for the first time the opportunity to use their own risk measurement and risk management procedures for the prudential limitation of liquidity risk, subject to prior approval by supervisors. This individualized approach, however, must meet rigorous requirements with compliance assessed by the supervisory authorities through appropriate examination.

Additionally, a process of harmonization in risk reporting has taken root in the European Union with the advent of an EU-wide *solvency reporting system* known as *Common Reporting* (COREP), developed at the level of the Committee of European Banking Supervisors (CEBS). Traditionally, the rules of solvency reporting had been established by national supervisors. With COREP there will be a common frame of reference, even if bank supervisors retain national discretion regarding the amount of detail in the specific information to be provided by institutions.

A QUADRILLION IN DERIVATIVES EXPOSURE

Implicit in the discussion in the preceding section is the notion that regulatory authorities worry about liquidity, solvency, and systemic stability because large and complex credit institutions, as well as nonregulated hedge funds, are rapidly increasing their use of derivatives. In many jurisdictions, risks are augmented by the facts that

- There are no explicit provisions governing situations that result from market strains.
- The methods and tools for gauging their impact for supervisory review are not in place.

Concentrations of derivatives exposure strain the market. Therefore, systemic concerns promoted by OTC trades feature high on the list of factors examined in the approval of bank mergers (more on this in the later section "Impact of Megamergers on Exposure"). On June 18, 2004, the Office of the Comptroller of the Currency (OCC) suggested that roughly 90 percent of bank-held derivatives are over-the-counter instruments specially tailored to financial institutions and featuring exotic, complex features.[2]

---

[2] News item, *Executive International Report* (EIR), July 2, 2004.

The same OCC reference stated that the top seven American derivatives banks hold 96 percent of the U.S. banking system's notional principal amount—which means plenty of trillions. It needs no explaining that both the absolute level of derivatives exposure and the pace at which this is growing will impact on

- The institutions' solvency
- The likelihood of systemic risk

According to figures provided by the Bank for International Settlements (BIS), at the end of 2000 there was a worldwide exposure of $109 trillion in derivatives, which had grown to $450 trillion by the end of 2006—an increase of a little less than 30 percent per year. Part of this rapid growth has been propelled by investors' betting on derivatives as a way for making extraordinary profits; look at Enron and Parmalat for evidence of the aftereffect.

Figure 5.1 gives a snapshot of derivatives exposure concentrated in the financial industry. It shows that JPMorgan Chase alone

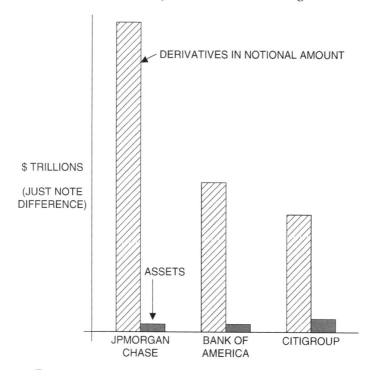

Figure 5.1 Derivatives exposure at top U.S. banks wipes out all of their assets

Source: Based on statistics by the Bank for International Settlements.

has in its portfolio a derivatives exposure that makes small game of its assets. Among American banks, the Bank of America and Citigroup come next. Taken together these three institutions account for a little over 30 percent of global derivatives exposure in notional principal amount—which speaks volumes in terms of leverage.

It is not that easy to arrive at exact figures on each individual bank's derivatives exposure because official information on this subject is intermittent; but extrapolation helps in closing some of the gaps. According to a December 21, 2004, report by the U.S. Controller of the Currency, as of September 30 that same year, JPMorgan Chase had a $43 trillion exposure in derivatives, expressed in notional principal amount.

Taking the rather conservative 30 percent annual increase in derivatives exposure (of which we spoke in the preceding paragraphs) by December 31, 2007, derivatives in JPMorgan Chase's portfolio should be an eye-popping $100 trillion in the notional principal amount. [Notice that the Comptroller of the Currency figures include holding company derivatives not counted by the Federal Deposit Insurance Corporation (FDIC).]

Some experts consider these figures to be too conservative, alleging that at the end of 2006 cumulative derivatives exposure was well beyond the aforementioned amounts. True enough, the $450 trillion (or more) in derivatives risk are in notional principal, which means that *if* the market operates normally and there is no nervousness among investors, bankers, and speculators, *then* the embedded *financial toxic waste* could be demodulated by a factor of 20.[3]

- Even this, however, will mean $22.5 billion, or nearly twice the gross domestic product (GDP) of the United States.
- Moreover, if there is a major crisis, then the demodulator shrinks to only 6 or even 5; resulting in about $82 billion in toxic waste, which is roughly three times the world's GDP.

Of this outstanding notional amount, an estimated 70 percent is in interest rate derivative instruments, 14 percent in foreign exchange, less than 3 percent in equities, a small part in commodities, and the balance in different other derivative products. These

---

[3] Dimitris N. Chorafas, "Stress Testing. Risk: Management Strategies for Extreme Events," *Euromoney*, London, 2003.

weights document that financial toxic waste is very sensitive to changes in interest rates and currency rates.

Some experts think that the notional principal amount is not necessarily a good indicator of exposure because it can be manipulated. For instance, leveraged swaps may make the notional principal look low, thereby artificially reducing exposure figures. That's true. The fact however remains that the notional principal

- Is a contractually established amount, and
- As such, it is a legal financial frame of reference.

These two contrasting opinions, for and against using the notional principal for risk control, can be brought together through a policy that analyses the risk embedded in every inventoried derivative instrument on its own merits, rather than as part of a larger number of transactions and positions that are not particularly homogeneous. Just tracking down the number of short swaps, long swaps, and offsets without analyzing their impact on exposure does not mean much except that somebody is active in the market.

Another reason given during meetings with experts as to why a summed-up notional principal amount may not be a good indicator of exposure is the difference that prevails between derivative instruments like swaps and structured notes. Structured notes have characteristics of significant leveraging with interest rates playing a very important role.

Because of all these factors, the derivatives portfolio exposure should be periodically reevaluated by looking individually at the risk embedded in each position. At the same time, when it is reduced to toxic waste, the total amount provides a snapshot of assumed risk, which can be most helpful for management decisions on whether the bank is in the right or wrong part of the balance sheet.

How far a market finds itself in terms of risks assumed in derivatives trades and how fast the latter grow also have an impact on assumed exposure. For nearly two decades the U.S. financial industry, as well as international banks working in America, were the big derivatives players. Not long ago in a meeting we had in London the president of an Australian bank said that his institution's branch in New York had more derivatives exposure than the parent company in Australia, which he headed.

These days, the United States is challenged in derivatives leadership, and the challengers are in Asia. The way a January 4, 2006, article in the *Financial Times* had it, South Korea's stock index futures and options boomed to $12 trillion in the third quarter of 2005, making South Korea "the world's busiest market for equity derivatives," overtaking the United States. That's how bubbles build up (Chapter 6).

According to some estimates, having passed the $400 trillion mark in notional principal amount, at the current rate of growth in exposure, the derivatives market is headed for the astronomical $1 quadrillion mark. How are the experts reacting to this forecast? Nobel Prize winner Dr. Merton Miller suggests that derivatives have made the world a safer place (though he does not explain how and why). But George Soros warns that, quite to the contrary, derivatives will destroy society (Chapter 3):

- The greater risk comes from the fact that very few people can see the further-out picture and its dangers, and
- Even those clear-eyed people who do see the picture have no hint of how far the damage could go if the derivatives market crashes.

Because, as we have already seen, derivatives instruments are traded for the most part outside of official exchanges, in the form of bilateral deals between two counterparties, nobody really knows the actual dimension of toxic waste in the banks' trading books. However, judging from the subprimes financial abyss, where losses of $5 million, $10 million, and $18 million became current currency, the amount of toxic waste must be very, very big.

Like debt, overexposure in leveraged financial instruments becomes burdensome when income is no longer available to service one's liabilities. *If* too many geared individuals, companies, states, or other debtors experience a cash squeeze while their credit deteriorates, *then* they will be forced to sell assets at distressed prices, while the banks that gave them loans will be doing the same with the collateral the borrowers have deposited.

UNEXPECTED CONSEQUENCES

The law of unexpected consequences says that unsettling surprises happen because of a nasty event that has not been foreseen in time to account for its effects. In finance, this often happens when the market unexpectedly turns south, reacts negatively to a novel instrument that is untested, or panics because a complex deal breaks down. The more sophisticated is a derivative instrument, the more prone it is to consequences not quite foreseen when the deal is made because of

- A sudden drop in liquidity
- An increase in market volatility
- A major bank's bankruptcy
- A significant stock market correction, or some other event

The aftermath of *event risk* is so much more pronounced when the product is not fully understood, as in the case of embedded options or an *underlying* combining equity indexes, debt instruments, commodities, or other benchmarks. Sometimes the doors to unexpected consequences open because the instrument's designer wants to increase its sophistication, reduce the likelihood that it is copied by competitors, or answer in the most accurate manner an important client's request.

All financial transactions are exposed to *event risk*. A credit downgrade is an example. Since the RJR Nabisco leveraged buyout (LBO), an increasing number of bond buyers are getting issuers to include new safeguards. The most popular is an implied covenant compensating investors in case the bonds drop to junk level due to a takeover or some type of credit event with unexpected consequences.

Known on Wall Street as *poison puts*, such covenants allow investors to get back their principal, and sometimes a few points more. Covenants usually kick in if a large chunk of a company's stock is bought by one buyer, or some other specified event occurs. As far as the issuer is concerned, there is also a silver lining in this deal. Because they ease buyers' fears, poison puts lower costs for issuers because

- They give the potential bond buyer some form of insurance.
- Investors are willing to give up a little in rate, something like one-third of a basis point in annual interest.

Of course, event risk is not the only reason for unexpected consequences. High gearing, too, has perils. A company that leverages itself to benefit from the good times may face hard times as the market turns against its bets and it can't buy any more cash to face its obligations. The near bankruptcy of Long Term Capital Management (LTCM), in September 1998, is an example.

LTCM was famous for its derivatives bets, but it was not alone in facing major losses. In mid-1998, at the time of the East Asia crisis, four U.S. banks—Bankers Trust, Chase, J.P. Morgan, and Citicorp—had more than $1 billion in nonperforming Asian derivatives (excluding Japan), out of a total of $5 billion in notional principal.[4] (This case proves that, under stress, the demodulator of notional principal amount into toxic waste, of which we spoke at the beginning of this chapter, is 5 rather than 20.)

Swap Monitor wrote that these four banks had written off $150 million, or 15 percent of their nonperforming derivatives. Wall Street analysts, however, said the $150 million was an understatement because J.P. Morgan alone had written off $489 million in derivative losses in South Korea—after SK Securities refused to perform. The unwillingness of a trading partner to face up to its obligations when the red ink is a torrent is one of the more glaring possibilities for unexpected consequences.

The reader should notice, as well, that the 1998 derivatives losses—from LTCM to the four aforementioned big banks—were not by any means a once-in-a-lifetime event. They have been preceded in a grand scale by massive bankruptcies and near bankruptcies of Japanese banks that in the late 1980s had become

- Overleveraged, and
- Overextended in wholesale and business loans.

Unexpected consequences see to it that financial might can quickly turn to ashes. In 1989, at the apogee of the Japanese banks' brief rise in the world's financial capitalization, they had an impressive $400 billion in unrealized profits. Then suddenly this became a $1.2 trillion torrent of red ink. The aftereffect has been very serious because

- Japanese banks were never strongly capitalized, and
- Their special reserves were trivial or outright nonexistent.

---

[4] News item, *Swap Monitor*, May 4, 1998.

Not everybody appreciates the importance of special reserves, and in some countries (the United States being an example), they are even illegal. Yet, when worst comes to worst, they can be life-savers. The last Louis (a French gold sovereign) wins the war, Louis XIV, the Sun King, once said.

LTCM and the majority of the big Japanese banks had spent their last Louis, and so did a number of other financial institutions. Special reserves, too, have limits. On November 15, 2002, after injecting another $1 billion in Winterthur, its insurance subsidiary, Crédit Suisse exhausted its special reserves. This completely changed its risk profile with the result that

- Its equity dived, and
- Independent agencies downgraded its credit rating.

Unwise investments, lightly screened loans, and heavy leveraging aside, there are as well other reasons why financial institutions bring upon themselves the aftereffects of unexpected consequences. Two of the worse exposures that arise in the banking business are

- Divergence risk, resulting from imperfect portfolio tracking
- Execution risk, which is largely an operational risk to which management pays scant attention

Divergence risk may be the result of the partial offsetting of futures-related arbitrage strategies. This usually happens either when an institution takes opposite positions in exactly the same index at different dates, but the timing difference turns against the firm; or two different indexes are used on the hypothesis they will move in price very closely but fail to do so. This unravels the hedging strategy (Chapter 4) of the bank.

Operational risk has many origins. Classically, the main reasons were internal and external fraud, lapses in security, and execution mistakes. To these have been added management risk, legal risk, technology risk (all of them major), and several other origins.[5] Belatedly, we have come to realize that every structure can be subverted.

---

[5] Dimitris N. Chorafas, *Operational Risk Control with Basel II: Basic Principles and Capital Requirements*, Butterworth-Heinemann, London and Boston, 2004.

THE CRITICALITY OF MARKET POSITIONS

To appreciate the magnitude of risk resulting from unexpected consequences, one should keep in mind that the most exposed banks in the United States and worldwide have a portfolio in derivatives that is more than an order of magnitude larger than their assets—which assets do not belong to their clients rather than to them. What belongs to the banks themselves is their equity capital (as described in the first section in this chapter), which nowadays tends to cover only some 0.5 percent of derivatives holdings.

A similar situation prevails in several countries in Europe, as well as in Japan. While bank equity remains more or less stable and bank assets increase rather slowly, derivatives are growing globally by leaps and bounds even by the relatively conservative estimates of the Bank for International Settlements. At the same time, derivatives losses mount, and these cannot be hidden forever.

For instance, on June 30, 2004, Freddie Mac shocked the markets when it reported that its 2003 profits plunged by 52 percent compared to a year earlier. This was due to losses on derivative instruments, which it used to hedge against interest rate swings. At the same time, Freddie Mac warned of more derivatives losses in the future.[6]

Several economists also worry about the use market makers and nonregulated institutions like hedge funds make of the privileges that they enjoy in the financial markets. To be able to quote two-way prices in securities, market makers have to buy lots of securities on which they trade. This is risky. Therefore, the market makers argue that they need a number of privileges. But both in the market and among regulators there is concern that the special privileges given to market makers are tilting the balance too far in their favor.

In theory, the market as a whole benefits from the liquidity that a market-making system tends to create. But the growth of derivatives has widened the scope for abusing privileges, by passing them on to companies that are not supposed to benefit from them at all. This is compounded by the fact that some countries have failed to create effective means of enforcing rules against insider trading.

---

[6] News item, *Executive International Report* (EIR), July 9, 2004.

Even in the United States where such rules exist, there is a good deal of insider trading as revealed in March 2007.

Therefore, regulators think of cutting back the privileges, without ending market making altogether, since market makers still stand to win other business from the firms whose shares they trade. Reducing the privileges would foster healthy competition since there is evidence that at least one of the market makers' many privileges—the ability to delay the reporting of large trades—gives them an unfair advantage over rival traders.

Beyond the preservation of a level playing field and of an appropriate degree of competition in the market, regulators are also increasingly concerned about the potential risks from a higher concentration of the exposure prevailing in the financial systems, particularly the risks assumed by a small number of interconnected credit institutions, which is reaching a level of criticality.

Criticality is a term associated to vulnerabilities, and it refers to a concept that is in its way establishing itself in finance. It's a concept that is well understood in engineering and physics. Criticality suggests that in extreme circumstances, certain infrastructures, entities, or products may change their status. Experts say that negative effects of criticality in finance are

- Excessive volatility
- A rather significant illiquidity (see the first section in this chapter)

Either or both can disrupt the efficient operation of financial markets because they alter the behavior of the players—hence the importance of defining what constitutes a critical level of behavior, what might be its impact on financial services' infrastructures, and what can be done in terms of countermeasures to stop the spread of vulnerabilities through the global economy.

Notice that threats propelled by vulnerabilities may at times be hidden, or their early effects might be disguised as good news. Figure 5.2 makes this point. In the last eight years of the twentieth century, bank failures became an extinct species while at the same time derivatives exposure zoomed. Some experts have suggested that exponentially increasing derivatives trades have been hiding bank failures at the expense of overleveraging the financial system.

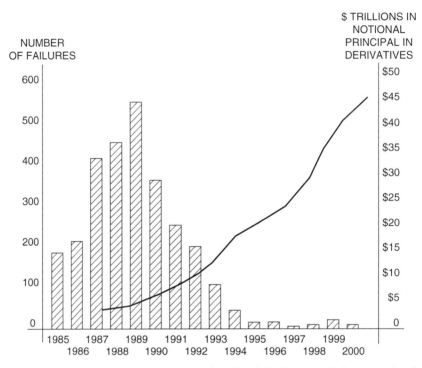

Figure 5.2 Shows an interesting trend on bank failures and the growth of derivatives in the U.S. market

The good news is that so far the derivatives markets have been sufficiently liquid to allow the unwinding of sizable positions without big dislocations. The case of the Bank of New England in 1991 is an example (as described in the following section). On the other hand, the events of September and October 1998 in connection to LTCM show that, under stress circumstances,

- The limits of the markets' resilience may be reached,
- Many unknowns persist because of the lack of transparency of OTC derivatives, and
- Even where transparency is acceptable, the accounting practices of many market players have not kept pace with product innovation and changes in financial markets.

Another concern of bankers and regulators is the impact of rapidly expanding derivatives trades on monetary policy; and the inverse of it: the use of derivatives in monetary policy decisions. With the exception of currency swaps, no major central bank is currently known to use derivatives as an instrument of monetary policy. Experts, however, suggest that it is conceivable that at some time in the future, central banks could use forward rate agreements and options to influence longer-term interest rates; and this may have unexpected consequences.

FREE FALL OF THE BOND MARKET IN 1994: A CASE STUDY

Dr. Murray Weidenbaum, chairman of the Council of Economic Advisors under President Reagan, claimed that too many companies may be looking to derivatives as a deus ex machina, sweeping in from the sky to save them from currency and interest rate changes: "I have a hunch that some of the less sophisticated businesses are jumping on the derivatives bandwagon. I am not knocking derivatives, but some companies just don't really know what they are getting into," Weidenbaum said.

- One major drawback with derivatives is the inherent complexity of several instruments.
- Another bigger concern regards the fact that derivatives make leveraging difficult to resist.
- A third risk is that because of leverage, and of the many design unknowns, it is almost impossible to compute liquidity, solvency, and capital adequacy for all derivatives trades.

Bubbles and wrong bets (see the section "Bubbles and Ponzi Games" later in this chapter) make a difficult monetary policy situation almost impossible. Betting that the Fed had no alternative but to lower interest rates, in 1991 investors and speculators took a huge position in Eurodollar futures that offer huge leverage. This was a way to bet on lower interest rates since the futures discount typically assumes a current interest rate.

In a way quite similar to what happens with other market bets, most of the big money that took part in this "sure-win" operation played the steep interest rate curve by loading up on short-term Treasury notes. It did so by borrowing the purchase price at a lower

cost of money than the Treasury was paying to hold them. By borrowing on extremely short term in a steep curve, these investors
were paying much less for money than they were earning on the
Treasury notes. Thus they were able to borrow money at less cost to
buy Treasury bonds that would pay at a higher interest.

Up to a point, this positive spread was money in the bank, even
if the notes did not improve in price at all. The risk was that rates
would spike up. They did not. As a result, the trade weighted heavily to the reward side once the economic recovery started to falter.

Panics often start with relatively small moves that, fed by
rumors, eventually reach the size of tsunamis. In spite of the circumstances the previous paragraphs briefly described, on Friday,
February 18, 1994, the world's bond markets fell sharply, as reports
of heavy selling by U.S. investors created nervousness among international investors, which led to the 1994 bonds bloodbath.

In a chain reaction, stocks, too, were hit on Wall Street by the
fall in the U.S. bond market. But while most investors were watching with gritted teeth as their bonds skidded in February and March
1994, speculators were getting rich by using intricate strategies to
take advantage of the market's turmoil. Aggressive traders willing
to accept huge risks were cleaning up the fallen debt instruments by
making bets on the future prices of stocks, bonds, commodities, and
currencies.

- This scenario is not new, even if it is inappropriate for
  nervous investors who like to sleep at night.
- What is new is the level of risk accumulated with
  potentially profitable but dangerous trades.

In Europe, the activity was mainly in the futures markets.
Bond dealers suggested that the motors behind the sell-off were the
American hedge funds. Economists advised that the European
bond market's fall ignored the economic background and the
prospect of lower interest rates on the Continent. But highly geared
hedge funds, which in the past were buyers of European government bonds particularly in the futures market, appeared to be liquidating their positions.

As it is always the case in panics and near panics, the bond
market's drop was aggravated by the fact that rumors had swept
the debt instruments markets of hedge funds being forced to close

out their positions in order to stem losses. Experts said that indeed some of the big funds appeared to be in trouble.

Commodities, too, underwent stress testing. On February 18, 1994, the sharp price decline in precious metals was primarily due to the perception of higher interest rates, which also impacted heavily on the U.S. bond and stock markets. Adding to the market's discomfort was a persistent rumor that one of the biggest U.S. investment banks

- Had been badly hit by the sharp retreat in bonds, and
- Was having to unload debt instruments and equities across international markets.

Stock market and bond market woes correlated because one of the frequently used strategies involved investing in options on stocks and stock indexes, as well as futures on stock indexes. These investments are bets on the directions of individual stocks or the entire market. *Short selling* on bonds was a parallel scenario, allowing investors to profit as bond prices fell. "In a weak market we benefit dramatically," said one of the players as the bond market sank.

Short selling is the flip side of buying and waiting for the price of a bond, a stock, or any other commodity to rise. A short seller borrows a stock or bond with a promise to return it at a later date. The trader then sells the stock and hopes it drops in price by the time he or she buys it back. The difference is his or her profit.

But short selling following a herd mentality can be extremely risky, and many investment advisors in private banking warn to avoid the practice. If an investor buys a stock at $15 and the stock goes to $7, the investor has a maximum loss of $8. However, if an investor has sold a stock at $15 and it rises instead of falling, the loss can be unlimited. Therefore, it is not without reason that some regulators and legislators are concerned with this practice, whose risks are compound by the bad disclosure rules prevailing in many countries.

BUBBLES AND PONZI GAMES

Speculative *bubbles* are defined as exponentially increasing deviations of the price of a commodity, such as an equity, index, barrel of oil, or ton of steel, from what is considered to be its real value level— the latter being determined by fundamentals and macroeconomic variables. Take as an example the currency exchange market. Once a bubble has formed in connection to a given currency, as happened with the dollar in the early to mid-1980s, this currency initially continues to appreciate because (for some time) market participants expect an increase in

- The currency's exchange rate, and
- The profit opportunities associated with it.

Up to a point, but only up to a point, because of such greater and greater expectations, market participants carry on investing in the currency, equity, oil, gold, or some other commodity, despite being aware that this is not consistent with the fundamentals. Typically, speculative bubbles are maintained

- By self-fulfilling prophesies, and
- By the disregarding of warnings provided by chartists and risk controllers.

Because, at least at their early stage, speculative bubbles are not easily distinguishable from other phenomena, there is a danger that they may be seen as the cause rather than the result of commodity price movements that cannot be explained by fundamental factors. Some economic researchers maintain that—from gold to equities and real estate—no empirical test so far has been able to conclusively prove the existence of a speculative bubble until it is almost too late.

In the end, bubbles burst, with the spot of any commodity whose price has been beefed up, collapsing to its level supported by fundamentals. The bubble phenomenon, of course, is not new; its first appearance dates to the time of the Dutch tulip mania, as well as the early eighteenth century, which saw the Mississippi bubble and South Seas bubble. "New" is the commodity chosen each time on which speculators make a kill, though many of them lose their paper profits as the bubble bursts.

One of the casualties of the real estate bubble in the late 1980s was the Bank of New England (BNE), which was a prosperous institution until the combined effect of bad loans and derivatives exposure brought it to its knees. At the end of 1989, when the Massachusetts real estate bubble burst, the Bank of New England became insolvent and bankruptcy was a foregone conclusion. At the time, BNE had

- $32 billion in assets, and
- $36 billion in derivatives exposure.

To keep systemic risk under lock and key, the Federal Reserve Bank of Boston took hold of the defunct credit institution, replaced its chairman, and pumped in billions in public money. Financial analysts said this was necessary because the risk was too great that a BNE collapse might lead to a panic. BNE's derivatives portfolio was in worse shape than its real estate loans:

- BNE lost $36 *billion* in notional principal.
- BNE lost $6 *billion* in derivatives.

This would make the demodulator of notional principal equal to 6 (see the first section in this chapter). The Bank of New England was closed by regulators in January 1991, at a cost of $2.3 billion. At that time, its derivatives portfolio was down to $6.7 billion in notional amount—with little over $1 billion in toxic waste, which represented pure and full loss.

Here is a more recent example. In September 2006, Amaranth Advisors' hedge fund speculated on the price of gas and lost $6 billion. This case, too, as true of so many other leveraged deals, has been one of *lottery,* which, etymologically, is the allotment or distribution of something by fate or chance. *Lottery* is as well an investment plan in which factors controlled only by chance play a key role in the outcome.

As it was pointed out by one of the experts who contributed to the research leading to this book, no gambler ever hankered for the feverish delight of the gaming table as much as some financial institutions are doing today in trading among themselves and with hedge funds, through processes having the essential features of a choice made more or less by chance. Typically, the instruments are novel, obscure, and highly risky—a sort of pyramiding scheme.

In 1920 Charles Ponzi invented a pyramiding game (known under the same name) that promised a return of 50 percent in less than two months. Ponzi must have been a master of herd psychology, not only an ingenious inventor who could take those trusting him to the cleaners. His plot was simple:

- He paid the early customers and himself with money from the later subscribers.
- As new subscribers showed up, this scheme worked, but by the time it folded, Ponzi was $3 million in arrears.

Convicted, Ponzi served a three-year sentence—one year per million dollars swindled. Paroled, he advertised a new scheme that promised 200 percent in 60 days. Rearrested he was deported to his native Italy, and not much is known about what has happened to him, but the term *Ponzi scheme* is still used to describe twisted methods of taking away the money of people who think they can get something for nothing.

Near the end of the go-go 1920s, some folks who specialized in leveraging were asking themselves the question: "If you can purchase a $1,000 car for $100 down, why can you not acquire stock the same way?" That kind of instant gratification was achieved by buying on margin, and financial history books tell what happened thereafter, as the economy slid down to the Great Depression.

But while the stock market crashed, the president of the New York Stock Exchange remained confident. Federal regulations were unnecessary, said Richard Whitney. "The exchange is a perfect institution." After he left office, Whitney was indicted for selling stock on insufficient capital. He was $6 million short, even after he dipped into the funds of the New York Yacht Club, where he was treasurer. Whitney was conveyed to Sing Sing.

A little over a generation later came Bernie Cornfeld. His company, Investors Overseas Services (IOS), specialized in mutual funds. We are in the business of totally converting the proletariat to the leisured class, Cornfeld said, while he played his sort of a highly leveraged game. In 1970, the vastly overgeared IOS fell victim to the bear market, and so did Cornfeld; but others followed up the practice in the 1980s with junk bonds, in the 1990s with overplaying one's hand with derivatives, and in the twenty-first century with an overleveraged global economy.

IMPACT OF MEGAMERGERS ON EXPOSURE

There is good news and bad news with the consolidation taking place in the banking industry. The good news is that mergers and acquisitions (M&As) create bigger entities better fit to a globalized economy. The bad news is that as the number of credit institutions shrinks because of M&As, the resulting entities not only get larger but also are loaded with exposures assumed in the past by the merged parties. Therefore,

- The derivatives risk increases, and
- Sometimes this increase is exponential.

The rationale for the wave of megamergers in the banking industry is to create global players and, at the same time, downsize the cost base. This, however, also reduces the number of counterparty names and leads to a concentration of highly leveraged portfolios, which increases by so much the amount of counterparty risk both in absolute and in relative terms.

There is as well the fact that big institutions are no less default prone than small institutions, and they are just as exposed to the law of unintended consequences (discussed earlier in the chapter). This makes regulators nervous. For instance, on June 18, 2004, a senior official of the Federal Reserve Bank of San Francisco warned of heightened "systemic risk concerns" due to stepped-up bank megamergers, by which a handful of giants have consolidated in their hands,

- A large amount of U.S. bank assets, and
- A sizable number of highly leveraged derivatives.[7]

What particularly worries many regulators with derivatives bets like 30-year-long forward rate agreements and other instruments is that these essentially are electronic bookkeeping entries. As such, unlike other more classical banking assets,

- They have no physical limits,
- They can escape management's attention if internal control is deficient, and
- Any big failure can spread around the world at the speed of light, as it happened in September 1998 with the LTCM crisis.

Plenty of examples document that the scale of bank megamergers now taking place, particularly in the United States and Europe, significantly increases the resulting entities' derivatives exposure. Until early 2004 Citigroup was the only trillion-dollar-asset banking organization in the United States. Then came others like the Bank of

---

[7] News item, *Executive International Report* (EIR), July 2, 2004.

America (itself the merger of BankAmerica and Nations Bank), which merged with FleetBoston; and JPMorgan Chase (the merger of Chemical Banking, Manufacturers Hanover Trust, Chase Manhattan, and J.P. Morgan), which merged with the Ohio-based Bank One.

Regulators' worries about overconcentration were expressed by Simon Kwan of the San Francisco Federal Reserve Bank when he asserted in the reserve bank's *Economic Letter* that "the ever-growing scale of bank mergers raises challenging policy questions, including banking concentration at the national level and systemic risk concerns."

> *If* banking activities are concentrated in a very few large banking companies,
>
> *Then* shocks to these individual companies could have repercussions throughout the financial system and the real economy.

It is not only the rapidly growing derivatives exposure that matters. Overconcentration is always bad, leading to unwanted consequences. Quoted in the June 17, 2004, issue of the *Financial Times*, Bill Gross, head of PIMCO, the largest bond-trading fund in the world, stated: "Too much debt, geopolitical risk, and several bubbles have created a very unstable environment which can turn any minute. More than any point in the past 20 or 30 years, there's potential for a reversal."

Nothing has happened since then to change this assessment. If anything, in the years that have followed since Kwan and Gross expressed their concerns, concentration in the banking industry has continued unabated—including the vastly increased derivatives portfolios. Nothing has been learned from previous misfortunes.

For instance, on January 1, 2002, JPMorgan Chase was America's second-largest bank, with $694 billion in assets, behind Citigroup with $1.05 trillion in assets but ahead of Bank of America. The three easily outdistanced the rest of the U.S. financial institutions; followed by Wachovia, Wells Fargo, Bank One, FleetBoston, U.S. Bancorp, National City, and SunTrust, in that order.

To the naked eye, no cracks were visible in this constellation, except the fact that at the end of the third quarter of 2001, JPMorgan Chase had reported $799 billion in assets, a drop of more than

$105.7 billion in its assets base. JPMorgan Chase's explanation for this serious drop was that the majority of the reduction reflected the resolution of the industrywide clearing and settlement problems experienced in September 2001. The existence of major industry-wide derivatives problems was denied before and after the tragic events of September 11, 2001.

This discrepancy in JPMorgan Chase's explanation gave analysts food for thought, with the result that the bank's market capitalization dropped sharply. On December 31, 2000, when the acquisition of J.P. Morgan by Chase Manhattan was completed, the newly christened JPMorgan Chase & Co. had a market capitalization of $86 billion, of which

- $26.5 billion came from Morgan and
- $59.5 billion from Chase Manhattan.

Fourteen months later, on February 22, 2002, the combined institution had a market capitalization of $57 billion, less than Chase Manhattan's alone at the time of the merger. Some Wall Street bank watchers attributed this major drop to the staggering amount of derivatives, an exposure well beyond that of other banks, amounting to roughly half of all U.S. commercial bank derivatives portfolios. Others suggested the troubles were much deeper because

- A loss equivalent to just under 0.2 percent of its derivatives portfolio would be sufficient to wipe out every penny of the bank's $42.7 billion in equity capital.
- Beyond this, there was JPMorgan Chase's exposure to the failed Enron, Kmart, and Global Crossing, also to the troubled Tyco, in addition to its losses on loans to Argentina.

One of the interesting hindsights is that JPMorgan Chase had a polyvalent sort of exposure to bankrupt Enron: Beyond loans to the energy company, it was an investor in some of Enron's partnerships, it had bought Enron stock for investment funds it managed, and it had entered into derivatives deals with Enron as a major player in the credit derivatives market. JPMorgan Chase was also selling credit derivatives with guarantees if Enron defaulted on its bond payments.

These complex financial interconnections to a failed company amounted to an extraordinary toxic waste. In early December 2001, shortly after Enron's bankruptcy, JPMorgan Chase put its loan exposure to the company at $900 million, but a few weeks later, it was revealed that it had also incurred $1 billion in losses on deals it had made with Enron through Mahonia Ltd., an offshore Morgan affiliate on Britain's Jersey Island.

According to an article published in the *Wall Street Journal* at the time of these happenings, the Federal Reserve Bank of New York was investigating these Mahonia transactions, particularly the fact that they were effectively loans to Enron disguised as energy trades. This sort of financial alchemy made it possible for Enron to get the money but keep the debt off its books.

Theoretically, JPMorgan Chase protected itself against a possible Enron default on the Mahonia transactions by buying credit guarantees from insurance companies. Practically, when Enron filed for bankruptcy and Morgan tried to collect, the insurance companies refused to pay, claiming that the deals were shams, not legitimate transactions. This case went to court with a first ruling against JPMorgan Chase. But following the unexpected appearance of a witness with damaging evidence for the insurance companies, prior to the second instance the case was settled out of court, and consequently,

- The insurance companies paid 60 percent of the disputed amount, and
- The banks that were in the litigation wrote off the balance.

This, experts said, fairly represented what was due to each party in an unorthodox deal that blew up. Along with this, an often-heard opinion has been that the extent to which the *Wall Street Journal*, *New York Times*, *Financial Times*, and other major financial newspapers were reporting the problems at JPMorgan Chase was an indication that the troubles were serious. The market's response was shown in the price of credit derivatives that would have paid off, in the event of a default, on a $10 million Morgan bond.

The option went from $35,000 at the end of January 2002 to $80,000 in late February 2002. This 228 percent change in one short month was interpreted as a clear sign that institutional investors were growing increasingly nervous about the survivability of a credit institution overexposed to all sorts of derivatives deals and a good part of the toxic waste coming from banks that had gone through the megamergers.

CHAPTER 6

The Daunting Task of
Capital Adequacy

CAPITAL ADEQUACY DYNAMICS

A statement was made in Chapter 5 that equity capital is first on the line in satisfying an entity's solvency challenges. In Basel II terms, this is *Tier 1 capital* (*core capital*) available to management to fence off a crisis. To this mission also contribute some other eligible funds (*Tier 2, Tier 3*).[1] With Basel I, the basic algorithm has been

$$\frac{\text{Core capital} + \text{other eligible own funds}}{\text{Risk} - \text{weighted exposure from (credit risk} + \text{market risk)}} \geq x \text{ percent} \quad (6.1)$$

This x percent ratio has been given by the regulators. Basel I set $x = 8$ for internationally active banks and $x = 4$ for national banks. The Basel Committee's 1996 market risk amendment established a market risk factor. The more advanced versions of Basel II (A-IRB and F-IRB) addressed the risk weights associated to credit exposure and added operational risk reserves, but so far, these versions did not materially alter the market risk factor—while the obsolete value at risk (VAR) remains the regulating model for its measurement.

The integration of balance sheet and off-balance-sheet items—realized through the SFAS 138 in 2000 in the United States and the

---

[1] Dimitris N. Chorafas, *Economic Capital Allocation with Basel II, Cost and Benefit Analysis*, Butterworth-Heinemann, London and Boston, 2004.

IFRS/IAS 39 in 2005 in Europe—has brought into perspective the need for dynamically adjusted capital requirements connected to market risk, specifically to derivatives exposure. This brings into perspective the need to rethink not only the classical definition and allocation of assets but also the dynamic capital adequacy (see also "The Origin of Legislation for Marking-to-Market" at the end of this chapter).

An integral part of the redefinition of market exposure is the fact that some derivatives trades can be either assets or liabilities depending on which way the market goes and, therefore, is subject to change on a moment's notice. An example is an interest rate swap (IRS; see also Chapter 14). An IRS is typically constructed with zero market value. But right after the deal has been made, it may become to its holder an asset or a liability. For the bank entering into an interest rate swap,

- The trade will be an *asset* if the market moves in the direction the bank thought it would move.
- But this same trade will be a *liability* if the market moves in the opposite direction.

No player really exercises control on which way the market goes. However, banks that are technologically advanced and use high-frequency financial data (HFFD) are well positioned to track present value change in a derivatives position from asset to liability (and vice versa), which can happen several times *intraday*. Such tracking requires

- Real-time system solutions
- Solid *management accounting rules* (discussed in the following section)

Management accounting is not regulatory accounting. Instead, its aim is to reveal to the bank's executives the exceptions, such as limits that do not correspond to the institution's risk appetite, drawdown rates that escape control, various types of unwanted trends, risk concentrations higher than were planned, and much more.

Through experimentation, modern management accounting must account for the fact that the more concentrated is a big institution, the greater is its relative impact on the market and the less it can get out of its positions without wrecking the price structure.

Exception reporting should as well qualify reasons for miscalculating capital adequacy for derivatives exposure such as

- Poorly done portfolio hedging (Chapter 4)
- Too optimistic an outlook that misses economic conditions that are worsening
- An instrument, customer, and/or industry concentration
- The existence of different types of exceptions to risk limits

Similar issues are as well found with credit risk control. Key among them are outdated borrower ratings; reporting lag on adverse financial conditions of the counterparty; wrongly calculated collateral; the likelihood borrowers pledged the same collateral to different banks (Maxwell risk); the fact that collateral value and audited value do not correspond; the long time it would take to recover funds through court action; and, quite often, less money recovered at liquidation than was expected.

Neither are the Basel II rules for capital adequacy perfect. The effect of correlations, for example, is downplayed. Covariance becomes important if we wish to reach a dependable estimate of probability of bankruptcy, but the study of covariance in banking is still in its beginning. This being the case, financial organizations have every interest to provide for themselves the added value of exposure, a good example being the level of confidence α chosen for the representation of risk factors (see the section "Capital at Risk and Level of Confidence").

Additionally, people knowledgeable of the intricate issues associated with the fine-tuning of capital adequacy suggest that current models should be refined to be in line with risk sensitivity, and they should also reflect the varying degrees of complexity characterizing the evolving notion of position risk. The approach must as well be developed to pay greater attention to

- Sophisticated elements of banks' internal risk management methods, and
- Their effect on the institutions' capital adequacy in the short, medium, and longer terms.

For credit institutions increasingly engaging in banking and trading across borders and providing financial services in several jurisdictions, management reporting should as well reflect an existing cooperation among supervisory agencies. National banking acts have to be revised to address cross-border market practices. Up to a point, this is in the process of happening in the European Union, with directives published by its Brussels-based executive in connection to uniform financial reporting norms. An example of such a directive would be a banking license granted by the bank's country of origin that will be recognized throughout the European Union.

Finally, with few exceptions—one such exception being the Financial Services Authority (FSA) in Britain—there is no supervisory authority responsible for the *consolidated regulation* of all types of financial institutions. Thus a dynamic approach to capital adequacy must be enriched by rules establishing the bank's connection to the different responsible agencies and their supervising procedures. This must be done under the perspective of a two-way consolidation on matters concerning capital adequacy: domestic and cross border.

MANAGEMENT ACCOUNTING FOR RECOGNIZED BUT NOT REALIZED GAINS AND LOSSES

Management accounting measurement and reporting practices that dominated the decades after the end of World War II are no longer adequate for novel and complex financial instruments, intensive trading business, and globalized financial operations. Innovation, deregulation, and the internationalization of markets, as well as the need for rigorous risk control, require that much greater attention be paid to fair value of trades and positions whether gains and losses have or have not yet been realized.

Using the rules and principles outlined in the U.S. GAAP and IFRS, the solution adopted by Tier 1 financial institutions for internal management accounting has been specifically designed to contribute to better governance. Two real-time tools have been put in place, aiming to inform, on request, at the level of an order of magnitude:

- The *virtual balance sheet* (VB/S), which shows the status of the business at any given moment in time, insofar as accounting figures can show its status

- The *virtual income,* or *profit and loss statement* (V/P&L), which reflects profits or losses arising from operating events and inventoried positions

Both are available in real time to authorized managers and professionals, for all of the entity's assets, liabilities, positions, and operations. While the VB/S shows status, the V/P&L emphasizes differences. Notice that because this is not regulatory reporting, approximations of 3 to 4 percent are acceptable as the price to be paid for the speed of response.

The thinking behind this approach is that senior management must be able to know the balance sheet position in an accurate way (albeit not precise), including recognized but not realized gains and losses. The following ratio is an important modern tool for revealing a company's financial staying power:

$$\frac{A}{L} \hspace{4cm} (6.2)$$

where

A = the assets estimated at market value, through the entity's capitalization

L = the company's liabilities (equity and debit) at book values

Capitalization is in essence the value of an entity's assets, which at any moment is given by the market. Moody's KMV model uses capitalization as a proxy of the company's assets value that otherwise would have been fairly complex to compute, and not so reliable. If the ratio $\frac{A}{L}$ falls below 1, the distance to default shortens. Evidently, volatility matters because it affects the value of the numerator in Equation 6.2.

In the typical case, the problem is that the book value of liabilities can be arbitrary, underestimating the effect of debt covenants and other commitments. A good alternative is *interest cover,* defined as underlying operating profit divided by net interest. This captures the interest rate paid, and using depreciation as proxy, it includes maintenance reinvestment. Since the 1990s, the markets are also using *earnings before interest, tax, depreciation, and amortization* (EBITDA):

- The net debt to the EBITDA, and
- The EBITDA to the net interest.

However, the EBITDA has a big theoretical caveat because it fails to capture *capital intensity*, the proportion of profit that must be reinvested to maintain the business. Because capital intensity varies among industries and because it is better to use a rich financial instruments panel when making an analysis, many analysts say they do not use the EBITDA metrics in isolation.

Additionally, in connection with internal management accounting reporting procedures, rules should exist for appreciation of exposure related to forward positions in currency exchanges, interest rates, precious metals, and equities. These should be valued at market rates with adjustments for appropriate forward premiums or discounts affecting the balance sheet.

For management reporting purposes, capital gains and losses arising from an ad hoc valuation should not be presented alone but rather entered in the profit and loss account and integrated into the balance sheet. Positions in derivatives must be accounted for with positive and negative replacement values.

A virtual balance sheet must as well account for gains and losses connected to interest rate derivatives used to manage the interest basis of flexible-rate borrowings, fixed-rate borrowings, and currency borrowings. It should as well integrate currency derivatives used to manage foreign exchange risk. This bypasses historical costs and leads to a distinction in reporting requirements depending on whether an item is

- In-current earnings, or
- Out-of-current earnings, as indicated in Table 6.1.

In Table 6.1, the first bulleted item includes derivatives designated as hedges of cash flow exposures—for instance, hedges of uncontracted future transactions and floating-rate assets or floating-rate liabilities. In these cases, the gain or loss on the derivative should be reported to management in comprehensive income but outside of earnings. The gain or loss would be recycled to the account, which essentially means it would be transferred from other comprehensive income into profit and loss.

This is an out-of-current-earnings classification. The same applies if the derivative is designated as a hedge of foreign currency exposure associated with a net investment in foreign assets. In this case, too, the gain or loss on the hedge should be reported

TABLE 6.1

Measuring Derivatives at Current Value and Reporting Gains and Losses

---

Out-of-Current Earnings

- Hedges of cash flow exposure from uncontracted future transactions or floating-rate liabilities
- Hedges of foreign currency exposure associated to net investment in foreign currency

In-Current Earnings

- Hedges of *fair value exposure*, like hedges of assets, liabilities, firm commitments
- All trades other than the above three bulleted trades

---

in comprehensive income, but outside of earnings, where it would offset the transition loss or gain on the foreign assets.

In contrast, in-current-earnings accounting regards derivatives designated as hedges of fair value exposures—which means hedges of assets, liabilities, or firm commitments. The gain or loss on the derivative should be included in the profit and loss account. The offsetting loss or gain on the asset or liability must as well be recognized and included in earnings.

The knowledgeable reader will appreciate that the suggested approach to management accounting for derivative instruments devices utilizes several concepts from the Statement of Recognized but Not Realized Gains and Losses (STRGL)—partly adopted from the rules of the U.S. GAAP. The basic principles are these:

- All derivatives should be recognized in the balance sheet as assets or liabilities and measured at current value.
- Whether realized or unrealized, gains and losses should be reported in a way conforming to management's stated reason for holding the instrument, in other terms to *management intent.*

In conclusion, the production of timely on-demand virtual balance sheets and virtual income statements requires both a first-class organization and high technology (Chapter 3). A few credit institutions have been leading in this domain, the described approach being also known as *process reengineering*. For instance, Deutsche Bank has created a department focusing on restructuring business processes.

Correctly implemented, a business reengineering process defines core businesses, establishes solid ways and means for valuing gains and losses, maps key processes into advanced information technology, and provides managers with split-second responses.

CAPITAL AT RISK AND LEVEL OF CONFIDENCE

Capital at risk (CAR) is the cushion against losses from credit risk as well as adverse events in interest rates, currency exchange rates, equity indexes, commodities, or other volatile assets to which the institution is exposed. As we will see in this section, this cushion should be computed at a level of confidence that corresponds to a chosen probability of the institution's solvency.

Capital at risk is *economic capital*. Its computation is based on individual risk calculations followed by risk aggregation, with CAR providing quantitative assurance that the entity will be able to face credit risk with market risk *if* worst comes to worst. While the financial literature examines many alternative and incompatible approaches to calculating CAR, to my judgment only one cuts new ground.

In his lecture at the First International Conference on Risk Management in the Banking Industry,[2] Dr. Werner Hermann of the Swiss National Bank explained how the concepts of accounting and capital at risk can be integrated into a single framework. As shown in Table 6.2, this integrative approach

- Displays all assets and liabilities at their fair value,
- But sustains the concept of prudence through confidence intervals implying different levels of capital as reserve.

This ingenious approach helps senior management in capital allocation for solvency reasons; it is not a supervisory directive. At least at present, there is no regulatory requirement in reporting capital at risk. Its calculation is an internal management accounting

---

[2] London, March 17–19, 1997.

TABLE 6.2

A Capital at Risk with Confidence Intervals for a Restructured Balance Sheet

Assets	100	Liabilities	50
		90% reserve	10
		90–99% reserve	10
		99–99.97% reserve	15
		Safe capital (>99.97%)	15
			100

challenge, and it should be seen as an integral part of a forward-looking governance. In essence, transparency in reporting (Chapter 5) is enriched with

- Accuracy and timeliness of financial information (as discussed in the first section of this chapter)
- An analytical approach to satisfying economic capital perspectives, using well-established statistical tools

Here is, in a nutshell, what the term *level of confidence* means. With the exception of destructive testing, statistical evidence is based in sampling. But any sampling plan is conditioned by an *operating characteristics (OC) curve*, which impacts on the assurance we can assign to the measurements we make. For instance, the risks embedded into the tests a loan office makes prior to granting credit are that of

- Rejecting a client of good credit quality
- Having to give a loan to a client of poor credit quality

This is also true of the results of a sampling of manufactured goods for inspection, not only a sampling of loans. The first risk is α, also known as a *Type I error*, or the *producer's risk*. That's the case of rejecting a good loan application. By expressing the likelihood of an unwanted but often unavoidable happening, α defines the kernel of *significance* in test results; hence the *confidence* that is attached to test results.

The challenge presented by the second bulleted point is β, also known as a *Type II error*, or the *consumer's risk*. (This β should not be confused with its other use, to indicate volatility.) In the case of loans, β is the likelihood of accepting a poor credit risk; in the case of manufacturing, it is the likelihood of accepting a lot of bad quality.

The reader should appreciate that α and β are risk indivisible from any statistical inference. One way of improving the operating characteristics of a test is to increase the size of the sample being tested, both in absolute terms and in the percent of the population from which it is derived. An alternative way of improving the operating characteristics is to improve the population's quality. Because the variance around the mean represents variability in the measurements that we make, high quality has a small standard deviation:

- High quality usually results in fairly uniform items, but not in clones.
- Low quality is characterized by significant differences among crucial dimensions of items, and their measurements.

Figure 6.1 presents two OC curves: *A* and *B*. As the reader will easily observe, α and β in *A* are smaller than those corresponding to *B*. The smaller is the α, the higher is the level of significance since it is equal to $1 - \alpha$.

Economic capital computed at $\alpha = 0.0003$ gives a level of confidence equal to 0.0097, which roughly corresponds to an AA credit rating by independent rating agencies. Over the last few years, the concept of α has been used extensively in connection with the distribution of risks. Its importance does not escape the market's attention. Correspondent banks, knowledgeable shareholders, and regulators are interested to know the probability distribution of capital at risk by

- Level of confidence
- Degrees of variance
- Existing correlations
- Simulations focused on future events under stress conditions[3]

---

[3] Dimitris N. Chorafas, *Stress Testing for Risk Control under Basel II*, Elsevier, Oxford and Boston, 2007.

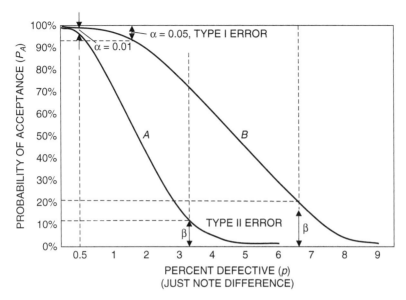

Figure 6.1 Operating characteristics curves for sampling plans

The emphasis on future events is crucial because even if we know today's capital adequacy of the company, the solvency requirements and their level of confidence change over time. Prognostication is important in providing lead time to react to stress conditions. Rigorous analysis helps in gaining a better appreciation of the probability distribution of capital adequacy, in conjunction to assumed risks. As it is to be expected:

- Finding the stochastic behavior of a complex portfolio of assets and liabilities is no easy task, and
- The difficulty is compounded by the problem that future transactions alter the portfolio's composition.

The notions underpinning α and β risks associated to a sampling plan and statistical testing are valid all over science, even if many traditional types of tests fail to account for the level of confidence associated to a testing procedure and statistical inference. Another shortcoming is the failure to account for the very significant effect on exposure by *correlation coefficients*. Their impact on the results of testing is very often terribly underestimated.[4]

------

[4] Dimitris N. Chorafas, "After Basel II: Assuring Compliance and Smoothing the Rough Edges," Lafferty/VRL Publications, London, 2005.

- The mean, standard deviation, skewness, and kurtosis are interesting statistics, but they give only half a message.
- The other half is provided by the correlation, covariance, and level of confidence associated with reported statistics.

In Figure 6.2, the expected value of the correlation coefficient is never negative. But at the 95 percent level of confidence, which corresponds to $\alpha = 0.05$, the two key variables of the model correlate also negatively. This happens practically all the time at the 99.9 level of confidence interval. When senior management decisions on capital at risk account for negative correlation, the quality of governance is significantly improved. While negative correlations may be low frequency, when they happen, they can turn risk management plans on their head.

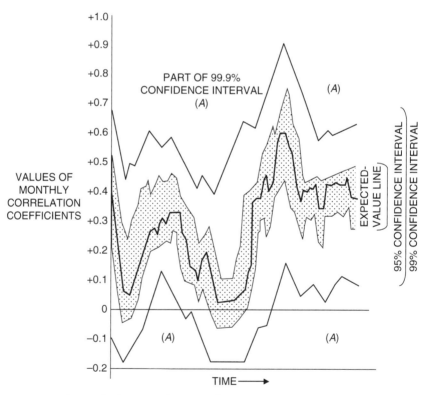

Figure 6.2 A graph showing how confidence intervals of correlation coefficients improve the accuracy of a financial risk model

By using correlation and levels of confidence, we relieve a good deal of uncertainty regarding the fitness of economic capital in regard to prevailing exposure. Supervisors are increasingly using confidence intervals to determine if a bank has a well-tuned risk management function that is able to assist the board and senior executives to take charge in managing exposure.

Therefore, confidence intervals associated with the computation of risk capital are destined to play a significant role both in regulatory reporting and in the institution's management accounting (as discussed in the preceding section). Because it affects the required amount of capital, a higher confidence interval is also a stress test, providing management with assurance on the population of risk events covered by the results.

QUANTITATIVE IMPACT STUDIES, AND SECOND THOUGHTS ABOUT CAPITAL ADEQUACY

As with any new system, the output of models associated with the advanced internal-rating-based (IRB) methods of Basel II had to be tested. This was done under regulatory supervision by means of quantitative impact studies (QISs). The first four—QIS 1.0, QIS 2.0, QIS 2.5, and QIS 3.0—provided input for rethinking the models and procedures. By contrast, QIS 4.0 and QIS 5.0 have been Basel II's (specifically, IRB) output tests.

The results of QIS 4.0 and QIS 5.0 can in no way be described as successful as far as the banks' capital adequacy and stability of the financial system are concerned. Following QIS 4.0, American regulators took a second look at Basel II and its aftereffect on the credit institutions' capital adequacy. Their analysis showed that QIS 4.0 has resulted in

- Material reductions in minimum capital requirements for banks
- Significant dispersion of results across institutions as well as portfolio types

It needs no explaining that both results are very negative references as far as the new Capital Adequacy Framework is concerned. Either the model *and* the method are inadequate, respectively, in a mathematical and procedural sense, or many of the banks participating in QIS 4.0 have been gaming the system. Therefore, as could reasonably be expected, U.S. regulators have insisted that further analysis is necessary to define whether QIS 4.0 results reflect one or more of the following:

- Differences in risk among banks
- Limitations of the method
- Uneven data availability
- Variations in stages of bank implementation
- Needs for adjusting the Basel II framework

Additionally, the Office of the Comptroller of the Currency (OCC), the Federal Deposit Insurance Corporation (FIDC), the Office of Thrift Supervision (OTS), and the Federal Reserve expressed doubt over the merits of Basel II *if* the new capital rules apply to only the 10 biggest U.S. banks while all other American banks are spared these compliance burdens. (It was therefore decided by the regulators that other banks in the United States will follow Basel 1A, an approach that fits somewhere between Basel I and Basel II.)

Given this need for deeper examination of Basel II methods, models, and rules prior to further experimentation, American regulators and commercial banks did not participate in the Quantitative Impact Study 5.0. Conducted by the Basel Committee on Banking Supervision, this study took place in 2005 and 2006 with credit institutions from 31 countries, including G-10 countries (except the United States where the Federal Reserve and other U.S. regulators are conducting, and will continue to conduct, their own Basel II tests) and 19 non-G-10 countries. In connection to QIS 5.0, the Basel Committee received data from

- 56 Group 1 banks in the G-10 countries
- 146 Group 2 banks in G-10 countries
- 155 banks from other non-G-10 countries

Beginning with QIS 3.0, Group 1 banks are defined as being those fulfilling all of the following criteria: Tier 1 capital of more than €3 billion ($4 billion), diversification of assets, and international banking activities. Limited data from the U.S. QIS 4.0 exercise, representing an additional 26 institutions, were also partly included. For participating G-10 and non-G-10 banks, the QIS 5.0 workbooks reflected changes that over time affected the Basel II framework—in particular, the

- Treatment of reserves
- 1.06 scaling factor applied to credit risk–weighted assets
- Recognition of double default (wrong-way risk)
- Revised trading book rules for credit institutions
- Move to an unexpected losses-only basis for computing risk-weighted assets (more on this later)

For the above-mentioned reasons, a comparison of the results from QIS 5.0 and previous quantitative impact studies is unwise. Scientifically speaking, a major flaw lies in the fact that the successive QIS tests have not observed the rules of experimental design but instead took place as more or less independent (if sequential) events, in order to help in tuning up the mathematics of capital adequacy requirements.

The second weakness is that macroeconomic and credit conditions prevailing in most G-10 countries at the time of QIS 5.0 and QIS 4.0 were more benign than during QIS 3.0 and previous tests, with an evident impact on needed capital. During QIS 5.0, a low volatility had also had a significant impact on the downsizing of capital requirements while its effects were not algorithmically compensated, as it should have been the case.

All in all, it has been *as if* central bankers who participated in QIS 5.0 wanted commercial banks to significantly reduce their capital adequacy, which of course is irrational. Abstaining from volatility has also been unwise because as everybody in the banking industry is expected to know, it does not take much for volatility to rise. For instance, according to Goldman Sachs, the February 27, 2007, jump in the volatility index (VIX) has been

8 standard deviations from the mean

Poor planning and (probably) little appreciation of levels of significance (as described in the preceding section) saw to it that all quantitative impact studies from QIS 1.0 to QIS 5.0 tested only the mean value of capital adequacy. Conveniently (and irrationally), they forgot to test for standard deviations from the mean, which dramatically changes the banks' capital requirements.

Using only mean values has the nasty habit of bringing to bankruptcy institutions that are weakly capitalized, and after they take big risks, they have to run for cover. The late 2006 move in energy prices that caused the collapse of Amaranth—the hedge fund that bet on gas prices—was

A 9 standard deviation VIX event

Neither is there the excuse that the above events happened after QIS 5.0 and therefore could not be integrated into the testing plan. Way prior to it, indeed prior to the establishment of the VIX, in October 1987 the NYSE stock market crash was

A 14.5 standard deviation event

Why was this not taken into account in the Basel II methodology? its models? and the way the quantitative impact studies were done? Lapses, conflicts of interest, or lack of experience in the way scientifically valid tests should be done?

To my book, the inadequate choice of correlation coefficients has also played a role in the weak results because a great deal of difference in capital requirements is created precisely by the choice of correlations. The lower is the correlation coefficient, the lower the resulting capital needs; and with this the door is wide open for gaming the system.

BASEL II'S UNEXPECTED HEADWINDS

Basel II's latest (and most inherent) version has been criticized in many quarters for its mixing of expected and unexpected losses and its uncertainty about capital for operational risk. "Minor work of major artists or major work of minor artists," said one of the critics, while another one commented that the post-QIS 5.0 revisions are not good enough for a system aiming to bring finance into the twenty-first century.

Several negative opinions reflected the fact that in the aftermath of QIS 5.0, in which neither U.S. regulators nor U.S. commercial banks participated, by changing the rules the Basel Committee lowered the defenses against systemic risk. While till then the results of the IRB methods represented capital adequacy needs for credit risk—and to this had to be added 12.5 percent (originally 20 percent) for operational risk—in one stroke credit risk and operational risk were merged and allocated minimalist figures, thereby raising eyebrows in regard to "capital adequacy."

In the aftermath of QIS 5.0, the Big Banks were to reduce their capital adequacy by 7.1 percent, 26.7 percent, and 29.0 percent, depending on their classification (see the preceding section). As if this was not enough, while the IRB and standard Basel II methods were designed to address *expected losses* (EL), the new minimalist numbers will be all inclusive for all sorts of losses, covering as well *unexpected losses* (UL) and *extreme events*—a disservice to the very notion of regulatory capital. As Figure 6.3 shows, unexpected losses find themselves at the queue of the loss distribution, and include a great deal of spikes.

One lesson learned from risk control in engineering, which modern finance aims to emulate, is that understanding physical systems well enough is fundamental to predicting and controlling their behavior. Figure 6.4 helps to illustrate the default frequency's statistical behavior by bringing once more to the reader's attention the difference between an average and a 90 percent level of confidence.

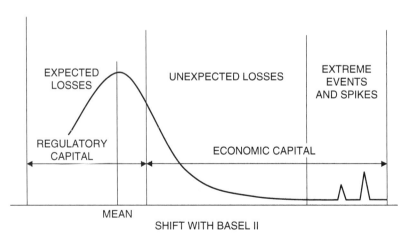

Figure 6.3 In the extreme aftermath of QIS 5.0, the Russian salad of expected losses, unexpected losses, and extreme events and spikes

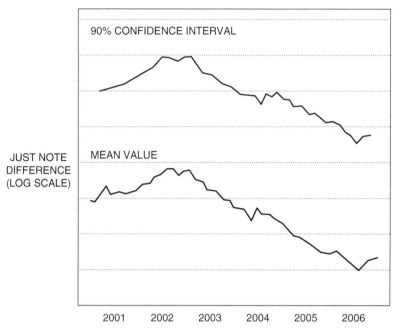

Figure 6.4 Expected default frequency of quoted European enterprises
Source: Statistics by Deustche Bundesbank.

A bird's-eye view suggests that while in the 2001 to 2006 time frame the mean value of the expected default frequency of quoted European firms has decreased quite significantly, there has always been an important gap between the average and the trendline of the 90 percent confidence interval. The shape of the practically unaltered default distribution is better understood by noticing that

- The 90 percent confidence interval is expressed by the mean plus 1.65 standard deviations.
- The gap in Figure 6.4 becomes huge if instead of 90 percent (which leaves 10 percent of all cases out of control), we use the 99.9 percent or 99.97 percent confidence interval.

Table 6.3 presents a numerical example taking as the reference nonperforming loans. In a baseline scenario of a 90 percent confidence level, the 1.80 percent mean value of nonperforming loans increases to 2.70 percent, but it rises to 4.03 percent at the 99.97 percentile (statistics are from a project on nonperforming

T A B L E 6.3

Nonperforming Loans in the Banking Book; Baseline Scenario and Stress Test

| | Percentiles | | | | | |
	50%	90%	99%	99.9%	99.97%	Standard Deviation
Baseline	1.80*	2.70	3.25	3.53	4.03	0.545
Stress test @	3.00	6.00	7.73	8.64	10.23	1.820
Stress test @	5.00	13.11	17.88	20.35	24.81	4.954
Stress test @	11.60	27.44	36.56	41.35	50.00	9.600
	$\bar{x}$	$\bar{x} + 1.65s$	$\bar{x} + 2.6s$	$\bar{x} + 3.1s$	$\bar{x} + 4.0s$	

*Percent of nonperforming loans.

loans in the European financing environment). As Table 6.3 shows, the aforementioned reference numbers zoom under stress testing conditions.

The subprimes crisis of July–August 2007 and subsequent months is an outlier of the third stress test in Table 6.3.

The Basel Committee says that stress tests have now become the province of national regulators under Pillar 2. This, however, should not mean that global QIS and other experimental findings must be deprived of stress tests. *If* this were the case, *then* Basel tests would end by being half-baked because a method that fails to use confidence intervals is a very weak one, indeed—and it cannot be trusted in decision making.

Let me put it in another way. When systems are simple, simple equations and elementary approaches can produce results that are more or less acceptable. But with complex systems like Basel II, we need to stress test and carefully consider different levels of confidence. We have to incorporate stress tests, no matter who has the final responsibility for their execution. Short of this, we don't know what we are doing.

All this means that in its current status as a method, Basel II is incomplete, characterized by both *methodology risk* and *model risk*. Concomitant to the shortcomings is a question of *data quality*. While national supervisors reported that data survey quality has significantly improved since the previous QIS, the Basel Committee thinks that there still exist two important issues:

- Implementation of economic downturn loss-given-default (LGD) estimates
- Issues relating to trading book positions, a subject always in need for further improvement[5]

This is an additional reason why I do not consider the outcome of the QIS 5.0 test conclusive, but only an interim, poorly executed exercise. The Basel Committee's Madrid meeting of late 2003 dropped the expected losses (EL) formula and converted it to one for unexpected losses (UL) because of the argument made by commercial banks that they keep the credit risk provision for EL. Subsequently, in 2006 the published results of QIS 5.0

- Made the reference that this particular test regarded the UL,
- But this exercise was done without the benefit of testing the long leg of the credit risk distribution and its spikes.

Looking back to Basel's discussion document of 1999, the ingenuity of Basel II's original version rested on differentiating between expected losses whose distribution was nearly normal and unexpected losses due to low-frequency–high-impact events. This was a brilliant idea that, without any reason or explanation, was abandoned in 2006.

The very weak and unreliable results of QIS 5.0 should be interpreted with these facts in mind. They are unreliable because they show that the minimum required capital under Basel II in G-10 countries would *decrease* relative to the Capital Accord of Basel I. For Group 1 banks, for instance, the minimum required capital under the most likely approaches to credit risk *and* operational risk would, on average, decrease by 6.8 percent. In financial stability terms, that's a big and dangerous drop in financial staying power.

The 9.6 percent in capital adequacy for credit risk *and* operational risk for international banks under Basel I shrinks to 6.8 percent under Basel II. Since only half of it is Tier 1 capital, this drop is tantamount to opening Pandora's box in exposure to adversity,

---

[5] Basel Committee on Banking Supervision, "Results of the Fifth Quantitative Impact Study (QIS 5)," Bank for International Settlements (BIS), Basel, Switzerland, June 16, 2006.

preparing for major bank failures and for taxpayers' money to salvage overleveraged and overexposed credit institutions.

THE EFFECT OF LEVERAGING ON CAPITAL ADEQUACY

Instead of fusing (and confusing) expected and unexpected losses, a sound regulatory plan for assessing the capital adequacy of globally operating institutions, evaluators should definitely consider the effect of leveraging, as well as the likelihood of chain events. This latter issue goes well beyond the now classical stress testing.

On May 7, 1998, Dr. Alan Greenspan admitted in a lecture that with leveraging, there will always exist a possibility, however remote, of a chain reaction—a cascading sequence of defaults that will culminate in financial implosion if it proceeds unchecked. Only a central bank, the then chairman of the Federal Reserve suggested, with its unlimited power to create money, can with a high probability thwart such a process before it becomes destructive.

This statement was wrong. The government as well as the central bank have no money of their own. The money the government obtains is taken from its citizens and from the companies in its jurisdiction. This is done in two ways:

- Through taxation
- By means of inflation, the worst taxation of them all

A small part of that government money is available to the central bank, if one abstracts the possibility that the monetary institution "prints" lots of money—which means inflation.

Greenspan suggested that, presumably with the government's agreement, the central bank can print all the money it needs. That's true. "What creates inflation?" Arthur Burns, the former chairman of the Federal Reserve, asked his students at Columbia University—and he answered his own question by saying, "Government deficits create inflation."

> *If* systemic risk is to be controlled, and the large majority of people agree that it should,
>
> *Then* the financial players themselves should provide the capital for the system's salvage, and the central bank must not have to intervene except in an extreme case.

Under normal conditions the money a central bank has at a moment's notice is a small fraction of the huge amount that will be necessary to stem the tide if the checks and balances of the banking sector's capital adequacy are no longer able to hold huge exposures in loans, derivatives, and other risks. Experts say that, day in and day out, the money the Fed has available is between $250 million and $300 million. What is this amount compared to the trillions and quadrillions of derivatives (Chapter 5)?

This issue evidently goes well beyond capital adequacy for credit risk and operational risk, which was the theme of the preceding section, because it brings into perspective one of the big motors propelling market risk. In the general case, today

- Derivatives exposure is underestimated by more than an order of magnitude.
- Some institutions, like hedge funds, don't even have the minimal obligation regarding capital adequacy for the risks they are assuming.

Cool heads see the perils. In a 1994 survey, the Group of Thirty (G-30) found that 96 percent of dealers and 99 percent of end users who participated in this project believed they should measure both *actual* and *potential* exposures due to derivatives. Furthermore, 87 percent of dealers surveyed had established or planned to establish in the near term credit limits reflecting the sum of current and potential exposures.[6] Not all of these plans materialized.

In January 1995, in the wake of the $2 billion loss and bankruptcy filing by Orange County, California, Alfonse M. D'Amato, then Senate Banking Committee chairman, called for a hearing to look into the use of derivative investments by municipal and corporate investors. In his testimony to the Senate, Greenspan said that derivatives are a bit like electricity: dangerous if mishandled but bearing the potential to do tremendous good.

It is indeed a sad irony that the Orange County's managers have learned nothing from this 1994 debacle. On December 5, 2007,

---

[6] Global Derivatives Study Group, *Derivatives: Practices and Principles, Appendix III, Follow-up Surveys of Industry Practice*, Group of Thirty, Washington, D.C., 1994.

it was announced that out of its $2.3 billion fund, Orange County had $860 million in subprimes—or 37.4 percent—and of this it lost $460 million, which amounts to 53.5 percent of its subprimes exposure.

The reaction of several economists has been that derivatives could be used for good reasons *if* the primary aims were hedging and *if* inordinate risks were kept under lock and key. The questions, however, were and still are these:

- Which risk is inordinate?
- How can a potentially limitless exposure be kept under control?

Focused legislation and regulation are the answers, but new derivatives legislation is by no means an easy issue nor one rapidly done. Banking industry lobbying against such a bill is a steady problem, and another deterrent is the sheer complexity of the subject. As a derivatives dealer said in a meeting: "You can't pass a law that prevents people from taking the wrong risks." In my opinion, to avoid taking the wrong risks, investors should never deal in derivatives unless they understand

- The nature of the contract they are entering into, and
- The projection of exposure they are assuming, not just today but all the way until it matures.

Investors also should be satisfied that the contract is suitable for them in light of their circumstances and financial position. While different derivative products involve different levels of risk altogether, a study done by the London-based Center for the Study of Financial Innovation (CSFI) in October 2003 found that, in that particular year, complex financial instruments, like credit derivatives, came at the No. 1 position in the list of instruments it calls "Top Banana Skins."

"I do not for one moment wish to suggest that you have got it all wrong. What I do ask is, are you quite sure you have got it all right?" said R. Farrant, then deputy head of banking supervision, Bank of England, in March 1992, in an address to participants at the International Swaps and Derivatives Association (ISDA) conference.

THE ORIGIN OF LEGISLATION
FOR MARKING-TO-MARKET

One of the early events of legislators' preoccupation with the management of derivatives exposure was the October 1, 1997, hearing by the U.S. House Banking Committee Subcommittee on Capital Markets, Securities, and Government-Sponsored Enterprises. The focal point was the then proposed new rules formulated by the Financial Accounting Standards Board (FASB). Effective January 1, 1999, these rules required that all publicly traded corporations and banks report their derivatives holdings on their balance sheets at fair market value (see Chapter 2).

The then FASB chairman, Edmund Jenkins, testified that the primary preoccupation was to put into effect rules that would require all corporations, whether financial or industrial, to report their derivatives holdings on their balance sheet by marking them to their current market price. As Jenkins put it: "If ever a case can be made for reporting something in more detail, it is for derivatives" because

- "Different companies may report very similar activities differently, and
- "Even an individual company may report similar activities differently. . . ."[7]

The U.S. House hearings exposed the fact that several companies had adopted the curious way of reporting derivatives *losses* as *increases* in the valuation of their assets. Backing this statement was the reference that until the late 1990s, gains and losses on derivatives were not explicitly disclosed, and their effect on earnings was difficult, if not impossible, for an investor or creditor to determine. Yet the public had the right to know the companies' financials.

Edmund Jenkins also pointed out that "gains and losses on derivatives that qualify for *hedge accounting* should have little or no effect on a company's earnings because they will be offset by comparable losses or gains on the thing that is being hedged—and the result is little or no volatility in earnings." By contrast, if the hedge is not matched by, and does not move in the opposite direction

---

[7] News item, *Executive International Report* (EIR), October 17, 1997.

from, the underlying instrument, then "maybe the hedge operation was not an effective hedge" (see also Chapter 4).

Testifying at the same hearing, Arthur Levitt, then chairman of the Securities and Exchange Commission, said that the SEC will enforce the FASB accounting rules for the 15,000 American companies that were public. He also warned that the FASB must remain independent and that he was there to shield it from political pressure: "It is very inappropriate for the Congress to suggest any further delays. I believe that we would be playing Russian roulette with our markets."[8]

Just a day prior to these hearings, on September 30, 1997, the *Wall Street Journal* reported that during the third quarter of that year, Salomon Brothers, the investment bank, had lost at least $200 million in derivatives. On Wall Street it was said that the actual money lost could be much higher, even if Salomon was not one of the top eight U.S. financial institutions active in derivatives.

Some other facts pertinent to that time frame, which by now have been magnified, help in appreciating the environment of derivatives deals and the need for rigorous financial reporting. Banks tend to allocate about two-thirds of their credit line toward counterparties, to off-balance-sheet operations, and there is a concentration in OTC derivatives trading:

- In notional principal amount, each of the 30 largest banks in the world has trillions in derivatives exposure.
- About 50 percent or more of derivatives trades made by banks are made with corresponding banks, not with corporations or other clients.

It has been already brought to the reader's attention that *concentration* is a most significant risk. In its January 2003 monthly report, the Deutsche Bundesbank noted that fewer than 10 percent of OTC derivatives are handled outside the financial sector, and over half of the OTC transactions in interest rate derivatives take place among 60 banks, 7 of them in Germany.

Apart the galloping exposure created by overconcentration of toxic waste due to derivatives, there is a potential for Ponzi schemes

---

[8] Ibid.

(Chapter 5). "In recent years some large-scale frauds, and near frauds, have been facilitated by derivatives," said Warren Buffett in 2003 in the *Fortune* article "Avoiding a Megacatastrophe." "We view them [derivatives] as time bombs, both for

- "The parties dealing in them, and
- "The economic system."[9]

Buffett pointed out that "derivatives contracts are of varying duration, running sometimes to 20 or more years. Their value is often tied to several variables, and their ultimate value also depends on the creditworthiness of the counterparties to them."

"True, there are methods by which the risk can be laid off with others," Buffett suggested. "But most strategies of that kind leave you with residual liabilities . . . [while] derivatives generate earnings which are to a significant extent widely overstated. They are based on estimates whose inaccuracy may not be exposed for many years."

In Buffett's opinion, errors will be usually honest, but the parties to derivatives also have enormous incentives to cheat in accounting for them. There are as well correlations because derivatives create what he called "daisy chain risk, and pile-on effect."

The pile-on occurs because many contracts require that a company suffering a credit downgrade immediately supply collateral to counterparties. Yet, while they have a significant impact on exposure, pile-ons and daisy chains are not included in the models typically written to handle derivatives risk.

These comments saw to it that "Avoiding a Megacatastrophe" created intense discussions in the financial industry. In the course of one of our meetings, the director of asset management of one of the largest global investment banks commented that Buffett "is right in some respects. Unless you are aware of pitfalls you can fall into crevasse."

"The greatest risk," this expert said, "lies in the fact that investors are unaware of implications, rather than in the instruments per se." This is precisely the thesis this book supports.

---

[9] Warren Buffett, "Avoiding a Megacatastrophe," *Fortune*, March 12, 2003.

PART THREE

Options

CHAPTER 7

The Use of Options

THE STRATEGIC USE OF OPTIONS

Chapter 2 briefly defined an option as a contractual agreement between two parties, a buyer and a writer (seller). For the "right to choose" that this contract conveys to him or her, the buyer pays the seller a one-time fee, or *premium*, that also serves as the payment securing the buyer's claim to the contract. There are no margin payments, and the premium paid for the option is the maximum loss to the option holder. Other characteristics include the following:

- The price at which the option can be exercised is the *strike price.*
- The day on which an option can be exercised, or *offset*, is known as its *expiration date.*
- The *premium* is the means by which the buyer compensates the writer for his or her willingness to grant the option and assume the associated risk.

For instance, an option on a given property gives the buyer the right, but not the obligation, to purchase that property at a stipulated price during a stated period of time. If the buyer decides to exercise his or her option, the seller is obliged to turn over the property at the agreed-upon price. However, unless an option is exercised, it expires worthless after the stated time period.

- An option is *exercised* at the sole discretion of its buyer, who will tend to exercise only when it is in his or her interest to do so.

- If an option has not been exercised prior to its expiration, it ceases to exist, and the option holder no longer has any rights, and the option seller no longer has any obligation associated to that contract.

What an option is worth is calculated by a *recursive pricing methodology* (Chapter 8) that considers *intrinsic value* and *time value* (discussed further in the following section). The latter is a function of the time remaining to the option's expiration date.

In principle, the writer of an option has unlimited risk, but this exposure could be hedged. For instance, a financial institution that writes currency options for its customers could use options on currency futures to make a profit on its trading, provided the price it pays in the market to buy options on futures is less than the premium it receives for writing options.

- A *credit spread* is a spread in which the value of an option sold exceeds the value of an option bought.
- A *debit* spread is the inverse case.

Most options are written using standardized terms like the nature and amount of underlying interest, style of the option, expiration date, exercise price, whether the option is a call or a put (more on this later), and whether the option is a physical delivery option or a cash-settled option, as well as whether the option has automatic exercise provisions, adjustment provisions, and so on.

Ordinary options typically have a longer life cycle than *exotic options* (see "Complex Options" later in the chapter) that are often custom-made and have a life cycle that depends on client needs. Usually, though not necessarily always, the more custom-made features it has and more unusual the instrument is, the shorter will tend to be its life cycle.

A simple kind of option is one that gives the right to buy or sell a share of common stock: other things being equal, the higher the price of the stock, the greater will be the value of the option. *If* the stock price is higher than the strike price of the option, *then* it is almost certain to be exercised. When the stock price is lower than the strike price of the option, its holder will forgo his or her right to exercise it, and at the same time he or she will forgo the premium paid to the writer.

As the careful reader will recall from Chapter 2, a *call* option gives the holder the right—but not the obligation—to enter a *long* futures position at a specific price. A *put* option gives the holder the right to enter a *short* futures position, while the writer will be obliged to enter a *long* futures position should the option be exercised.

There are two different kinds of delivery:

- Cash settled
- Physical

A *physical delivery option* gives its holder the right to receive physical delivery (if it is a call) or to make physical delivery (if it is a put) of the underlying interest when the option is exercised. A *cash-settled option* gives its owner the right to receive a cash payment based on the difference between

- A determined value of the underlying interest at the time the option is exercised, and
- The fixed exercise price of the option.

The cash settlement being received is known as the *exercise settlement value*. For instance, a cash-settled put conveys the right to receive a cash payment if the exercise settlement value is less than the exercise price of the option.

A call option may be long or short. A *long call* reflects a bullish opinion, and it is taken when a market is expected to rise. The buyer pays a premium in exchange for receipt of potential upside in the market. A *short call* is essentially a bearish position taken when a market is expected to fall.

- The word *long* refers to a person's position as the holder of an option.
- The word *short* refers to a person's position as the writer of an option.

A *long put* corresponds to a bearish position taken when a market is expected to fall; a *short put* reflects bullish investor sentiment, and it is entered into when a market is expected to rise. These four positions are known as *directional strategies*; each has potential upside and potential downside in the market.

In a way, an investor's strategy reflects the notions connected to these terms. Andrew Carnegie, the nineteenth century's king of steel, provides an excellent example on smart use of options for strategic purposes. To purchase property and construct his new home on Ninety-First Street, New York City, he hired a broker to quietly buy options on all the ploys on the Fifth Avenue block between Ninetieth and Ninety-First Streets insisting that the expiration date for each be set for the same day.

On that day, Carnegie emerged from the shadows and bought them all, catching the various owners by surprise. His Scottish-Georgian mansion cost $1.5 million to build, not much more than the option money won from Frick, Phipps, and Moore in 1900, when the firm bet on a leveraged buyout for Carnegie Steel—and failed. Options may indeed be ingredients of low-cost strategies for people and corporations.

INTRINSIC VALUE AND TIME VALUE

Theoretically, the price buyers and sellers of options are willing to accept at a particular time is influenced by two primary factors: intrinsic value and time value of the option. Practically, like any other commodity, apart from these two factors, options are subject to the law of supply and demand:

- When demand is low and there is plenty of supply, prices go down.
- When demand is high and writers are risk averse, prices go up.

Intrinsic is the value of the option if it were to expire immediately. Essentially, this is the amount the futures price is higher than a call's exercise price or lower than a put's exercise price. For a call option, the *intrinsic value* is the amount of premium by which the futures price is above the option's strike price. For instance, at a time when the current market price of Microsoft equity is $28 a share, a Microsoft put at $32 would have an *intrinsic value* of $4 a share.

- An option that has an intrinsic value is said to be *in-the-money*.

- The option is *at-the-money* if the futures price is the same as the strike price.
- If the futures price is below the strike price, it is *out-of-the-money*.

Some investors buy out-of-the-money options in the expectation the market will turn around. These are contracts with a low purchase price because what is acquired is the right to buy or sell at a price removed, or even far removed, from actual market values. However, if the market swings in a favorable direction, the profits can be quite important (Chapter 8).

A call option that is at-the-money or out-of-the-money has no intrinsic value. By contrast, a put option has intrinsic value if the current future price is below the option's strike price—a statement reflecting the condition of a buyer's option.

Extrinsic value of an option is its current price less its intrinsic value. Extrinsic value is also called *time value* because the time remaining for the option to make a move is key to its worth. Time value is a risk premium demanded by the option writer, and it depends on

- The relationship of the futures price to the exercise price,
- The volatility of the futures price, and
- The amount of time remaining until expiration.

A definition easy to remember is that the extrinsic value of an option is the amount of its value that is not in-the-money. By contrast, the intrinsic value is the amount an option is in-the-money. Intrinsic values are determined by the underlying market. Extrinsic values are determined by the options market. Notice that the two are loosely coupled: when one changes, the other may or may not change.

If the market price of Microsoft stock is still $28 a share, a call at $28 may have a current market price of, say, $1 a share. This is entirely *time value* (see also Chapter 8). An option with intrinsic value may often have some time value as well, which means the market price of the option may be greater than its intrinsic value. This could occur with an option of any style (see the following section).

One way of looking at time value is as the portion of an option's premium in excess of its intrinsic value. The amount of time value in a premium depends to a large extent on how much time is left until the option expires: the longer is that time, the greater the time value will be. Time value is a *wasting asset*, which is why

> Many options traders prefer to sell calls and puts rather than to buy them. But astute investors can make time work in a way that will be favorable to them.

One example of using derivatives in the over-the-counter market is that of *long-dated options*. If an investor has a portfolio of American convertible bonds that were issued in the mid-1980s and are deep out-of-the-money, the portfolio is behaving as if it were a portfolio of bonds. If the investor's view is that the equity market is cheap compared to bonds but he or she does not want to sell the convertibles, he or she could

- Write long-dated interest rate swaptions (Chapter 13), and
- Use the proceeds to invest in equity warrants.

Warrants are options in securitized form that can be traded on exchange or OTC. Over-the-counter options are neither securitized nor traded on exchange. They are agreed directly off exchange between the writer and buyer.

The use of long-dated options is a process of transferring long-term exposures with the effect of converting interest rate exposure to equity market exposure without altering the underlying assets. Basically, it is a means for optimization of portfolio value by swapping different types of exposures.

Optimization capitalizes on the fact that, as stated in the introductory paragraphs, a major factor that moves prices is supply and demand. When a market starts to move or heat up, traders are more uncertain about what might happen. Because of this, options become more valuable and their prices go north. As option prices change, their extrinsic value increases.

Implied volatility is a measure of the extrinsic value of an option price. In addition to the close relationship between option prices and implied volatility for a given underlying price, a one-to-one relationship exists between option prices and extrinsic values for a given underlying price.

An interesting issue is a bank's or investor's exposure to credit risk associated with counterparty nonperformance. Options written involve no credit risk because of nonperformance of counterparties in fulfilling their contractual obligations. The opposite is true of options bought.

STYLES OF OPTIONS: AMERICAN, EUROPEAN, ASIAN, AND OTHERS

The term *style of an option* refers to the way in which it is exercisable. There are five different styles of options: American, European, Bermuda, Asian, and capped:

- An *American option* may be exercised by the holder at any time on or prior to its expiration.
- A *European option* may be exercised only during a specified period before the option expires—typically on its expiration date.
- The style of a *Bermuda option* is between the American and European.

This distinction refers to when an option is exercisable, and it has nothing to do with the geographic location of the markets in which the options are traded. Since European-style options may be exercised only during a limited period before expiration, other things being equal, their cost is lower.

From the viewpoint of the holder of a European-style option, the limited period in which to exercise it means that the only way of recovering its value prior to maturity is by selling it, at its then market price, in the secondary market. During the time when a European-style option cannot be exercised, it has no intrinsic value and its market price depends only on the likelihood that the option may ultimately be exercisable at a profit.

- For *Asian-style options*, an average value is derived from the market value of the underlying over a specified time period.

This average is used to fix the underlying's value for an *average rate option* and for calculating the strike price for an *average strike option*. Such averages may be arithmetic or geometric. Notice that the calculation of such average values for the underlying may result in the value of the option on expiration date being considerably lower for the buyer and considerably higher for the writer than the difference between

- The strike price, and
- The current market value on expiration date.

For an average strike call option, the average strike price can be higher than the price originally agreed, while for an equivalent put option the strike price can be lower than that originally agreed. In short, the pricing of Asian-style options may involve different surprises.

- A *capped option* will be automatically exercised prior to expiration if the market on which it is trading determines that the value of the underlying interest at a specified time on a trading day "hits the cap price" for the option.

Capped options may also be exercised, like European-style options, during a specified period before expiration. However, if a secondary market is not available during this time, it will not be possible for the holder to realize his or her profits.

Unlike a conventional option, a *binary option* is a derivative instrument providing the holder with a discontinuous payoff depending on the position of the underlying price in relation to the strike price. These options are used by entities that require building blocks of other instruments like day-count notes and accrual notes. The payoff for the in-the-money binary puts and calls is a preestablished amount unrelated to the specific value of the derivative. Two binary options examples are

- Cash-or-nothings
- All-or-nothings

Because of the binary nature of the payoff, these instruments are relatively straightforward to analyze in credit risk terms. The buyer of a long cash- or all-or-nothing option expects to receive a fixed amount from the seller as the strike is reached. Therefore, he or she faces credit risk exposure to the seller, while having paid up front a rather substantial premium.

A *contingent premium option*, also known as a *cash-on-delivery* or a *pay-later option*, allows the buyer to defer payment of premium to the writer if and until the option moves in-the-money (see the preceding section). If it remains out-of-the-money over the life of the transaction, the buyer makes no premium payment to the seller. However, if it moves in-the-money at expiration, the buyer is obliged to exercise the option and pay the writer a premium, regardless of the intrinsic value of the option at that time.

Stated otherwise, buyers of a contingent option must pay the premium only if the market value of the underlying reaches or exceeds the strike price during the life of the option in the case of American-style options or on expiration date in the case of European-style options. However, the holder will have to pay the entire premium even if the option is only just at-the-money or just in-the-money.

Options on options are *compound instruments* that allow the holder to buy or sell an underlying option. A compound option gives the buyer the right, but not the obligation, to buy or sell an underlying put or a call. To gain that advantage, he or she pays the writer an initial premium payment on the trade date. If the original option is in-the-money at expiration, the buyer can exercise into the underlying option, settling the additional premium at that time. If the original option is out-of-the-money, he or she simply lets it expire. Examples are

- European on European
- European on American
- Call on a call
- Call on a put
- Put on a call
- Put on a put

As these examples suggest, compound options have an option as their underlying. They also have an especially large leverage effect, which means that the writer can be faced with big obligations. In contrast, the buyer buying an option on an option locks in a certain level of protection without committing to a transaction he or she may not actually require. It also makes it possible to save on premium payments for a contingent event that might not occur.

Cliquet (or *ratchet*) *options* are memory independent permitting an investor to lock in profits at fixed points in time. *Shout options* are similar to ratchet options, with the choice of optimal versus nonoptimal exercise. *Barrier options* are memory dependent. They become activated or extinguished when an underlying price crosses a barrier. The four main barrier categories include the following:

- *Up-and-out option*, whereby an option is canceled (out) if the underlying price rises above a certain barrier (up)
- *Down-and-out option*, whereby an option is canceled if the underlying price falls below a specified barrier (down)
- *Up-and-in option*, with an option created (in) if the underlying price rises above a certain barrier (up)
- *Down-and-in option*, whereby again an option is created if the underlying price falls below a certain barrier (down)

Puts and calls are available within each of the four categories, providing for different barrier combinations. Exercise rights for *knock-in barrier options* arise only if the market value of the underlying reaches a fixed threshold (*barrier*) within a specified period. Exercise rights for *knock-out barrier options* expire if the market value of the underlying reaches the specified barrier during the given time period.

Double-barrier options are extinguished if the underlying does not stay within a collar defined by the knock-in and knock-out barrier options. *Partial barriers* are hedged barrier options. As a derivative instrument, a barrier option either creates or extinguishes an underlying European option when a market price reaches a predetermined level (the barrier).

Moreover, there exist multiple barrier options that, as the name suggests, contain more than a single knock-in or knock-out option. *Multiple-barrier packages* are those which feature knock-ins or knock-outs around the strike price and have become quite common. More complex options are discussed in the following section.

COMPLEX OPTIONS

Some examples of complex, or exotic, options were given in Chapter 2. The terms are often, though not always, employed with the newest derivatives in the market, whose underlyings may be interest rate, equity, currency, other commodities, or credit. (A similar statement is valid in connection to complex swaps.)

In the background of designing and marketing complex options is the extra value they might offer. *Outperformance options,* for example, allow the holder to exchange one asset for another. The downside is exposure because the tools like the determination of the Greeks on two assets (see Chapter 10) are too complex.

Every exotic product has its problems. With *rainbow options,* which target the best of two performing assets in a market, the challenge is estimating correlations. Here are some other examples. The object of *spread options* is the spread between a so-called refined product and an unrefined product. *Payoff-to-hold power options* are based on the underlying price raised to a power. With a *log contract,* the payoff is computed by the log of the underlying price.

However, while a power option generates an exponential payoff, it also engenders a high amount of credit risk that—given the large potential payoff of the transaction—must be recognized in advance by the investor. Another element of credit risk is the potential intrinsic value of the transaction:

- The more rapid is the increase in credit exposure,
- The greater the likelihood of default by the seller of a power option, once it is in-the-money.

Many traders say that *combination instruments* make it feasible to take positions in more than one option at the same time. What is not talked about is their risk. Spreads and straddles are examples. In a *spread* the investor is both buyer and writer of the same type of option (puts or calls) on the same underlying, but the options have

- Different exercise prices, and/or
- Different expiration dates.

As we will see in the following section, a *straddle* consists of writing or buying both a put and a call on the same underlying. In this case the options have the same exercise price and same expiration date. In hedging equity risk, for instance, a popular approach is to combine a put and a call on the same underlying stock, with the same striking price and the same expiration date (more on this in Chapter 9).

The term *embedded options* (*embeddos*) is typically used in connection to tailor-made derivatives deals. Among embedded-options features are callable debts, convertible bonds, delivery options, limited liability, and putable bonds. The notion underpinning *callable debt* is that some debt can be prepaid at face value, as it happens with personal mortgages. The writer holds a call option on the debt with the exercise value equal to the face value of the debt.

- With a putable bond, the holder can ask for early redemption at a predetermined price prior to maturity.
- To materialize this transaction, he or she holds a put on the bond in addition to the bond itself.

Termination options permit the writer to make a noncollateralized transaction in exchange for the opportunity to exit this transaction at a future point if the counterparty's credit quality deteriorates. This takes place primarily between counterparties of equal credit rating, entering into longer-term derivatives transactions. For instance, either or both parties may negotiate the right to

- Terminate a transaction at specified times and
- Do so without specifying their reason(s) to the counterparty.

The implicit understanding may be that the termination clause specifies that the option is only exercisable if an independent credit agency downgrades the counterparty. Or there is an alternative clause: instead of a public rating downgrade, the derivatives instrument may be structured to terminate on deterioration of a specified financial ratio, below a defined threshold. This has similarities to covenants in loans.

As the careful reader will appreciate, in all these examples, and those that follow, the emphasis is on design and marketing issues underpinning the modeling and structuring of a pricing approach. An example is a path-dependent structure like the average rate Asian options (discussed in the second section of this chapter), and *lookback options*, also known as *no-regrets options*. With lookback options the market value of the underlying is recorded periodically over a specified time period.

- With a *strike lookback option*, the lowest value of a call option and the highest value of a put option of the underlying become the strike price.

- With a *price lookback option,* the highest value of a call option and lowest value of a put option are used in calculating the value of the underlying, while the strike price remains unchanged.

A particularity of lookback options is that both the calculated strike price and the calculated value of the underlying can vary considerably from market prices prevailing at the expiration dates. Sellers of lookback options must be aware that in all likelihood their options will be exercised at what may be the most unfavorable time for them.

A *payout option* provides the buyer with the right to payment of a fixed amount agreed in advance. With a *binary* or *digital option* (see the preceding section), payment occurs if the market value of the underlying reaches a fixed value once during a specified time period in the case of a one-touch digital option—or precisely on the day of expiration with an all-or-nothing option.

The seller of payout options owes the buyer the full amount of the fixed payment if the barrier is reached, regardless of whether or not the option is in-the-money when exercised, or on the expiration date. Therefore, compared to the option's intrinsic value, the amount owed can be

- Considerably larger for the writer, or
- Considerably smaller for the buyer.

A *multiple strike option* generates a payoff on the best performing of a number of assets, each with its strike price and underlying price. Such instruments can be viewed as a portfolio of individual call or put options. A *basket option* permits the buyer to obtain in a single structure a payoff based on the performance of a combination of related or unrelated assets. Combining a series of underlying assets into a basket, which is usually done on a weighted basis, generates a payoff based on

- Appreciation in the case of a call, or
- Depreciation in the case of a put, of the group of assets against a predetermined strike level.

A *chooser,* or *preference, option* provides the purchaser with flexibility in selecting specific characteristics of an underlying option within a given time frame. For instance, the buyer is given the ability to select between a put and a call when both options have identical strikes and maturities. Once the selection is made, the buyer pays the writer the required premium and assumes a long position in a European-style option.

The payoff the buyer expects to get from a floating-strike lookback option is based on the maximum market movement experienced during the instrument's life. This maximizes profits but also engenders large credit risk at maturity. Both writers and buyers must be aware of timing differences that exist between lookbacks and conventional options.

A *forward start option* is contracted between writer and buyer at a time T and commences at time $T + 1$. The buyer is required to pay the seller a premium on the contract date, even if the transaction will not start until some future time because all terms were agreed upon and contracted at the time the premium was paid. An investor or entity may wish to hold a forward start option to match expected flows connected to assets or liabilities occurring at a future date.

STRADDLES, STRANGLES, AND BUTTERFLIES

A *straddle* consists of the purchase or sale of both a put and a call, on the same underlying futures contract, with the same expiration date and the same exercise price. In this sense, it is a put and call with everything else the same. The breakeven is determined by adding the premium paid to the call and subtracting it from the put exercise prices.

A trader, banker, or investor might purchase a long straddle if he believes the underlying futures contract is going to make a sizable move but he is not sure in which direction. Therefore, he buys both a put and a call and hopes to make money in either direction. Long straddles are taken in anticipation of significant volatility, and they are positive gamma strategies (see Chapter 11):

- If the market moves by an amount greater than that dictated by the volatility reflected in the price of the options, then the position will result in a gain.
- But if the market remains rather stagnant, then the long straddle position will not be profitable.

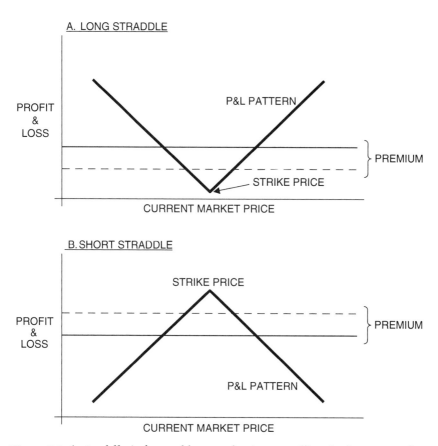

Figure 7.1 A straddle is formed by purchasing or selling both a put and a call of identical characteristics

The payoff of a long straddle position is shown in Figure 7.1A. A short straddle is the inverse of a long straddle; it is taken by traders and investors who believe that volatility will remain relatively low for a period of time. The pattern of a short straddle is shown in Figure 7.1B.

A *strangle* consists of the purchase or sale of both a put and a call on the same underlying futures contract, with the same expiration date but different exercise prices. The call is above the market and the put below the market—hence the exercise prices bracket the market. Strangles are more aggressive than straddles, but they are very similar in terms of design:

- Long strangles are made by buying puts and calls with same expiration date but different strike levels.
- As with straddles, short strangles are taken when market volatility is projected to be very low.

A trader would purchase a long strangle if she believes the underlying futures contract is going to make a sizable move but she is not sure in which direction. The buyer's risk is limited to the total premiums paid, and the buyer would be hurt by time delay in a nonvolatile or stable market. Her hope is that her potential profit is unlimited—this being somebody else's risk.

As with straddles, a trader would sell a short strangle if he or she believes there was going to be little or no movement in the price of the underlying futures contract. Breakeven is determined by adding the premiums collected to the call and subtracting it from the put exercise prices. In this case, the seller's maximum profit is limited to the premium collected. In contrast, his or her risk is unlimited.

A *butterfly* is a combination of four separate puts and calls. A long butterfly is quite similar to a short straddle but tends to have somewhat more limited risk; it is structured by buying the low and high strikes and selling the middle strike price. A butterfly's payoff profile is shown in Figure 7.2.

A short butterfly is the inverse of a long one, generated through the writing of options with low and high strikes and the

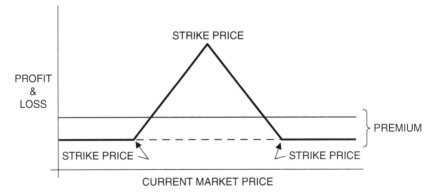

Figure 7.2 A butterfly is a combination of four puts and calls

buying of options with middle strikes—all with the same expiration date. This approach is followed when the trader or investor believes volatility will increase. A sharply higher volatility renders the package of options worthless, but the seller gains premium income.

Moreover, when strikes of the different options are further apart, traders talk of a *condor*. As a structured instrument, the condor has the potential for greater profits, but it is also open to more significant losses. As these examples demonstrate, there is plenty of room for creativity in the financial markets.

INTEREST RATE, YIELD-BASED, AND FOREIGN CURRENCY OPTIONS

Interest rate options include caps, floors, collars, corridors, and power caps. Also part of interest rate options are synthetic instruments like swaptions, when-in-the-money options, compound (nested) caps and floors, preference options, and others. Figure 7.3 gives a snapshot of the impact interest rate caps and collars have on effective borrowing cost.

- In the upper half of the figure, a cap keeps the interest rate at 9 percent while the market rate zooms.

Cap protection has a cost: the premium the buyer will pay to the writer. To reduce the cost of the protection he or she provides, the seller needs a way to benefit too. This is provided by the floor of the collar.

- In the lower half of the figure, a collar's cap protects the borrower from the interest rate rising above 9 percent, but the collar's floor does not allow him or her to benefit from an interest rate below 6 percent.

Because caps and floors are widespread, many analysts have investigated if and how hedging transactions by options dealers could have feedback effects on the market. A frequently reached conclusion has been that the markets for hedging are generally sufficiently liquid to absorb the demand for hedging created by changes in interest rates. Typically, though not always, in recent years the balance between sales and purchases of interest rate options by options dealers fluctuated only marginally. However, in

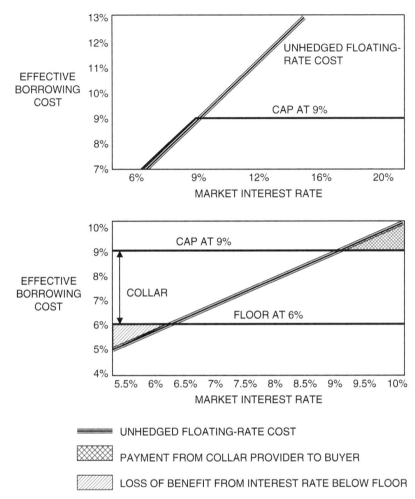

Figure 7.3 Interest rate costs can be managed through caps and collars

mid-2003 market liquidity problems occurred due to demand for hedging instruments following a sharp rise in yields leading to

- Trading in a broader class of debt-based options, and
- An increase in the use of interest rate swaps for hedging purposes.

Yield types of options are a vibrant class of derivative *debt* instruments—mainly cash-settled European-style options. Their underlying yield is the annualized yield to maturity of the most recently issued U.S. Treasury security of a designated maturity, such as 30 years, 10 years, or 5 years. This follows public quotations or prices determined in accordance with a method specified by the market on which the option is written:

- The underlying yield is stated in terms of a *yield indicator*, equal to the percentage yield multiplied by 10.
- The designated maturity of the Treasury security from which the underlying yield is determined is a standardized term of yield-based options.

Because newly auctioned securities having the longest remaining life replace old issues on the first trading day following their auction, the specific Treasury security from which the underlying yield is derived may change during the life of the option. However, given that yield-based instruments are European-style options, investors often, but not always, know prior to the time an option is exercisable the specific Treasury security from which its exercise settlement value will be determined.

Exercisable settlement values for yield-based options whose underlying yields are derived from Treasury securities are based on the spot yield for the security at a specified time on the last trading day of the option, as published by the Federal Reserve Bank of New York. The aggregate *cash settlement amount* to which the assigned writer of a yield-based option is obliged is the difference between

- The exercise price of the option, and
- The exercise settlement value of the underlying yield on the last trading day before expiration.

Generally, yield-based options are cash settled based on the difference between the exercise price and the value of an underlying yield. There is, however, another major class of debt options that are price based. These give their holder the right either to purchase or sell a specified underlying debt security or to receive a cash settlement payment based on the value of an underlying debt security. The choice depends on whether the options are delivered physically or are cash settled.

Many of the elements we have examined at the beginning of this section with interest rate options are also found with *currency rate options.* Examples are caps, floors, collars, and corridors. There are as well currency swaptions, path-dependent and path-independent options, preference options, and outperformance currency rate options, as well as combinations of equity and forex options such as the following:

- Foreign equity options struck in domestic currency
- Equity-linked foreign exchange rate options
- Fixed-exchange-rate foreign equity option

A currency option operates in different jurisdictions and trades in a market that is very large (over $1 trillion per day); and, contrary to equities, its market is decentralized. These three issues see to it that it is essentially free from government regulation, even if governments may take various actions that affect their own currencies and the markets on which they are traded.

The exercise price of a physical delivery cross-rate option is denominated in the trading currency, and it is the price at which the underlying currency may be purchased or sold upon exercise of the option. Exercise prices for cross-rate options are generally expressed in terms of units, or fractions thereof.

Dollar-denominated foreign currency options allow investors to purchase or sell underlying foreign currencies for dollars. Cross-rate currency options make it feasible to buy or sell an underlying currency at an exercise price that is denominated in another foreign currency.

A *quanto*, also known as a *guaranteed-exchange-rate contract*, permits the buyer to fix a foreign exchange rate, thereby eliminating currency risk from a given transaction such as payoff of an underlying index or foreign investments currently being made. For instance, if a manufacturing company that is building a factory abroad fears that currency movements are likely to alter its payoff plans when it is turned back into its base currency, the company can hedge through currency options.

Other derivative instruments for foreign exchange are baskets of options that allow the holder to buy or sell a basket of underlying foreign currencies.

In all these cases, the function provided by currency options is that of enabling an investor to purchase or sell one currency at a price denominated in another currency or currencies.

- The exercise price of a currency option essentially represents an exchange rate.
- The currency to be purchased or sold at the exercise price is the *underlying currency*.
- The currency in which the premium and exercise price are denominated is referred to as the *trading currency*.

If the value of an underlying foreign currency rises in relation to the trading currency, *then* the call premiums will normally increase while the put premiums decrease. *If* the value of an underlying foreign currency decreases in relation to the trading currency, *then* the call premiums will normally decrease while the put premiums increase.

Currency options are traded in a major exchange like the Philadelphia Exchange (PHLX), London Stock Exchange (LSE), and the London International Financial Futures Exchange (LIFFE). Typically, they are written against major currencies such as the American dollar, the British pound, the euro, or the Japanese yen. Moreover, a significant amount of trading is done off-exchange over the counter, between two counterparties.

OPTION SPREADING; LONG CALLS, SHORT CALLS[1]

The term *spread* refers to the difference in premiums between the purchase and sale of options. An *option spread* is the simultaneous purchase of one or more options contracts and sale of the equivalent number of options contracts, in a different series of the class of options. A spread could involve the same underlying:

- Buying and selling calls, or
- Buying and selling puts.

Combining puts and calls into groups of two or more makes it feasible to design derivatives with interesting payoff profiles. The profit and loss outcomes depend on the options used (puts or calls); positions taken (long or short); whether their strike prices

---

[1] See also Chapter 9 on spread trading; Chapter 11 on credit spreads and option spreads; Chapter 13 on swap spreads; and Chapter 14 on credit risk spreads.

are identical or different; and the similarity or difference of their exercise dates. Among directional positions are bullish vertical call spreads, bullish vertical put spreads, bearish vertical spreads, and bearish vertical put spreads (more on this later).

If the long position has a higher premium than the short position, this is known as a *debit spread*, and the investor will be required to deposit the difference in premiums. If the long position has a lower premium than the short position, this is a *credit spread,* and the investor will be allowed to withdraw the difference in premiums. The spread will be *even* if the premiums on each side results are the same.

A potential loss in an option spread is determined by two factors:

- Strike price
- Expiration date

If the strike price of the long call is greater than the strike price of the short call, or if the strike price of the long put is less than the strike price of the short put, a margin is required because adverse market moves can cause the short option to suffer a loss before the long option can show a profit.

A margin is also required if the long option expires before the short option. The reason is that once the long option expires, the trader holds an unhedged short position. A good way of looking at margin requirements is that they foretell potential loss. Here are, in a nutshell, the main option spreadings.

A *calendar, horizontal,* or *time spread* is the simultaneous purchase and sale of options of the same class with the same exercise prices but with different expiration dates. A *vertical,* or *price* or *money, spread* is the simultaneous purchase and sale of options of the same class with the same expiration date but with different exercise prices.

A *bull,* or *call, spread* is a type of vertical spread that involves the purchase of the call option with the lower exercise price while selling the call option with the higher exercise price. The result is a debit transaction because the lower exercise price will have the higher premium.

- The maximum risk is the *net debit*: the long option premium minus the short option premium.
- The maximum profit potential is the difference in the strike prices minus the net debit.

- The breakeven is equal to the lower strike price plus the net debit.

A trader will typically buy a vertical bull call spread when he is mildly bullish. Essentially, he gives up unlimited profit potential in return for reducing his risk. In a vertical bull call spread, the trader is expecting the spread premium to widen because the lower strike price call comes into the money first.

Vertical spreads are the more common of the direction strategies, and they may be bullish or bearish to reflect the holder's view of market's anticipated direction. *Bullish vertical put spreads* are a combination of a long put with a low strike, and a short put with a higher strike. Because the short position is struck closer to-the-money, this generates a premium credit.

Bearish vertical call spreads are the inverse of bullish vertical call spreads. They are created by combining a short call with a low strike and a long call with a higher strike. Bearish vertical put spreads are the inverse of bullish vertical put spreads, generated by combining a short put with a low strike and a long put with a higher strike. This is a bearish position taken when a trader or investor expects the market to fall.

The bull or sell put spread is a type of vertical spread involving the purchase of a put option with the lower exercise price and sale of a put option with the higher exercise price. Theoretically, this is the same action that a bull call spreader would take. The difference between a call spread and a put spread is that the net result will be a credit transaction because the higher exercise price will have the higher premium.

- The maximum risk is the difference in the strike prices minus the net credit.
- The maximum profit potential equals the net credit.
- The breakeven equals the higher strike price minus the net credit.

The bear or sell call spread involves selling the call option with the lower exercise price and buying the call option with the higher exercise price. The net result is a credit transaction because the lower exercise price will have the higher premium.

A bear put spread (or buy spread) involves selling some of the put option with the lower exercise price and buying the put option with the higher exercise price. This is the same action that a bear call spreader would take. The difference between a call spread and a put spread, however, is that the net result will be a debit transaction because the higher exercise price will have the higher premium.

- The maximum risk is equal to the net debit.
- The maximum profit potential is the difference in the strike prices minus the net debit.
- The breakeven equals the higher strike price minus the net debit.

An investor or trader would buy a vertical bear put spread because he or she is mildly bearish, giving up an unlimited profit potential in return for a reduction in risk. In a vertical bear put spread, the trader is expecting the spread premium to widen because the higher strike price put comes into the money first.

In conclusion, investors and traders who are bullish on the market will either buy a bull call spread or sell a bull put spread. But those who are bearish on the market will either buy a bear put spread or sell a bear call spread. When the investor pays more for the long option than she receives in premium for the short option, then the spread is a *debit* transaction. In contrast, when she receives more than she pays, the spread is a *credit* transaction. Credit spreads typically require a margin deposit.

OPTION HEDGES

Hedging was the theme of Chapter 4. Options are one of the most important hedging instruments. An equity hedge combines an option with its underlying stock in a way that the option protects the stock against loss, and the stock protects the option against loss. In this sense, an option hedge combines a long position in the stock with a written position in calls or a purchased position in puts. One of the popular hedges consists of writing one call option against each share owned of the underlying stock.

- To have a protected call, the investor buys one share and writes one call in a one-to-one hedge.
- To have a protected put, the investor would buy one share and also buy one put.

A *reverse hedge* combines a short position in the stock with a purchased position in calls or a written position in puts. A *wrapped hedge* is a defensive strategy that locks in the gains made on a stock, while letting the investor share in some of the upside potential that may be left in the issue. This technique involves buying a put option on, say, shares of Johnson & Johnson as a form of insurance when the market price is $60.

- The put allows the holder to sell the shares to the writer of the option at $60 at any time until it expires.
- If the price of Johnson & Johnson erodes before then, losses to the investor will be offset because the put will gain in value by a similar amount.

But is it really so? The second bulleted point states the theoretical concepts surrounding option hedging. Real life does not always work like that. As it has been already shown in other occasions, quite often returns are asymmetric and therefore deviate significantly from theoretical results.

The other half of the hedge in this short case study involves selling, or writing, a call to recoup some of the cost of buying the put option. The call may let the buyer purchase Johnson & Johnson at a price higher than $60. In this way, the owner of the shares is capping his or her potential profits at that price, up until the option's expiration.

Using as an example the fact that at year's end stock prices tend to slump because of window dressing by institutional investors, many experts advise that the wrapped hedge is a good way to carry gains into the next year to defer taxes, while also eliminating the risk that one might lose the profits in a December correction. This argument should be seen through the prism of a theoretical approach that may not be sustained in real life. December 2006 saw no correction.

Covered call writing, which is a more aggressive options technique, works best in gradually rising markets. It concentrates on the second half of the wrapped hedge, in which the investor sells call options on shares he or she owns in order to gain premium income. However, unlike a wrapped hedge, downside protection is not on hand:

If a given stock on which he or she was betting tanks,

Then the investor bears all the losses, offset only by the amount of premium income taken in.

This strategy also can backfire spectacularly if the stock zooms because it is a takeover target (as it often happened in 2007) or for other reasons.

Index options are another class of hedgers. An *index* is a measure of a group of securities or other assets. Stock indexes are compiled and published by a number of sources.

A stock index is typically designed to be representative of the stock market of a particular country as a whole or a broad market sector such as transportation, or of securities traded in a particular industry such as electronics. Such an index may be based on the prices of all or only a sample of the securities whose prices it is intended to represent. Like a cost-of-living index, a stock index is usually expressed in relation to a base established when the index originated.

The value level of an index underlying an option is the value of the index as reported by the authority designated by the options market where the option is traded. Every value initially reported by this authority is

- Presumed to be accurate, and
- Deemed to be final for the purpose of calculating the cash settlement amount, even if the value is subsequently revised.

However, from time to time this base may be adjusted to reflect events like capitalization changes affecting the index securities or to maintain continuity when securities are added to or dropped from the index. Securities may be dropped from an index in the aftermath of mergers or because a particular security is no longer representative of the types of stocks constituting the index. Trading strategies include purchases and sales of

- Index options
- Index futures
- Options on index futures
- Portfolios of some of the securities in an index

Can these transactions affect the value of the index and prices of index futuresl In principle, changes in the prices of index options impact upon the volatility of the stock and derivative markets. Traders holding positions in expiring index options or futures contracts hedged by positions in securities included in the index may liquidate their positions, and this can result in significant changes in the level of the index.

All this is most pertinent to the use of options for hedging. As the April 2007 Monthly Report of the European Central Bank (ECB) points out, option prices contain useful information about market players' risk perceptions. A contract such as a call option can be seen as a bet that, at some point in the future, the underlying asset will exceed a certain level.

- By combining the information from several options that give a positive payoff for different levels of the underlying, one could recover the set of probabilities the market assigns to possible future stock price developments.
- By estimating the price distributions that have become known as *option implied*, it is possible to derive the probabilities assigned by investors to possible future stock price developments.

As the aforementioned ECB study suggests, these price distributions can reveal potential asymmetries and, therefore, the balance of risks the market may perceive in connection to future asset price movements. Additionally, by comparing the shape of the option-implied density functions before and after a specific event, it is possible to determine the way in which a given event shaped market participants' views about the future.

The aim of this analysis is that of deriving a chart that reflects the distribution of future stock price developments as perceived by the market.

RISKS ASSOCIATED WITH OPTIONS

It seems very difficult to convince bankers, traders, and investors, even though they should know better, that trading in options is full of hidden exposures—and, therefore, it's a game that should be reserved only for courageous people and knowledgeable institutions with deep pockets. With derivative products, not only is in-depth market information not available as readily as it is for shares but also price movements can be magnified.

Serious brokers advise that unlike share portfolios, which can be left in the care of a broker, options are too risky to devolve. "They are far too volatile and speculative to leave to a broker, and people should follow them closely," said an executive of Killik & Co, a London-based broker.[2] In spite of what was written in the closing paragraphs of the preceding section, there is little the investor can learn from prices and spreads on options if he or she does not have the skills and the technology to do the analytics.

Several risks, for example, are associated with index options. One of the major risks is that a writer of cash-settled index call options cannot provide in advance for potential settlement obligations by acquiring and holding the underlying interest. While a call writer can theoretically offset some of the risk of his or her position by holding a diversified portfolio of securities, similar to those on which the underlying index is based, in practice this is not doable with broad indexes.

Additionally, the case of asymmetry is always present. Writers of cash-settled index calls, who also hold positions in securities, bear the risk that the market prices of those securities will not increase as much as the index. There is, furthermore, *timing risk* inherent in writing cash-settled options.

As with many other types of options, the writer will not learn that he or she has been assigned until the next business day at the earliest. This creates a time lag during which the index may decline, and there may be a corresponding decline in the value of the securities portfolio. Timing risk and other exposures associated with index options, and a long list of more complex derivative financial instruments, can hit not only speculators but also legitimate investors like companies who labor to hedge themselves.

A most important risk with options is *right pricing* (Chapter 8). Many financial losses sustained by investors and intermediaries have been caused by mispricing complex structures, because of

- Misunderstanding the risk and return profiles of the options,
- Being too optimistic about future volatility, or

_____
[2] News item, *Financial Times*, July 23–24, 1994.

- Circumventing the internal controls that could put a break on promoting options sales by assuming more and more exposure.

The way to bet is that transactions involving buying and writing multiple options in combination present major risks to both bankers and investors. For instance, option spreads (discussed earlier in the chapter) are more complex than buying or writing a single option, and option complexity in itself is not well understood.

All participants in the options market must strive to understand the upside and downside of transactions, no matter how straightforward or esoteric, as well as the limits that exist in an open market. But control issues increase exponentially with the complexity of the issue. Writers and buyers considering strategies with combination options should appreciate that it may at times be impossible to simultaneously execute transactions in all of the options involved in the combination.

There are times when options prices do not maintain their anticipated relationships to the prices of the underlying. Changes in volatility or other factors or conditions might adversely affect market liquidity, efficiency, continuity, or even the orderliness of the market for particular options—resulting in pricing asymmetries brought to the reader's attention.

Alternatively, the options market might discontinue the trading of a particular option (or options). It may as well impose restrictions on certain types of options transactions, such as opening transactions or uncovered writing transactions, therefore providing for discontinuities. If an option is exercisable while trading has been halted in the underlying, option holders may have to decide whether to exercise without knowing the current market value of the underlying, which may become an important exposure if an option is close to expiration. Failure to exercise will mean that the option will expire worthless.

If exercises do occur when trading of the underlying interest is halted,

Then the party required to deliver the underlying interest may be unable to obtain it, which may necessitate a postponed settlement or the fixing of cash settlement prices.

Generally considered as being "safe," cash-settled options may have special risks. For instance, if the option is in a different currency than the investor's base currency, buyers and writers will be subject to exchange risks with respect to the foreign currency. Even though the intrinsic value of an option is determined by the value of the underlying currency relative to the trading currency, investors may not only be affected by changes in the exchange rates, but also by other factors.

For instance, given that foreign currency transactions occurring in the interbank market involve substantially larger amounts than those likely to be required in the exercise of individual foreign currency options, investors who buy or write foreign currency options may be disadvantaged by

- Having to deal in an odd-lot market for the underlying foreign currencies, and
- Accepting prices that are less favorable than those for big lots. This price differential may be significant.

In conclusion, derivative instruments have changed from relatively straightforward transactions, like currency exchange forwards, to very complex transactions, like compound options and swaps based on sophisticated payoff formulas. The way to bet, however, is that the more complex are the derivative products, the greater will be the potential for losses—hence the need not only to understand the instrument but also to study market trends and pricing structures prior to making a commitment.

CHAPTER 8

The Pricing of Options

PRICING DERIVATIVES: A GENERAL PERSPECTIVE

With an option on olives, Thales might have started the derivatives business in the sixth century BC, but it was only after the options pricing theory of the early 1970s met the volatile financial markets of the deregulated 1980s that options took off. So did futures, forwards, swaps, swaptions, caps, floors, collars, and a score of other more sophisticated financial instruments.

The ability to price a financial product in a way acceptable to the market is, in the general case, the most important asset to its marketability. Pricing derivatives can be a detailed job that requires

- A methodology
- Analytical financial thinking
- Market data
- Models acceptable to market players

For its part, the development of a pricing methodology cannot be dissociated from trading conditions such as arbitrage, the stochastic processes underpinning the dealers' actions, and the effects of liquidity and of volatility, as well as the rules and principles characterizing the behavior of market players.

Rules are a methodology's pillars. In the nineteenth century the Chicago commodity futures markets were the scene of tugs-of-war between longs and shorts, in which the outcome was determined by the exhaustion of financial resources of one or the other party. An epic story is that of Joe Leiter who began a famous attempt to corner the December wheat contract and become the Wheat King.

He bought all stocks and futures he could get, and

Then, he forced those who had sold futures to cover their positions by buying from him at inflated prices.

Leiter used common sense plus analytical financial thinking. The important part of analytical finance is not mathematics but the key assumptions we make. Can we assume constant volatility? Constant interest rates? If not, which is the pattern of volatility and of interest rates we should project and adopt?

Sometimes analysts make a great deal of simplifications, like costless trading with no taxes or restrictions frictionless, or no underlying cash flows over the option's life (more on this when we talk of the Black-Scholes model's strengths and limitations). Quite often, this has been misleading. A more sophisticated approach

- Will pay attention to the term structure of volatility
- Will measure prevailing correlations, which is indeed a tough problem

Beyond these prerequisite conditions, the pricing of derivative financial instruments uses *number theory*—that is, the science of inventing new analytical ways to manipulate whole numbers. Number theory originated in ancient Greece, but for centuries it provided material for intellectual games rather than business results. This has changed, and for the last 40 years number theory and numerical models have left a growing footprint in finance.

Rigorous mathematical analysis is necessary to study the behavior of financial products whose value is tied to the fluctuating price of an underlying. Pricing derivatives is a challenge, particularly when clients of investment banks are waiting online to get a quote on what it costs to invest in a derivative such as collateralized mortgage obligations (CMOs) whose value is linked to mortgage interest rates.

Moreover, as pointed out in Chapter 3, in connection to the strategic use of derivative instruments, real-time response is important because the client demands it. Also, a numerical calculation can be obsolete in an instant if rates or the slope of the yield curve change. Computing the value of a pool of mortgages entails solving an equation with many variables, such as:

- The monthly mortgage payments
- Information on how rapidly people refinance or pay off mortgages

Most derivative financial instruments have their particular pricing characteristics. Contrary to a future that is bought or sold in the exchange at the market price, a forward transaction is done over the counter at a price agreed between counterparties with payment and delivery taking place at an agreed future date. The option resembles a forward with a difference: the buyer does not have to carry out the transaction.

The challenge is to properly price the option premium whose value is derived from the underlying spot transaction and the risk being assumed. The general lines were explained in Chapter 7, and they like being simple:

Option value = implicit value + time premium

The problem is to estimate in advance the future volatility, implicit value, and time value. To appreciate the challenge, we should look at the way forward contracts are priced, based on the terms of the transaction that will take place at a later date. For instance:

A result fairly similar to the one achieved by buying an asset forward can be had by borrowing the money to buy immediately the asset.

The key difference is leveraging. The investor can buy a futures or forward contract by depositing only a margin requirement that is a small part of the cash part.

The interest paid for the rest of the capital is not transparent to most investors because they do not appreciate that it is embedded into the quoted futures prices. Pricing options is a conceptually more involved issue than this example because capital claims can be interpreted as options. On this notion rests much of the work done by Franco Modigliani and Merton Miller.

Briefly, the Modigliani-Miller theory says that the equity of a firm is a call option on the assets of this firm. According to this hypothesis, buying a gold producer's stock is akin to buying an option on gold (which in practice is not true because of asymmetries). Similar to what was said about futures, the payoff of a call or put option could be emulated by buying the asset and borrowing money. But this involves a dual transaction rather than a single transaction as with forwards:

- Making the initial transaction in the trade,
- Then, adjusting it as the spot price of the asset changes.

In simple terms, that's what the Black-Scholes option pricing formula is all about (discussed later in this chapter). The formula includes one additional piece of information: the underlying asset's volatility. A higher volatility implies a higher price for the option, which is a pragmatic approach because the writer assumes higher risk.

OBJECT OF PREDICTION AND EFFECT OF VOLATILITY

Analysis is a compelling metaphor for the way the modern financial industry works. We examine the key instrument's variables, sensitivities, and potential for reward, as well as its market volatility, liquidity, and embedded risks not only through spot but also, if not mainly, through predictions of future behavior. Whether in finance, or any other business sector,

- Forecasting and planning are not really concerned with future decisions.
- The object of prediction is the future impact of current decisions.

Basic parameters in modeling the future impact of current decisions include the volatility of underlying assets, the variance of volatility, and the correlation between option price and volatility. Experimenters with experience in the modeling of derivatives use sophisticated techniques to estimate model parameters, devise figures of merit based on the bid-ask spread, and gauge model performance.

- This approach permits them to improve the results of existing pricing models.
- It leads toward a trading strategy enriched with predictive capabilities.

Prediction is a challenging task made so much more complex in times of turbulence. By definition turbulence is nonlinear, irregular, and erratic—hence, very difficult to predict and map onto an analytical model.

The most important analytical models are those that help to evaluate the financial market at some future date and allow experiments on markets and on products and their prices. For instance, we may wish to know about trends, study pockets of inefficiency, flesh out short-lived anomalies, or test prevailing hypotheses on risk and return.

- The key to financial analysis is nontraditional research.
- Hence, there exists the need for the new methods and tools we put in place for reasons of prediction.

Some banks are outsourcing the prediction process, but this has several risks. An example is *volatility smiles*, a term that stands for predicting low volatility while a higher one would have been more realistic. To sell more options and make bigger commissions, sometimes business partners find a way of convincing the bank's management that in the coming weeks or months, volatility is going to be lower than it has been so far. In 1995 NatWest Markets priced its options based on a volatility smile, and a year later it went bankrupt.

- Using brokers as consultants presents problems of conflicts of interest.
- Brokers have incentives to lean toward volatility estimates that assist in making deals.

To avoid the conflict of interest associated to external inputs affecting financial instruments, some companies prefer internal prediction. At least in theory, this harnesses the collective brainpower of employees who are expected to come up with forecasts on issues as varied as volatility or an industry sector's development.

The idea is that by participating in a structured game through virtual trading accounts with virtual money, knowledgeable employees will gain insight into specific projects, realistically project next quarter's sales, or provide input into other selected issues. These are, in effect, elaborate computer games that might help firms spot trends and make more acceptable forecasts based on their employees' collective brainpower, but they are not a sort of financial penicillin.

Intel and Hewlett-Packard pioneered the corporate use of pre-diction markets, but neither seems to be using them for anything more than experiments. Where internal prediction seems to help is in capturing employee sentiment on project deadlines or product quality more accurately than other measures. Practically, where it is used,

- Internal prediction helps in foretelling internal matters, rather than broader trends,
- But it may also assist in challenging "the obvious," which is a major contribution in volatility studies.

Whenever internal prediction is used for option pricing, the cardinal principle is that front-desk and backoffice opinions should not be averaged but tested against one another and with outsourced predictions of volatility. Internal prediction is not free of conflicts of interest.

As the careful reader will remember from Part 1, the Risk Council at Bank X was characterized by conflicting duties. The Risk Council had four members: the director of treasury and trading (later president and chairman of the bank), the chief credit officer, the assistant director of trading, and the chief risk manager, report-ing to the director of trading. This violated two cardinal rules at the same time:

- Traders and loan officers should never be entrusted with risk control.
- The functions of the front desk and the backoffice should be separated by a thick wall.

Financial analysts also said that the creation of another risk control function, undertrading, diluted rather than strengthened the bank's risk management. When this happens, the sky can break loose because predictions are biased, the estimation of future volatility is given short shrift compared to other interests, and the proverbial long, hard look takes a leave.

Independence of opinion is instrumental in providing solid pricing premises and better control over exposure. Both are important issues with derivatives because of the leverage factor: considerably less capital is required to participate in the options market than in the stock market. Moreover, bankers and investors are often present in the options market with two contradictory objectives:

- Hedge risk.
- Optimize profits derived from their portfolios.

We can use a valid option pricing formula to calculate the fair value of a derivative, but if our hypotheses and forecasts are wrong, the result will be unreliable no matter how good the model has been. Option positions can change in value, and this is true even though the underlying instrument may not change.

It is interesting to notice that thoroughly studied and tested models, based on factual hypotheses and sound appreciation of the prevailing market situation, can also be used in reverse to find a volatility level that makes a certain option worth a given price, such as the current market price.

- Originally, option pricing models were designed to produce a computed, and therefore theoretical, value or price for an option,
- But their greater worth proved to be in calculating implied volatility, as well as in providing a common frame of reference—which essentially constitutes the value of the Black-Scholes options model.

Financial analysis done at the edges of our know-how in terms of instruments and market behavior plays another important role, beyond simulation and optimization. The prediction of the future aftermath of current decisions helps in developing dissension among decision makers.

In his book *My Years with General Motors*,[1] Alfred Sloan recounts how as chairman of the board of GM he "never accepted an important proposal without having dissension, hence critical discussion about its merits and demerits." And Dr. Robert McNamara, the former U.S. Secretary of Defense and president of the World Bank, advises: "Never go ahead with a major project unless you have examined all the alternatives. In a multimillion dollar project you should never be satisfied with vanilla ice cream only. You should have many flavors."

---

[1] Alfred P. Sloan, Jr., *My Years with General Motors*, Pan Piper, London, 1967.

OPTIONS PREMIUMS AND OPTIONS PRICING

Chapter 7 made reference to the option premium as the price that the buyer of an option pays and the writer of an option receives for the rights conveyed by the instrument. This price is negotiated by the holder and writer, or their brokers, in the market where the option is traded. The premium

- Is not a standardized term of the option.
- Does not constitute a down payment. Rather, it is a nonrefundable payment in full.

Since an option's premium is its cost, it is essential to understand how it is determined, as well as the factors that influence its value. First and foremost, option premiums are a function of supply and demand for option contracts, for any commodity at any particular time. Typically,

The demand for calls is stronger when a commodity's price is rising,

While the demand for puts is stronger when the commodity's price is falling.

Therefore, premiums are subject to continuous change in response to market and economic forces, including changes in trading conditions in the market(s) where a particular type of option is traded. Among key factors that generally affect the pricing of an option are the following:

- Style of the option (Chapter 7)
- Depth of the market for the option
- Effect of supply and demand in the option's market and underlying
- Relationship between an option's value and exercise price
- Current values of related instruments like futures on the underlying
- Critical ratio equal to strike spot price
- Strike price of the option relative to the price of the underlying
- Days remaining before an option contract expires
- Historical volatility of the underlying

- Individual estimates of market participants of future volatility of the underlying

For instance, in the case of an option on a given equity, the higher is the volatility, the higher the likelihood that the stock does very well or very poorly. These are offsetting effects on the stock's owner, but not to the call's owner, since he or she enjoys the upside potential without facing the full risk of the downside. If he or she does not exercise the call, he or she only loses the premium. Other crucial factors affecting an option's premium are these:

- Prevailing interest rates in the case of interest rate options
- Cash dividends payable on the underlying in the case of stock options
- Current currency exchange rates in the case of foreign currency options
- Individual estimates of market participants of future developments that might affect any of the foregoing

Other factors, too, can affect the price of options. As a general observation, options premiums do not necessarily conform to or correlate with any theoretical options pricing model, and this reference includes Black-Scholes. As we will see in the section on the Black-Scholes model later in the chapter, most of the latter model's value derives from its general acceptance.

Wise investors track the price of an option to its expiration date. Usually the interval is taken equal to be one year although most options, particularly those that are exchange traded, have less than a year's lifespan. In contrast, over-the-counter interest rate options have long maturities.

The way a call option's value relates to its future price is shown in Figure 8.1. Simply stated, this value is the amount by which the option premium is above the option's intrinsic value, defined in Chapter 7. The remaining premium is the time value. (As a reminder, *intrinsic value* is the value of an option at any time it is exercised, depending on the condition: in-the-money, out-of-the-money, or at-the-money.)

- The premium declines steadily until the final few days of the option's life.

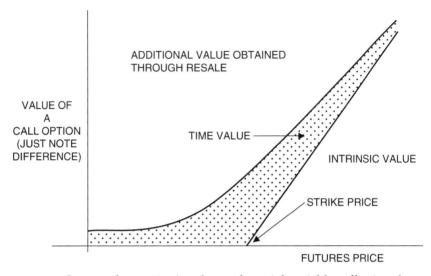

Figure 8.1 Spaces of an option's value and crucial variables affecting them

- During these final days before expiration, its value drops sharply to its intrinsic value.

Time value, the other major variable in Figure 8.1, has been also defined in Chapter 7. It is a function of the time to maturity, volatility, interest rate, and critical ratio. The time value reflects any additional amount that buyers are willing to pay in the hope that changes in the underlying futures price prior to expiration will increase the option's value.

The premium of an out-of-the-money option is thus largely, if not entirely, a reflection of its time value. Moreover, an option that is deep out-of-the-money, which happens when a substantial difference exists between the strike and futures prices, will have less time value than an option that is only slightly out-of-the-money. Barring extreme events, it is less likely that the former will ever become profitable to exercise.

The third important variable in Figure 8.1 is the strike price. Taking equity options as an example, the value of different option positions at expiration depends primarily on two variables: the current stock price and the strike price even, as we have seen, if other variables also contribute to determining the option's value—for instance, the cash dividends, time to expiration, stock volatility, and interest rate.

All told, the premium is really a market price. When a new option is introduced, the premium will be established by the sellers and the initial exercise price will emulate the current expiration month. However, as the future price fluctuates, additional exercise prices will be opened by the exchange.

Up to a point, the buyer and writer of an option have a common interest in connection to the option's premium. The buyer pays a premium he knows in advance but loses the premium he paid if he does not exercise the option. The seller benefits from the premium she gets for writing the option but also takes unlimited risk. For instance, if over time the interest rate exceeds the cap, she must make up the difference.

Notice that for both parties to this transaction, benefits and risks depend on the prognostication about volatility—for example, its impact on the behavior of interest rates. For the writer, the forecast must be accurate not only in terms of the direction interest rates will move but also in terms of the amount of change during the life of the option. Indeed, for some exotic options like lookbacks (Chapter 7) the curve this movement will take is, as well, very important.

Precisely because an option's premium is its cost, its establishment is the key to options trading. Option buyers must see the premium being paid under the light that an option is a wasting asset; when it expires it becomes worthless. The buyer retains the right to exercise the option by acquiring a futures market position, but if he or she does not exercise the option, he or she gets nothing in return for the premium paid.

A long call option offers the opportunity to weather pullbacks without additional exposure beyond the initial premium. If the market advance continues, a long option position would give the investor a profit from a rising market. The risks to an outright long option position arise from time decay, decreasing implied volatility, and falling futures prices.

BINOMIAL AND LOGNORMAL MODELS

Understanding a number of statistical distributions is quite essential to option pricing. The *binomial model* is a numerical method often used with calls and puts. This distribution is essentially an approximation to the hypergeometric distribution, just like the Poisson distribution is an approximation to the binomial.[2] (Hypergeometric and Poisson distributions are outside the scope of this book.[3])

One of the advantages of the binomial in the study of option premiums is that it is a discrete probability distribution. The time value is addressed with time to expiration divided into small time slots. The price of the underlying, for instance, an equity, is assumed to go up or down with a given probability in each step.

The study of probabilities associated to each time slot and its price is a compelling metaphor for the way the financial markets work. The binomial approximation allows us to incorporate stochastic volatility in American-style option trading, using a set of fixed input parameters such as these:

- Stock price
- Stock price/exercise price ratio
- Volatility
- Variance of volatility
- Correlation between parameters

This option pricing approach assumes that the asset price follows a binomial process over the time slots taken as discrete periods. Here is an example of how the underlying's value is assumed to go up or down by a specific amount in the next slot. Say that an equity with a current price p will either increase to p^{+} with probability P or decrease to p^{-} with probability of $1 - P$.

---

[2] The binomial distribution is expressed as

$$P(x) = \frac{n!}{x!\,(n-x)!}\; P^{x}\, Q^{n-x}$$

$$= 0$$

for $x = 0, 1, 2, \ldots, n$

One approximation to $n!$ is

$n! \cong (2\pi)^{1/2}\, e^{-n} n^{n+(1/2)}$

The error:

$$\frac{\left|\, n! - (2\pi)^{1/2}\, e^{-n} n^{n+(1/2)}\,\right|}{n!} \;\to 0,\ \text{for } x \to \infty$$

[3] Dimitris N. Chorafas, *Statistical Processes and Reliability Engineering,* Van Nostrand, Princeton, N.J., 1960.

Assume also that a call option on the stock expires at the end of the next slot.

The option value at expiration will depend on the value of the stock at expiration. Since the value of p at expiration is uncertain, in a frictionless environment (known as a *Brownian motion*), the value of a call option with one period to expiration is obtained by discounting the expected terminal values of the option to the current period.

What has been described so far is a one-period model. The same pricing principle can be applied to a multiperiod approach, starting with an extension of the one-period model to a two-period case, assuming that the equity price follows the same binomial process for price changes in each period.

Notice that this binomial pricing approach can be used with various time periods—minutes, hours, weeks, or months. As the time slot becomes smaller, the number of periods to expiration increases for an option with a given life cycle. This is the process followed by so-called continuous-time option pricing formulas such as Black-Scholes:

- They are binomial pricing approaches.
- They are derived for an infinite number of arbitrarily small time slots.

In its basic structure, the binomial option pricing model uses a decision tree approach. The life of the option is divided into the afore-mentioned discrete time slots, each characterized by upper and lower bounds on price movements derived from an assumed volatility.

- There are two possible values for the option—hence the binomial label.
- The price can move up or down, but there is more upward than downward pull due to the lognormal distribution underpinning the model (more on this later).

A decision tree is extended over many time periods forming a binomial lattice. For each of the possible up and down price move-ments, there are two possibilities at the end of a time slot that constitutes a node of the lattice. When the so-described path is followed, it is always possible to return to the original price.

The reason why a distribution of prices is not normally distrib-uted lies in the fact that market and other factors tend to impede price movements in the downward direction. Therefore, the assumption of a lognormal distribution of prices seems to be reasonable.

The accuracy of this model significantly depends on the fine grain of the time slices. Coarse-grain time slicing will result in very approximate estimates of the exercising of American-style put options, or call options with dividends. However,

- The amount of possible routes through the lattice doubles for each new time interval, and
- As the number of time slices increases, there is an exponential increase in complexity and in computational requirements.

Part A of Figure 8.2 presents the normal probability distribution; Part B, the lognormal distribution. A random variable has a

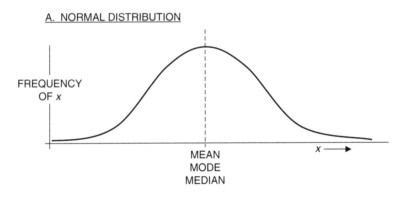

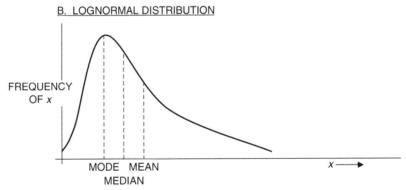

Figure 8.2 Normal and lognormal distributions

lognormal distribution if the natural logarithm of the variable is normally distributed.

- Different option pricing models assume that stock prices are lognormally distributed.
- If stock prices were normally distributed, then this would imply that it is equally likely for a stock price to move up or down.

Understanding normal and lognormal distributions is essential for options pricing. As long as the natural logarithm (ln) of a given variable—for example, the interest rate—is linear, there is a lognormal distribution for its possible values. Assuring a different lognormal rate distribution for each future time slot permits both the mean and the variance to depend on time.

The Black-Scholes model, discussed in the following two sections, uses a more general lognormal distribution than others because it allows the local process to change over time. On the other hand, one of the advantages of the binomial approach over the Black-Scholes model is that by valuing the option through a lattice, using well-defined time slots that run through the options lifespan, it is possible to assess the case of the option being exercised:

- This can be realized through a Monte Carlo simulation,[4] and
- It is done through hypotheses made on prevailing circumstances that warrant or do not warrant the decision to exercise.

On many occasions, Monte Carlo models have proved to be more accurate for option pricing purposes than alternative approaches. They make it feasible to directly incorporate volatility and assets price changes, as stochastic processes, and they are easy to parallelize. The downside is that the Monte Carlo models are computationally intensive, and, as noted on several occasions, many banks lack the high-tech capability to use these models.

---

[4] Dimitris N. Chorafas, *Chaos Theory in the Financial Markets*, Probus, Chicago, 1994.

THE BLACK-SCHOLES MODEL

All models have advantages and disadvantages as well as constraints. The Black-Scholes option pricing model assumes constant volatility and European type of pricing. It is a fairly approximate method, making many assumptions and employing a stochastic equation for call price. There are other models that treat volatility as a stochastic process, but they have other shortcomings depriving them of general acceptance.[5]

The Black-Scholes model concentrates on a *cap curve*.[6] In the path to maturity, this cap curve gives the price of an at-the-money differential cap—which maps a rate to the positive difference between the short rate and the strike price. For any maturity, an at-the-money cap has a strike equal to the forward rate for that maturity.

Contrasted to the use of binomial distribution for option pricing, the Black-Scholes formula has been designed specifically for calculating the price writers and buyers are willing to accept in a transaction. This perception of a custom-made algorithmic representation in connection to products and services of the financial systems is rather recent. It comes from a steadily evolving experience with

- Mathematical modeling
- Pricing mechanisms that help to expand the market appeal of novel instruments

The reader should, however, notice that mathematical modeling of observed phenomena has been used in the physical sciences for centuries[7]; and it has also served for the development of different scientific theories. Models have to be accurate, but the large majority of them are not precise. The price we pay for their usage is approximation, and this is perfectly true in finance.

Even if approximation is the name of the game, modeling helps the financial analyst in getting a better perspective. However,

---

[5] The original paper by Dr. Fischer Black and Dr. Myron Scholes was submitted for publication in 1970. After answering the editors' remarks and conforming to their suggestions, the paper was published in 1972. In 1994 Dr. Black received the Chorafas Foundation award for his contribution to analytical finance.
[6] By Black and Karasinki (1991).
[7] D. N. Chorafas, *Systems and Simulation*, Academic Press, New York, 1965.

how good this is going to be largely depends on his ingenuity and the data he has available. It also depends on how well he exploits the potential this model is offering in terms of insight and foresight.

The human element is at the roots of strengths and weaknesses of all models. Though universally accepted as a valid tool—which constitutes its main strength—it should always be kept in mind that the Black-Scholes options pricing model is an approximation of what really happens in the market. In intraday trading, as well as within any other time frame, the price of the derivative vehicle may move away from what Black-Scholes indicates. Moreover, the model

- Does not measure risk
- Underestimates maximum volatility (more on its weak spots in the following section)

Furthermore, as all models written for pricing and for risk management, Black-Scholes has a problem with implied volatility because it is at the same time a most crucial factor and an unobservable quantity. A similar statement is valid in connection to the use of the binomial model (as described in the preceding section). Indeed, the two are not so dissimilar. If in the binomial model we make the grid of time slots really fine, we obtain the Black-Scholes formula that assumes that asset prices follow a geometric Brownian (frictionless) motion.

With this background, let's take a closer look at the nearly 40-year-old structure of the Black-Scholes algorithm. The model specifies that market prices of stock options and warrants on a stock follow, or at least approximate, the following algorithm:

$$F(x, y, T, r) = xN(d_1) - ye^{-rT} N(d_2) \qquad (8.1)$$

where

x = price per share of underlying stock

y = strike price of the option

$T = t^* - t$ = time to expiration (in fraction of years)

t^* = expiration date

t = today's date

r = annualized short-term risk-free interest rate

N = cumulative normal density function

e = Euler's number equal to 2.7182818 . . .

The cumulative normal distribution function is tabulated in most statistical texts, and it can be approximated using a simple algebraic expression. In this option pricing formula, $F(x, y, T, r)$ estimates the value of an option (or warrant) on the stock, with d_1 and d_2 given by the following equations:

$$d_1 = \frac{\ln (n(x/y) + (r + 1/2\ s^2)\ T}{s\sqrt{T}} \qquad (8.2)$$

$$d_2 = d_1 - s\sqrt{T} \qquad (8.3)$$

where

> $\ln$ = natural logarithm
>
> x = price per share of underlying stock
>
> s = annualized standard deviation of stock's return
>
> s^2 = annualized variance of the stock's return
>
> y = strike price of the option

The annualized deviation of the stock's return is essentially the volatility of the price of the underlying equity. $N(d_1)$ and $N(d_2)$ are lognormal distributions (see the previous section). Using logarithms to the base e ($\log_e$ or $\ln$), known as *natural* or *Napierian logarithms,* lead to a significantly simplified formula.

The better way of looking at the Black-Scholes model is as an attempt to specify the equilibrium value of a call option as a function of outlined parameters. Equations 8.1 to 8.3 illustrate the steps needed to obtain a numerical option price. There are no problems associated with the price per share of the underlying stock, the strike price of the option, or the time remaining to the option's expiration date.

However, as already brought to the reader's attention, the tough parameter is the volatility of the price of the underlying equity, which must be estimated and which plays a crucial role in option pricing. A classical method for estimation of volatility uses observations of the stock price at fixed time intervals—days, weeks, months—with the mean rate of return.

A larger sample size (in absolute terms and as a percent of the population) contributes to greater accuracy. The argument that large n also means that the variance may have changed is only partly true.

Last but not least, while in practice many analysts use closing prices from daily data over the most recent 90 or 180 days, one should appreciate that such data may be old because the market has indeed changed. Statistical theory permits testing for this, dividing the larger sample into subsamples that are then subject to t tests (tests of the mean) and chi square tests (analysis-of-variance tests).

ADVANTAGES AND SHORTCOMINGS OF THE BLACK-SCHOLES MODEL

Models are not made to be effective forever. This is true of any construct including the popular Black-Scholes formula for pricing options. Whether or not, as some analysts say, it is overpricing or underpricing options, the fact remains that models have a lifespan, and they start getting unstuck as structural changes alter the behavior of the market.

In spite of this, models are crucial to the attempt by interactive computational finance to apply to the markets some of the complex mathematical techniques developed in physics and in engineering. Behind this effort has been the fact that there exist striking similarities in the idealization of

- The behavior of financial markets
- The astronomical events in the cosmos
- The patterns of weather systems

Indeed, the early 1970s' breakthrough in financial modeling by Fischer Black and Myron Scholes was an adaptation of heat transfer equations from physics. At the core of it was a method of studying *Brownian motion*—that is, the movements of tiny particles buffeted by gas or liquid molecules.

Typically, the formulation of the problem into a modeling structure tries to classify information in a manner amenable to investigation and interpretation. To a substantial extent, this is done by identifying and then handling in an effective manner

- Independent variables
- Dependent variables

Engineers and physicists were the first to practice this approach. Therefore, it is not surprising that one of the basic Black-Scholes assumptions is that price movements in financial markets follow the same kind of a lognormal distribution that applies to natural sciences and their phenomena.

Not all financial distributions, however, can be studied through this model. Some exhibit frequent extreme outcomes, or *fat tails,* with outliers having a far greater impact than values around the mean. By consequence, in a universe of what some analysts consider to be "usual circumstances," there may be awkward price jumps, so that

- Volatility is higher than assumed under normal conditions.
- Risks cannot be entirely hedged away as implied by the idealized model.

The application of developments made in the natural sciences to financial markets is commendable as long as we remember that financial models are not just controlled by natural laws but as well, if not primarily, by human psychology of greed, lust, and fear. Hence, correct modeling requires understanding of the behavior of traders, bankers, and investors.

In spite of these reservations, by being one of the first successful and generally acceptable microeconomic models, the Black-Scholes formula has become a cornerstone to the growth of the options trading business. Even if it works through approximations, it has been instrumental in promoting new techniques for representing complex instruments performance and optimizing portfolio strategies.

At the same time, however, by tracking tick-to-tick behavior of prices and analyzing data streams, financial professionals have developed improved methods. New insight has been cast by awareness that there exist extreme events and their impact can be huge. Hence there exists the need to develop robust techniques for testing and experimentation, able to handle extreme circumstances.

The requirement to study the long leg of a distribution arose more than two decades after the Black-Scholes model was born, in the aftermath of the discovery that distributions of financial events may well be neither normal nor lognormal but leptokurtic with fat tails. The so-called *Hurst coefficient* comes from engineering science, following the observations of the floods of the Nile by a British engineer and agronomist.

Some of the shortcomings of the Black-Scholes model have also to do with its age and with the hypotheses made when it was originally designed. Developed in 1972 when pricing models were still in their early beginnings, the Black-Scholes model violated several basic market premises. Two of the most important are these:

- Asset price behavior is influenced by leverage, stochastic volatility, and excess kurtosis.
- Problems are embedded in derivatives pricing, such as volatility smiles and changing behavior of the price distribution.

When one asks the question "What's wrong with Black-Scholes?" it is not unusual to get as an answer: the volatility smiles; the probability of a stock market crash (which Black-Scholes assumes is close to zero, yet it happens); and the mixing of a discrete-in-time and continuous-in-price space; as well as its weakness in regard to the size of prevailing correlations.

Neither does the Black-Scholes model account for market liquidity. The fact that very little thought is given to liquidity in terms of its price impact is a common pitfall of practically all pricing models. Yet, it escapes nobody's attention that in the markets, liquidity counts a great lot—as illiquidity can happen in the wrong time, upsetting many detailed calculations.

Another shortcoming of the Black-Scholes model is that it abstracts another important market element: when historical volatility is high, hedging becomes practically impossible. Hence, trying to hedge leads to a significant hedging error whose likelihood has to be kept under perspective when using Black-Scholes. The net result is a negative impact on portfolio positions, even the more carefully chosen ones.

Some rocket scientists advise that the best strategy in overcoming the aforementioned facts is *superreplication*, which is based on self-financing using optimal decomposition theorems. Models developed along this line of thinking demonstrate that with a *short gamma* (see Chapter 10), which means a "convex space" in finance jargon, the investor is losing money when the actual volatility is greater than assumed volatility. In contrast, with a *long gamma*, which corresponds to a concave space of instrument prices, the investor makes money when the actual volatility is greater than the one being assumed.

TESTING THE BLACK-SCHOLES MODEL

What the preceding section brought to the reader's attention is not that the Black-Scholes model provides unreliable results. Rather the message is that, like all types of models, it has limitations which must be observed so that its usage is controllable and the dependability of its output properly appreciated. Modeling and simulation are great tools as long as

- We know what they can and cannot provide.
- We are always ready to provide model sustenance, as experience from its usage demonstrates what needs to be done to improve accuracy and performance.

For instance, the Black-Scholes pricing outcome can be improved through an optimization procedure aiming at generating more reliable estimators of volatility. Developed in conjunction to a project by the Swiss Stock Market Index (SMI), this volatility add-on has benefited from an extensive simulation to which were subjected 29,000 complex derivative strategies.[8]

The concept behind this research project came from a computer program developed to serve in the evaluation and behavioral analysis of derivative positions. Its algorithms are based on statistical movements both on the Black-Scholes and the Wiener process.[9] The researchers used high-frequency financial data of European-style options on the SMI. The time frame of the series started January 3, 1994, and ended July 7, 1995. The data set included the following:

- 107,000 information elements on options
- 92,000 underlying data elements
- 298,000 information elements on SMI futures

One of the interesting results of this Swiss study was that there was a decreasing efficiency in the effect of derivatives because of tariff structures (which is not reflected in the different current models).

---

[8] Konrad Baechler, "Black & Scholes-Analyse Optimieren," Schweizer Bank, Zurich, September 1996.

[9] Dimitris N. Chorafas, "How to Understand and Use Mathematics for Derivatives," Euromoney, vol. 2, London, 1995.

The researchers also found that the central factor influencing the Black-Scholes result was volatility. Hence, there exists the need for measuring volatility in an accurate manner:

- Volatility arises through historical and projected price movements,
- But projected price movements include information asymmetries, news, and psychological factors that make its estimates less than reliable.

Theoretically, implied volatility can be computed from observed options prices; also theoretically, as opposed to historical volatility, implied volatility is forward looking. Practically, psychological market factors and asymmetries raise major questions regarding estimates of implied volatility. Probably for this reason, the researchers have focused on two basic kinds of volatility estimation:

- Historical volatility, as ex post evaluation
- Ex ante evaluation of volatility, with an exponential moving-average model used in RiskMetrics, the credit risk model of Crédit Suisse

Part of the test procedure followed in the SMI study applied the aforementioned exponential moving-average volatility approach. Another part used historical volatility. All tests incorporated real dividend payments. Volatility results were plotted after weeding out anomalies. The root-mean-squared error method was used to measure how the model's results fit real market data. (This method reflects the differences between market price and model price.)

Improvements observed by the handling of anomalies ranged from a minimum of 64 percent to a maximum of 89 percent, which in the researchers' opinion opened up substantial application perspectives. One implementation of the method in reference has been the evaluation of risk in a derivatives portfolio as a function of time to maturity.

A total of 29,109 investment possibilities were simulated 10,000 times. Because each option strategy consists of two contracts, the computing environment included some 582,120,000 option prices. This corresponded to about the contract volume of the SOFFEX—the Swiss Options and Financial Futures Exchange—for nearly a decade (at the time this study was done).

To keep the estimation close to real life, as far as the market organization of the SOFFEX was concerned, 50 contracts were always simulated, though liquidity problems that may have existed with the contract size were ignored. Also, costs for margin calls were not taken into account—which demonstrates that even an improved method uses approximations.

These simulation processes produced a three-dimensional graphics output that helped investors and others to visualize the resulting risk strategy. An example was the profit and loss distribution over a 21-day period, taking into account the tariff structure of the market. Another test concerned a vertical spread. The SMI research project with the Black-Scholes model also provided a good example of back testing, which should accompany every simulation.

CHAPTER 9

Option Traders, Buyers, and Writers

TRADING DERIVATIVE INSTRUMENTS

The fast growth of derivatives markets, and the impact that they have on spot markets, has increased the interest traders have in using them for price discovery. It has also created new opportunities for hedging, though hedging, too, involves risk, and therefore measurement tools are necessary as we will see in Chapter 10.

Trading activities may take place for the bank's own account or for that of its clients. Part 1 made the point that derivative financial instruments that are traded in exchanges are standardized. They are products usually designed to be bought and sold in active markets.

Other derivatives are custom-made for individual counterparties, typically exchanged over the counter at negotiated prices. Because of its wide range, its leverage, and its capacity for personalization, derivatives trading can send signals to other markets, which may have a stabilizing effect *if* the future expectations of the market players are positive.

In contrast, if the derivative markets give a negative message or there is high volatility in prices, derivatives trading and associated dynamic hedging strategies can wreak havoc on illiquid spot markets. The extent to which derivatives create unwanted consequences for the entire financial system is closely tied to the question of how these instruments are used by their sellers and their buyers in specific market circumstances.

Most derivative transactions relate to selling and buying for profits, not to hedging as it is so often said. A majority of the counterparties are correspondent banks or hedge funds. Integral parts of trading activities are

- Market making
- Positioning
- Arbitrage operations

Market making involves quoting to other market participants ask and bid prices with the intention of generating revenues based on spread and volume. *Positioning* includes the identification and management of market risk positions, with the expectation of profiting from favorable movements in prices, rates, or indexes. An integral part of *arbitrage* is identifying and taking advantage from price differentials between

- Different markets for the same product or
- Similar products in the same market.

It is equally important to understand, when examining the behavior of markets, the way the trader makes money for the bank and for himself or herself. Human nature sees to it that prerequisite to such understanding is the ability to answer a number of critical questions:

- Has a trade created value?
- What were the fundamental assumptions? Were they correct?
- Was the business right for the bank? For the client?
- How did the trader leverage the instruments?
- What kind of commission did the trader derive from the transaction?
- What type and how much risk are the bank and its client assumed to have in the longer term?

If nobody in senior management is able, or wants, to understand how the trader makes the money, *then* nobody can control the exposure assumed with a given derivative transaction. This speaks volumes because, to a large extent, trading in derivatives essentially means trading uncertainty. Currently available models

- Make it possible to put a price on a contingent liability,
- But do not provide a way for measuring and pricing longer-term exposure.

Chapter 8 pressed the point that in trading options (and all other types of derivatives), understanding volatility is crucial to appreciating the uncertainty embedded into movements in the prices of securities. Part of the task is conceptualizing why volatility itself is so volatile. It was high in 2001 and 2002, it was very low in 2004 to mid-2006, and it started to rise again in late 2006 and early 2007.

Experts have suggested that one reason volatility was so low from mid-2004 to mid-2006 was that there were so many sellers of equity options. This practically meant that there were plenty of writers of insurance against falls in share prices, whose protection sales have driven down the price of implied volatility.

Hedge funds, commercial banks, investment banks, and fund managers have been selling lots of equity options—a profitable trade up to a point. Players in this popular game, however, have often forgotten that several banks have confirmed financial catastrophes by selling options. A most famous instance came in 1995, when Nick Leeson sold 34,000 options on Japan's Nikkei 225 Stock Average index:

- This drove implied volatility on the world's second-biggest stock market from 22 to 11 percent,
- But shortly thereafter the treasury of Barings Bank, the oldest merchant bank in England, ran into the ground, bringing the venerable bank to bankruptcy.

Some of the risks connected to derivatives trading are legal; others are not. On November 28, 2003, Japan's regulators asked for penalties to be imposed on Société Générale (SocGen), the French global bank, for a series of exchangeable bond transactions in November 2001 at its Japanese subsidiary that allegedly violated trading rules. This move was part of a wide-ranging investigation by the Securities and Exchange Surveillance Commission (SESC) into the activities of more than 100 domestic and foreign brokerages in Tokyo.

The SESC asked the Financial Services Agency (FSA), Japan's financial watchdog, to take action because SocGen's Japanese brokerage allegedly used exchangeable bonds designed to manipulate market prices and avoid making multi-million-yen payouts.[1]

---

[1] News item, *Financial Times*, November 29–30, 2003.

Beyond this incident, in March 2003, Japan's FSA ordered J.P. Morgan's Japanese brokerage to suspend stock trading for 10 days and to submit a business improvement plan as a penalty for similar illegal exchangeable bond transactions.

OPTIONS TRADING

When options started being traded in the early 1970s, they were highly regulated. In addition, transaction costs were high. The secondary market for options was started in 1973, by the Chicago Board Options Exchange (CBOE); a year later the volume on the CBOE was about 30,000 contracts traded per day (a big number at that time).

Within a few years, by December 1983, puts and calls were traded on an estimated 145 securities. This number grew exponentially during the following years, until the crash in 1987 when it tapered off. The following year the daily contracts on the CBOE dropped slightly, but the exponential growth curve started all over again; by 1994 it surpassed the 1987 level and kept on growing. At present, the volume in certain option markets is many times bigger than on the underlying stock. The main trading strategies include these:

- Write call
- Buy call
- Write put
- Buy put

Options are traded on an expiration cycle based on that of the underlying futures contract. Call and put options are traded in the same delivery months as the underlying futures contract. No certificates are issued to evidence options. Investors look to the statements and confirmation they receive from their brokers as evidence of their positions as option holders or writers. Authority is exercised by a system of rules.

An *options class* means all option contracts of the same type covering the same underlying futures contract—for instance, all Treasury bond call options, regardless of expiration date or exercise price. The term *options series* is used in connection to all option contracts of the same class, with the same exercise price and expiration date. Thus, a class of options can belong to different series.

A group of firms known as *clearing members* carries the positions of all option holders and option sellers in their accounts. To qualify as a clearing member, a company must meet financial requirements, provide collateral for the positions of the option writers that it carries, and contribute to clearing funds that protect against a clearing member's failure.

Indeed, a predominant opinion among experts is that the success of the organized options exchanges can be attributed to the creation of a central marketplace, with its attendant regulatory, surveillance, and price dissemination functions. This includes the capability of the Options Clearing Corporation (OCC)[2] that looks after the writers' obligations, financial strength of clearing members, collateral that they deposit, obligations of correspondent clearing entities, and the clearing of funds. Taken together, these functions make up the OCC system backing the performance of options.

Notice that without a system of clearers, credit risk would be an important exposure, even if derivative instruments were generally considered to involve mainly market risk. Creditworthiness is a significant factor in pricing and selling instruments, making it difficult for institutions with less than an AAA or at least an AA credit rating to have access to the international market (more on this in Chapter 10). The success of any derivatives market—indeed of any market at large—depends on the following:

• The trading entity's solvency
• Rules that are generally appreciated
• Restrictions on market makers
• A dependable clearing system

In options trading, the seller must be prepared to enter an appropriate futures position opposite of the option buyer if and when the option is exercised. All options transactions are either opening or closing transactions:

• An *opening transaction* is one in which a trader establishes or increases a position in an option.
• In contrast, a *closing transaction* is one in which a trader decreases or eliminates an existing option position.

---

[2] Not to be confused with the Office of the Comptroller of the Currency.

A trader who has made an opening transaction by selling a call might later buy a call on the futures contract with the same striking price. With this, he or she is offsetting the short call position, terminating his or her obligations as an option writer. It is, however, important to keep in mind that—because of price asymmetries—no trader can truly offset the purchase of a call with the sale of a put, as many people think. Quite similarly, the sale of a call option cannot be fully offset with a purchase of a put.

Adjustments may be made to some of the standard terms of outstanding stock options when predefined events occur, like stock splits, reverse stock splits, rights offerings, reorganizations, recapitalizations, or mergers in connection to the underlying. Or, alternatively, adjustments may be made in cases of dissolution or liquidation of the issuer of the underlying security.

Generally, no adjustment is made for ordinary cash dividends or distributions. A cash dividend or distribution is considered *ordinary* unless it exceeds an established *x percent* of the aggregate market value of the underlying security outstanding; this *x percent* often depends on the jurisdiction. On the other hand, precisely because stock options are not generally adjusted for ordinary cash dividends and distributions, writers of calls are entitled to retain dividends and distributions earned on the underlying securities during the time prior to exercise.

A call holder becomes entitled to the dividend if he or she exercises the option prior to the ex-dividend date. If an underlying security is converted into a right to receive a fixed amount of cash, options on that security will generally be adjusted to require the delivery upon exercise of a fixed amount of cash. Different jurisdictions, however, may have different rules.

Not only does the protection of investor interests have an impact on the rules written to regulate the deals being made but also, under certain conditions, it may necessitate compensation for some of the risks. The rules of options markets, generally, limit the maximum options on the same side of the market. An example of this type of rule is that the side of calls held plus puts written would be limited with respect to a single underlying that may be carried in the accounts of a single investor or group of investors acting in concert.

Known as *position limits*, these differ for options on different underlying interests. Information concerning the position limits for particular options is available from brokers or from the options market on which those options are traded. An options market has the privilege of stopping the introduction of new options on an underlying on which it has doubts. Also, in certain circumstances, it may impose restrictions on transactions that open new positions in options series that have been previously introduced.

Theoretically, internally traded options can be written and bought—and positions in these options can ordinarily be liquidated—in offsetting closing transactions in any of the options markets in which the options are traded. In real life, however, premiums are affected by market behavior conditions, and, therefore, prices may not be the same in all markets at any given time or place.

FLEXIBLY STRUCTURED OPTIONS

The first thing done by a rational financial institution that is *designing options* is to examine for which style and type (Chapter 7) there is demand. The next step is to select the *underlying security* on which the option will be based and traded in the market. Among the popular types of options currently available are those with underlying

- Interest rates
- Equities
- Stock indexes
- Government debt
- Foreign currencies

As derivative financial products steadily develop and new designs are introduced, options of other types of underlying interests also become available, first on a customized basis and then—if they attract investors' interest—in the wider market. It is a common practice that options traded in exchanges use *standard terms* regarding

- Whether the option is a call or a put
- Style of the option (American, European, Asian)
- Expiration date
- Exercise price
- Whether it involves physical delivery or cash settlement

- Manner in which cash payment and exercise value of cash-settled option is determined
- Different adjustment provisions
- Whether the option has automatic exercise clauses

Each option market publishes specification sheets setting forth the particular standards of the options traded on that market. However, an options market may also provide for trading in options whose terms are not all fixed in advance but subject to certain limitations. And the counterparties, too, may designate some of the terms.

In the past three decades, the rapid development of financial markets could not have been realized without deregulation and the growth of futures and options exchanges. As barriers between markets have fallen, international investors have turned their attention to new markets, and the proliferation of new instruments led to the promotion of trading opportunities.

The growth of trading in financial products has also been fueled by the increased sophistication and internalization of investors. On one hand, this has led to the standardization of exchange-traded instrument features; on the other hand, it has led to a proliferation of complex over-the-counter deals.

The terms of *flexibly structured options* are associated with those that are not all standardized. When such an option is sold in an opening transaction, the counterparties have the flexibility to set forth some of its terms within the rules of the options market on which the transaction occurs.

The terms that may be fixed by the parties are called *variable*. If many of these terms are not normalized, then it is less likely that there will be an active secondary market in which holders and writers of such options will be able to close out their positions by offsetting sales and purchases.

Usually, trading procedures established by options markets for transactions in flexibly structured options differ from the procedures for transactions in other options. An options market may fix the minimum sizes or minimum monetary values for transactions in flexibly structured options, but it will leave some freedom to sophisticated investors seeking to manage particular

- Trading risks
- Portfolio positions

The bottom line is that the parties to an opening transaction in flexibly structured options may designate the option's variable terms in accordance with the rules of the options market where the transaction takes place. Limits defined by the options markets may differ from option to option, though a given market may more generally require that positions in certain flexibly structured options be aggregated with positions in some other options (as discussed in the preceding section).

As a rule, the exercise, assignment, and settlement of flexibly structured options occur in the same manner as they do for other options of the same style with the same underlying. The method of determining the date of a flexibly structured index option is a variable term, fixed by the parties in their opening transaction.

Additionally, as explained in the preceding section, in the case of options standardized by the market, those with the same normalized terms comprise an *options series*. Options of the same series traded on more than one options market at the same time are known as *multiply traded options*. *Internationally traded options* are part of this class. Hedging-wise, positions in options can be liquidated in offsetting closing transactions. But there is a hitch: because premiums are affected by market forces, the premiums for identical multiply traded options may not be the same in all markets at any given time.

Chapter 7 brought to the reader's attention that the period during which an option is exercisable depends on its *style*. For instance, a capped option is subject to automatic exercise *if* the automatic exercise value of the underlying hits the cap price for the option. Other options are subject to automatic exercise at expiration if then they are in-the-money.

To exercise an option that is not subject to automatic exercise, the holder must direct his or her broker to give exercise instructions, before the firm's cut-off time for accepting exercise instruction on that day. A brokerage firm's cut-off time for accepting exercise instructions becomes critical on the last trading day before an option expires. Option holders and writers who actively manage their options positions need to understand the fine print of exercise procedures.

BUYERS' STRATEGIES

The way an adage has it, investors who buy options are either purchasing volatility to protect against market fluctuations or to speculate. The greater is the turbulence in the market, the more the option might be worth. This, however, does not exclude that (for a European option) market conditions might be unfavorable at maturity and that the option might expire without being exercised.

For hedging purposes investors may buy calls for several reasons. Most often, the objective is to take advantage of an anticipated increase in the price of an underlying futures contract. By purchasing the call, they hope for an increase in the value of both the underlying and the call option.

Contrary to the strategy of hedging, a speculator will buy a call to sell it at a higher premium. A trader may purchase calls to protect short futures positions. The same may be true for a mining, manufacturing, or agricultural company who oversold its produce. For all participants, when futures are rising, the purchase of calls presents a method of entering markets with risk limited to the premium paid:

- If the market continues to rise, then the calls can be exercised at a profit.
- If the market declines, then there is no margin call, the risk being the premium.

A manufacturer may buy options for physical delivery of raw materials to hedge an expected move in prices. Alternatively, a gold producer may use futures to hedge against market downturns in the price of bullion.

A speculator who believes that gold prices will rise sharply over the next few months might purchase call options on gold futures. If prices rise, he can then take profit by reselling the options, or he may hold the position in hope that prices will increase further.

- If, instead, futures prices decline during this period, he can sell back his options at a loss while they still retain some value.
- Or he may maintain his option position in the hope of a market reversal, given that the most he can lose is the initial cost of the option.

While calls provide the holder with the possibility of *preprocessing* by establishing a sales price in advance of an actual sale, puts permit to hedge long futures positions in portfolios. Buying put options can act as insurance against the depreciation of a long futures position, in the expectation that a futures loss would be offset by a gain on the put. This, however, is not mathematically precise.

By buying at-the-money put options on a given raw material, the investor hopes that he insures his ability to sell his produce at current market prices. This is true, but at the same time he will not be able to take advantage of a market decline of the material in reference, as we saw in Chapter 7 through practical examples.

A call writer will sell a derivative product for the premium he gains, given his expectation on price trends. The risk he is assuming is that he may be obliged to sell a given futures contract at the specific (exercise) price at any time prior to expiration, upon being notified that the call has been exercised (more on sellers in the following section).

There exist, as well, more complex strategies that use puts and calls in combination with each other and with futures. These are the *synthetic positions* discussed in Chapter 7 (see also the section "Trading in Synthetic Options" later in this chapter). There exist, as well, complex arbitrage strategies, known as *conversions* and *reverse conversions*, used to duplicate traditional cash-and-carry operations. We have already spoken of the covered call purchase that consists of

- A long call option, and
- A short futures position.

This is like buying a call option and selling a futures position. (A *covered put purchase* consists of a long futures contract and a long put, which means buying a futures position and buying a put option.) Covered purchases have risk and reward features that look like purchasing options outright, but the exposure is nonlinear, and risk management requires lots of knowledge and information.

There is no derivative instrument, or any other financial product, with unlimited reward potential and minimal risk. Among the better known, and simpler, risks for options buyers is that if they neither sell their option in the secondary market nor exercise it prior to its expiration, they will lose their investment in the premium. This may seem fair enough, but it also identifies the holder's inability to utilize the leverage of options to control a larger quantity of the underlying than he or she might have purchased directly.

An evident risk for the holder is that the more an option is out-of-the-money and the shorter the remaining time to expiration, the greater the price volatility necessary for the option to become profitable and the shorter the time within which this price movement must occur. Moreover, exercise provisions of an option may create risks for their holders. In spite of these exposures, *buying options* generally involves less risk than writing options.

WRITING OPTIONS

The writer of an option accepts a legal obligation to purchase or sell the underlying asset if the option is exercised against it, no matter how far the market price has moved. If the seller does not own the underlying that he or she has contracted to sell—a transaction known as an *uncovered call option* (Chapter 7)—the risk can be unlimited.

While this does not happen every day, it is nevertheless true that the exposure assumed in *writing options* is considerably greater than it is in buying options, and it is not always compensated by the premium. The seller may be liable for a margin to maintain his or her hedged position, and a loss may be sustained well in excess of what the hedge may offer. It comes therefore as no surprise that several conservatively managed firms have eliminated the practice of writing options. And if they buy options, they see to it that the counterparty risk is controlled by

- Strict limits on the size of deals
- A high credit rating (AAA, AA) of the counterparty

This section pays particular attention to the risks options writers face because the decision of *if* and *when* to exercise the option rests entirely with the buyer. In practice, few options are likely to be exercised before expiration since the buyer can usually obtain additional profits by selling the option in the market, but the fact remains that the option seller must be ready to face the eventuality that exercise could occur at any time prior to expiration.

The cost of option writing varies according to the amount of premium received for the options written. The premium received must be put up as the margin for the options, but it may be in interest-bearing form. In essence, this type of premium is like an interest-free loan and may reduce the cost of the transaction. Commissions will affect the cost and therefore gains or losses.

Like futures trading, but in contrast to buying options, selling options requires margin deposits that are adjusted daily in accordance with option premium fluctuations. Brokers are typically very careful in managing their clients' margin requirements—calling for more money when it is due because the market moved against the seller.

Since market prices are not truly predictable and may, for example, rise rather than fall as the seller had expected when writing the option, the risks involved in writing calls must be studied in advance at different levels of likelihood. This is true even if theoretically call sellers can offset their positions at any time through compensating operations.

To protect themselves, call writers follow different strategies. For instance, *covered call writers* own the underlying futures. A seller is employing a conservative strategy by seeking to reduce the risk of his or her existing long futures positions. If a call option is exercised by the buyer, the exercise serves to liquidate the covered writer's offsetting futures position—but that's an *if*.

Moreover, the fact that an option seller may not receive immediate notification of an assignment creates a risk for uncovered writers of physical delivery call stock options, exercisable when the underlying security is the subject of a tender offer. If the seller fails to purchase the underlying on or before the option's expiration date,

He may learn after the expiration date that he has been assigned an exercise filed with the OCC on or before that date,

But in the meantime commodity prices have changed to his disfavor, without relieving him of his obligation to perform.

Covered call sales are often used by professional portfolio managers to increase the yield on their securities, and under certain conditions this strategy might become profitable. Such conditions are characteristic of periods of relatively stable markets, when the lack of a definitive trend on movements would keep traders on the sidelines.

More precisely, covered call sales are done when the writer thinks that the price of the underlying futures will exhibit an upside bias; while covered put writes are used when the writer's outlook is neutral to bearish. One of the risks confronting the writer of a covered call is that he or she

> Forgoes the opportunity to profit from an increase in the value of the underlying above the option price,
>
> But continuously bears the risk of a decline in the value of the underlying interest.

Unlike the holder of the underlying interest who has not written a call against it in exchange for the premium, the covered call writer gives up the opportunity to benefit from an increase in the value of the underlying interest above the exercise price if he or she is assigned an exercise.

Uncovered, or *naked*, *call writers* are more risk prone. They have no underlying futures position but seek to gain from an expected weakening of the underlying futures. The risk of these sellers stems from the possibility that if the futures price significantly increases, the call will be assigned, with large net losses to the seller. Quite similarly, there exist covered put writers and uncovered put writers.

The distinction between covered and uncovered call writing positions should retain the reader's attention. Though a call option writer who is not covered may hold another option in a *spread* position and thereby offset some or all of the risk of the option he or she has written, asymmetries are always at work, and the spread may not offset all of the risk of the uncovered seller position.

Another seller strategy is *ratio writing*. It resembles collars (Chapter 7) in the sense that it permits the option writer to create a profit band of futures price movements. Multiple options are written against each underlying futures contract, simultaneously generating covered and uncovered option positions. This practice involves either

- Selling two or more puts against a short futures position,
- Or selling two or more calls against a long futures position.

Ratio writing may as well be employed in connection with existing futures positions, taking advantage of the fact that option premiums generally do not move with futures prices down to the last cent. Experts suggest that this is a good strategy when the option writer is not sure of the market's direction but expects futures prices to trade in a narrow range around current prices.

TRADING IN SYNTHETIC OPTIONS

Sophisticated option strategies employ a number of positions involving calls, puts, strike prices, and expiration dates as well as the alternatives of owing the underlying, being short of it, or playing on ratios. Examples of synthetic financial products created with options and underlyings are shown in Table 9.1. (See also the broader discussion on synthetic financial instruments in Chapter 2.)

Let's start with some examples. A long underlying short call position has the same effect as a short position. This has clear implications on the interdependence of put and call options of the same strike price and same expiration date, but as the market turns, profits and losses don't need to balance out. At any given time, however, and for a period that is reasonably short, the call, put, and underlying positions can be combined into an overall P&L framework. In principle,

- There is currently a wide range of synthetic options offered in the financial markets.
- Among the simpler are those that actively combine puts and calls in various combinations.

As a rule, credit risk and market risk with synthetic options are greater than those found in simple option positions. The problem starts with the very first basic step, that of taking a view of the financial market and its evolution and the impact of market changes on the instruments of a synthetic.

TABLE 9.1

Synthetics through Options and Underlyings

If You Are Exposed in Options	Then You Have a Synthetic
Long put at price P and long on underlying	Long call at price P
Long call at price P and long on underlying	Long put at price P
Short put at price P and long on underlying	Short call at price P
Short call at price P and long on underlying	Short put at price P
Long call at price P and short put at price P	Long instrument
Long call at price P and long put at price P	Short instrument

The next challenge is judging the sector of the market to which the option addresses itself in terms of actual versus projected price fluctuations that will cause a profit or loss. Price volatility is much more difficult to forecast in the case of synthetic derivatives, as the price-driven positions multiply.

Even a relatively simple case of synthetics may involve long calls, long puts, short calls, and short puts in some ingenious combination—which, superficially, a trader or investor may think of as being a sure profit. But when the market turns around, one position does not compensate the other. We have spoken several times of the result of asymmetries.

Synthetic financial instruments get increasingly complex as the number of combinations and permutations increases. Because in the general case synthetics are created by a combination of long or short options and long or short underlying financial instruments, for risk control purposes it is wise to unbundle a synthetic package to its atomic level. This permits an investor to

- Examine separately long and short positions
- Attribute risk factors by element, then integrate those risk factors into a comprehensive figure

Here is a simple example from real life that dates back some years. A manufacturer of gold jewelry made a large purchase of physical gold when the metal was at $400 per ounce. Because the drop in gold's value could force him to discount the retail price of his jewelry, he immediately established a short position in gold futures hoping to hedge his risk. The gold price collapse of 1992 saw to it that his hedge protected him from $72 per ounce in losses. Therefore, he continued his hedge.

As a contract approached final delivery, he would roll it into a later contract. Because the jewelry manufacturer's calculation showed that his exposure was equivalent to owning 200 ounces of gold, he maintained for some time a three-contract short position in gold futures.

Then came a projection of an uptrend. At the end of 1992 his broker advised him to buy gold as there was a long in gold prices. If gold rose in price, the extra profits from jewelry markups would be offset by losses from the short futures position. But if the manufacturer removed the futures position and gold prices fell again, he would have nothing left to offset his markdown losses:

- If he had a gold call position rather than owning physical gold, he would have control over losses.
- But he could not dispose of his physical gold unless he elected to go out of business.

As a solution, also on the advice of his broker, the gold jewelry manufacturer synthesized his position given that the physical gold price correlated well with the near-term gold futures contract. The principle was the following:

> *If* one is long on the underlying instrument and wishes to have the equivalent of long calls in options at the exercise price P,
>
> *Then* he needs only purchase puts of the exercise price P.

With this solution, the gold jewelry manufacturer's downside losses stopped at the level of the put options that he had bought. His profits, however, were open ended if gold prices rallied. His net position synthesized a long call with the price at the put options specified price. If gold prices rose, the risk faced by the manufacturer was the loss of the premium paid for each option. In spite of its constraints, the hedge was a good one; but notice how dynamic it had to be kept in order to deliver results.

SPREADS TRADING

Spreads represent the difference between the prices at which dealers are willing to buy and sell securities. Spreads trading provides much of the profits earned by bond dealers. However, there is evidence indicating that as markets become more transparent and prices become widely known to traders, spreads are reduced. (See also Chapter 7 for a general discussion on spreading and Chapter 11 on credit spreads.)

A *spread option* is a derivative instrument providing a payoff based on the spread between reference indexes. In a way not dissimilar to the examples given in the preceding section on trading in synthetic options, risk control with spread options is more complex than with traditional options. One of the reasons for complexity is that the underlying market variables are lognormally distributed, making it impossible to combine them to obtain a lognormally distributed spread.

Therefore, market players make assumptions regarding spread movement and its treatment. For instance, one hypothesis is that the spread itself has a price that is lognormally distributed. An alternative hypothesis is that the spread is distributed normally (or in some other fashion) rather than lognormally.

Both assumptions have limitations. A better approach is to employ a two-factor mapping that requires an examination of the distribution of each of the two variables enriched with the use of correlations. But as we have seen in several occasions, correlations and covariance in finance are notoriously difficult to compute and document.

If one abstracts from the challenges associated with the measurements necessary for risk control in spreads trading, the able usage of option spreads may mean attractive returns. Option spread strategies can be constructed to capitalize on an essentially neutral market where futures trades don't present great profits opportunities:

- In an option spread, a call or put can be bought at the same time another call or put is sold.
- The purchase and sale, however, cannot be of the same call or put or the net position would be nil.

Therefore, option contracts vary in regard to strike price, expiration date, or both. The most fundamental kinds of option spreads are vertical, horizontal, and diagonal. There are, as well, reverse spreads and other types. We will briefly examine some of them.

A *vertical spread* is the purchase and sale of calls or puts in which the two legs of the spread have different strike prices but the same expiration date. The term originated in the stock option market, where options were quoted in the financial press with expiration months running across a row and strike prices running downward in a column.

Vertical spreads may be constructed to take advantage of a sideways-trading market, generally classified as either bullish or bearish. Depending on their design, they may profit in advancing or declining markets. Since the strike prices of the two legs are different, these strategies also have been called *money spreads:*

- With a bull spread, the trader or investor buys a low struck option and sells a relatively high struck option.

- With a bear spread, he or she buys a high struck option and sells a relatively low struck option.

A *bull vertical call* is a combination of a long call with a low strike and a short call with a higher strike. Because the long position is chosen closer to the money, it is more expensive. This type of strategy is suitable when an investor is bullish and wants to generate market gains within a limited range.

To appreciate the difference between vertical, horizontal, and diagonal spreads, let's take as an example a spread with two contracts involving two different options: *buy* at the $6.25 strike price per bushel (usually written 625 as it is expressed in cents) one July call option; and *sell* a July call option at the 650 strike price. The spread, hence the difference between the two options, is 25 cents:

- If the contracts are exercised the same month, like the buy 625 and sell 650 example we have seen with July contracts, we speak of a *vertical spread*.
- If they are exercised in two different months but at the same strike price, like buy a July 650 call and sell a September 650 call, then this is a *horizontal spread*, or *time spread*.
- A *diagonal spread* will involve both different strike prices and different months, like buy one call July 625 and sell one call September 650.

A *long backspread* is generated when a trader or investor buys more put or call contracts than he or she is selling, all contracts having the same expiration. To remain delta neutral (see Chapter 10), this spread requires

- The purchase of calls with higher strikes and the sale of calls with lower strikes,
- Or the purchase of puts with lower strikes and the sale of puts with higher strikes.

As volatility increases, the value of the backspread moves higher. If the value moves south because volatility is low and the market remains stable, the long and short calls expire worthless but the writer retains his or her premium income.

The opposite of a long backspread is a *short backspread*, also known as *ratio spread*. This is somewhat more complex than other spreads because it does not involve a one-to-one correspondence between contracts.

For instance, we can buy one soybean call at 650 cents per bushel at the cost of 28 cents. But we can also sell two calls at 675 cents per bushel at 14 cents each to make up for the 28 cents and have no debit to our account. (Higher-price calls cost less money, as a higher price is less likely to be reached than a lower price.) This is, however, an imperfect hedge because it leaves the trader or the investor one call contract short. As a result,

If the market turns against the investor's view,

Then the risk taken by the investor can be unlimited.

The major holding costs in the government bond market are an example of *reverse spreads*. The term *reverse spread* identifies the difference between the lending rate on general collateral and the lending rate on specific collateral. The difference is usually positive because of

- Difficulties in finding the owner of a particular bond
- The likely attempts of other would-be shorters to find that same bond

The scenario translates into an opportunity loss on the money lent through reverses. Bonds are sold short through *reverse repurchase agreements* in which the short seller lends money and takes the security he or she wants to short as collateral.

EXERCISE, SETTLEMENT, AND TECHNICAL SUPPORT

Many option buyers and sellers close their positions through an offsetting transaction. Even so, they need not only know the action to be taken prior to exercise, as well as exercise procedures, but they also need to be able to determine whether exercise is or is not more advantageous than offsetting.

An option holder who decides to exercise his or her option before expiration must give exercise instructions to his or her broker before the firm's cut-off time for accepting such instructions. The limit is the last trading day before the option's expiration. An option that expires unexercised becomes worthless.

Brokers accept standing instructions to exercise or they have procedures for the exercise of options that are in-the-money by a specified amount at expiration. But investors should

- Discuss with the broker the potential consequences of such instructions
- Determine whether the exercise of their options is subject to standing instructions of their broker

Additionally, some options may be subject to automatic exercise. For instance, capped options are subject to automatic exercise if the value of the underlying interest hits the cap price for the option. Some other options are subject to automatic exercise at expiration, if at that time they are in-the-money.

In the United States, the Options Clearing Corporation (OCC) assigns exercises in standardized lots to clearing member accounts. The clearing member then assigns them to customers maintaining positions as writers of the exercised options series. The rules of the options markets require their member firms to allocate assignments to customers on a first-in, first-out (FIFO) basis or on a random basis.

On practically all exercised physical delivery transactions, stock options are handled through stock clearing corporations in the same way as ordinary purchases and sales of the underlying. After exercise and assignment of a physical delivery stock option, the OCC reports it to the designated stock clearing firm of the clearing members representing the exercising holder and assigned writer.

The way of determining the exercise settlement value for a particular option series is fixed by the options market on which the series is traded. However, as it has been already brought to the reader's attention, the exercise settlement values for options on a particular underlying traded in one options market may not be determined in the same manner as the exercise settlement values for options or futures on the same underlying traded in another market:

- On specified days or on all days, options markets may change the method of determining exercise settlement values for particular options series.
- An options market might phase in a change in the method of determining exercise settlement values by opening new series of options, different in the method for calculating

exercise settlement values, but otherwise identical to outstanding options series.

The *settlement currency* is the one in which the cash settlement amount is payable. Tax consequences of an options transaction depend on both the tax status and type of underlying because tax rules are not the same for each type of underlying asset. Other factors are whether an option is exercised, is allowed to expire, or is the subject of a closing transaction; whether it has been written covered or uncovered; and whether there are specific rules in the jurisdiction that pertain to the transaction.

As it easily transpires from these references, advanced information technology (IT) solutions are necessary not only for risk management—which is a "must"—but also for administrative duties connected to trading. Derivatives need high tech because they are a complex business involving

- Rapidly changing products
- A great variety of trading term structures
- A maze of taxation rules, even in the same jurisdiction

Technical support must more than match the institution's risk control culture. As I never tire of repeating, risk management strategies can make or break a firm. Information technology that supports options trading must be handled by avant-garde professionals. The support must be available in real time and be knowledge enriched, extensible, adaptable, and responsive to rapid changes. One of the major problems associated with the able use of IT in connection to derivatives is that technology specialists lack the domain expertise to make the system focused, to make the system react rapidly to changes by revamping it, and to never miss an opportunity to upgrade it.

PART FOUR

Risk Control for Options

CHAPTER 10

The Greeks:
Delta, Gamma, Theta, Kappa, Rho

THE CHALLENGE OF MEASURING
RISK AND RETURN

Derivatives are a game of risk. No policy and no model can eliminate that element. It is she who controls best her exposure who
wins. There are many reasons why exposure can go out of control,
ranging from too little attention paid to risk and return in the
design of the financial instrument to too little experimentation to
study aftereffects in the longer run. Very often

- More emphasis is placed on features promoting sales than
  on risk control.
- The internal control system is defective or nonexistent.
- There is poor top management oversight of what takes
  place on the trading floor.

One of the factors behind substandard management of
assumed exposure is *basis risk*, to which reference was made in
Chapter 1. As a reminder, basis risk expresses the relationship in
exposure between the underlying asset and the derivative product
(or reference asset), which is usually a publicly traded security.

- Bankers, traders, and investors do not properly track the
  real risk against which they hedge.
- Left to its own devices, basis risk becomes a major concern
  to everybody, from buyers to writers and regulators.

The first step to overcome the problems associated with deficient control of exposure is senior management's policies reflecting the awareness that risk is a dynamic entity that changes all the time for every position in the portfolio. This requires the development of a framework for accurate risk measurement and management, which in turn calls for tools and a methodology that permit us to

- Test our hypotheses connected to hedging
- Develop exposure-oriented scenarios
- Confront them with adversity
- Analyze the aftereffect of stress tests
- Reach timely as well as focused conclusions on risk control

Examining the reasons why exposure can go out of control, and experimenting on them, is a very instructive experience, especially to those bankers, traders, and investors who are branching out into all sorts of new financial instruments and new markets. For instance, to guard against the risk that she might end up with a load of bonds she does not want, the option writer typically tries to sell some bonds short, but

The more likely the option is to be exercised,

The greater the proportion of the nominal value the seller will try to dispose of in advance.

A scenario built along this frame of reference can theoretically tell how much a trader, investor, or speculator needs to sell short in order to cover herself. Since bond prices and volatility change constantly, the same is true of the required hedge ratio—which essentially means that option hedges must adjust the weights to balance risk.

Market characteristics play a major role in the act of rebalancing a portfolio. For instance, while it is fairly easy to buy bonds in emerging markets, it can be very difficult and expensive to sell them short. If bond prices fall too quickly, as they did in March 1994, those who have sold put options cannot dehedge fast enough. A similar problem created huge losses for currency options dealers in September 1992 when the European Union's exchange rate mechanism was derailed.

The best traders and financial analysts are aware of these facts; hence they try to rethink and revamp their hedges—sometimes instrument by instrument. This is, however, tough both because of the amount of work involved and because an estimate of future volatility is essentially a guesstimate.

The rebalancing of exposure is no easy business. To simplify matters, many traders (and, sometimes, risk managers) assume that the original hedge ratio was right and adjustments are needed only for market gyrations. This may not be so for two reasons:

- With little price history to show how volatile an asset has been in the past, it is more than usually hard to predict how volatile it may be in the future.
- Pricing models are based on the false hypothesis that the market behavior is generally symmetric and price variations are normally distributed—which is rarely the case.

Financial markets do not behave in a nice and neat manner, and some markets are particularly erratic. No wonder, therefore, that more often than not, a given hedge will turn out to be wrong, and the same is true of the classical way of revamping hedges. This further underlines the need for metrics and for test tools.

The so-called Greeks, which are the theme of this chapter, are among the better tools for measurement of exposure associated to a derivative instrument. The better method is that the results provided by the *delta*, *gamma*, and other tests discussed in the following section are not seen as standalone, scalar quantities. Rather, they should be added up into a pattern of exposure that is compared to capital levels, the better ones being these:

- Earnings at risk
- Capital at risk

Earnings at risk (EAR) measures the discounted pretax earnings impact of a given event or exposure over a specified time horizon—for instance, the exposure revealed by a delta test, or a defined shift in the interest rate yield curve, for a given currency. Earnings at risk must be calculated separately for each inventoried position, and they should reflect the repricing gaps in the position, both explicit and implicit.

Differences established by marking-to-market and marking-to-model should be added up into earnings at risk. The outcome of such evaluations is closely connected to risk and return. Limits may be set for earnings at risk on a desk, business unit, country-of-operation, and total entity basis, with exposures regularly reviewed in relation to limits and EAR targets.

Capital at risk (CAR), discussed in Chapter 6, is a concept based on the aggregation method that simulates allocation of economic capital[1] among competing objectives. The allocation of economic capital should be mapped onto a matrix: by business unit and product line—such as loans, investments, or trading. Changes in the value of the bank's portfolio are inputs to the CAR. Simulation and experimentation are the best way to evaluate EAR and CAR, both ex ante and ex post.

THE GREEKS IN A NUTSHELL

In the background of all hedging, as well as of metrics and tools used in the evaluation of hedges, is the price change relationship between the option and the underlying futures. The crucial question is: How will the changes in the price of an option relate to the changes in the price of the underlying contract? We know the relationship is usually not linear, but we do not necessarily know its exact pattern.

This lack of one-to-one correspondence leads to other queries: What kind of measurements can we use to gauge the change in the price of the derivatives vehicle for a given change in the underlying's price? Can our tools help in assuming neutral market positions? How polyvalent is our methodology, and how much can we depend on it? The answer is given in the following bulleted list:

- *Delta* is the expected change in an option's price as a proportion of a small change in the underlying. Mathematically, it is the first derivative of price change (as discussed in the following section, "Delta Hedging").
- *Gamma* is the partial derivative of *delta* and the second derivative of the price function identifying the speed of change or the slope of the curve (as discussed in the section "Gamma Hedging" later in the chapter).

---

[1] Dimitris N. Chorafas, *Economic Capital Allocation with Basel II, Cost and Benefit Analysis*, Butterworth-Heinemann, London and Boston, 2004.

- *Theta* expresses the rate at which an option loses computed value for each day that passes with no movement in the price of the underlying. Hence, it expresses decay (as discussed in the section "Theta, Kappa, Rho" at the end of the chapter).
- *Kappa* (or *vega*, *lambda*, or *beta prime*) addresses the impact of fairly small changes in a given position—for example, the impact of a 1 percent change in volatility (beta).
- *Rho* (or *phi*) measures the option's carrying cost. It tells the change in the option price for a 1 percent change in interest rates.

Taken together, the five Greeks provide a framework for risk measurement by means of *sensitivity analysis* that helps to quantify the risk of an option:

- Delta gives the sensitivity to the asset price.
- Gamma gives the sensitivity of delta to the asset price.
- Kappa gives the sensitivity to volatility.
- Theta gives the time premium connected to the option's expiration.
- Rho gives the sensitivity to interest rates.

For instance, an option with a delta of 40 can be expected to change its value at 40 percent the rate of change in the price of the underlying security. If the underlying security goes up 5, the option's theoretical value can be expected to go up 2.

With higher volatility, the delta is somewhat higher, and with a lower volatility, somewhat lower. One general observation is that if the underlying price is about the same as the strike price, the options premiums will vary by about half the change in the underlying contract.

Delta is also known as the *hedge ratio* because it expresses the ratio of the underlying to the option contract, for reasons of neutral hedge (see "Delta Hedging"). Delta-neutral, gamma-neutral, and other positions in relation to the aforementioned metrics are established through hedging, but not all of the above metrics can be hedged at the same time.

To appreciate the Greeks' background, one must bring back into perspective the fact that the option's price consists of its *intrinsic value* (if any) and its *time value*. As the careful reader will recall, the intrinsic value is the value of the option if it were exercised immediately. The time value is the time to the option's maturity. The greater the intrinsic value, the more responsive the instrument is to change in the futures' price. As a metric, delta addresses itself to this price dependency.

For a different way of looking at this issue of price dependency, let's take as an example foreign exchange. Delta measures the sensitivity of the option's price to a variation of the currency's price. To be market neutral in terms of delta, the trader must take in the underlying currency the inverse position than that characterizing her option. In this case, at least theoretically, if her original option position depreciates, she will be compensated by the appreciation of the opposite position.

This thesis rests on the link between derivatives and spot markets, and, to a large extent, it is centered on the distribution and processing of information by market players. There has been little research on transactions not induced by new information—for instance, the fact that option writers insure themselves against losses from their open options positions by

- Spot buying and spot selling the underlying,
- Or by acquiring new calls and puts positions.

Backspreads provide an example. They are established when the bank buys more contracts than it writes, whether these are puts or calls. While all contracts may have the same maturity, for delta-neutral reasons the bank may have to buy a different number of puts and calls at higher and lower strike prices that have different premiums. Options can be replicated by spot market transactions. Standard call and put options can be priced through replication by

A portfolio composed of the underlying, and

A loan taken or investment made, at a risk-free rate of interest.

In this case, the delta of the option is used to determine the quantity of the underlying, as practiced in delta hedging. Like the Black-Scholes algorithm itself (see Chapter 8), this approach rests on the hypothesis of efficient markets, which assumes that the replication of options has no effect on the price of the underlying. This is too much of a theoretical assumption because the trade in the underlying asset induced by dynamic hedging affects spot market prices, particularly under tight liquidity.

Moreover, since an option's delta fluctuates steadily during its life cycle, there is a need for continual adjustments to the replicated portfolio by buying and selling options or underlyings, which evidently impacts upon the spot market. Added to this is the fact that spot markets are not always liquid enough to permit such multiplicity of hedging transactions without affecting spot prices.

One of the advantages of derivatives contracts is that they tend to promote liquidity, and in the general case, liquidity in derivatives markets is not nearly as fragmented as it is in the spot markets, so constraints always exist. Ironically, one of the aftereffects of derivatives-induced liquidity is that it reduces the market's price sensitivity, particularly when settling large transaction volumes.

Though not part of the Greeks, the metrics of volatility should be integral parts of the analyst's toolkit. *Beta* measures the volatility of a security relative to a benchmark. For instance, the S&P 500 Index has a beta of 1; any security with a higher beta is more volatile than the market represented by this index. Any security with a lower beta is less volatile than the market. The first will rise, and the second will fall more slowly than the S&P 500 Index.

DELTA HEDGING

The preceding section brought to the reader's attention that *delta* is the measure of percentage change in the price of an option for a unit change in the price of the underlying. The value of delta ranges from 0 to ± 1. A value of 0 would result from a far out-of-the-money option for which there is no need to hold a hedge in the underlying asset since the probability of exercise is virtually nil.

In contrast, a value of 1 would come from a deep in-the-money option that is virtually certain to be exercised. Therefore, the option writer would have to hold the underlying as a hedge against the option he or she had sold. In real life, delta measures are typically midrange like the two examples in Figure 10.1. A value of 0.66 would arise from an option at-the-money with a 66 percent probability of being exercised.

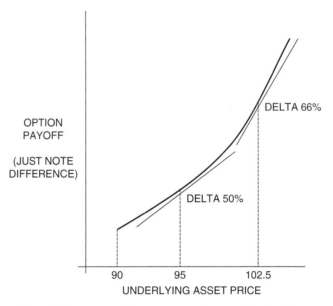

OPTION
PAYOFF

(JUST NOTE
DIFFERENCE)

DELTA 66%

DELTA 50%

90   95   102.5

UNDERLYING ASSET PRICE

Figure 10.1 Payoff diagram of the target option and delta slope

If a trader buys a call with the delta of 0.25, in theory he or she is long 0.25 of an underlying futures contract. The delta identifies the theoretical or equivalent futures position and therefore the change in the theoretical value of an option with respect to the change in the price of the underlying contract.

An option whose price changes, for instance, by $10 for every $20 change in the price of the underlier, has a delta of 0.5, or 50 percent, as shown in the lower part of Figure 10.1, while the upper part of the option payoff is 66 percent. Mathematically, delta is the first derivative of the payoff function $F(x)$.

$$\frac{dF(x)}{dx} \qquad\qquad (10.1)$$

This is considered to be one of the first practical applications of the calculus of variations in finance. The slope of this option's price diagram at a given *underlying asset price* is its delta, which expresses the rate of price change with respect to the price of the underlying asset.

Options at-the-money usually have a delta of 0.5, which means that for a price change of 1 in the underlying instrument, the option price moves by 0.5. Options further in-the-money have deltas greater than 0.5, converging on 1.0 as time to expiry approaches. In contrast, options out-of-the-money tend to have deltas of less than 0.5, and they converge on 0.0 as expiry draws closer. Moreover,

- Long calls have deltas that are positive, as do short puts.
- Long puts and short calls have negative deltas.

For instance, in a deep-in-the-money call where the spot price is far above the strike price, the delta is 1. When this happens, the change in the option's value corresponds to the absolute change in the underlying's price.

In an at-the-money call where the spot price is close to the strike price, the delta will rise with the spot price. The delta increases more rapidly as the expiration date approaches. With deep-in-the-money options, where the spot price of the underlying is far below the strike price, the delta is -1. When this happens, the option's value falls by the same amount as the increase (fall) in market prices.

If the spot price of a put option is far above the strike price, which means a deep-out-of-the-money put, the delta is 0. Market movements in the underlying have no impact on the value of the option since the option will not be exercised, expiring worthless.

As the foregoing examples document, delta is a metric often interpreted as the likelihood that a given option will end in-the-money, which implies that it is connected to the level of volatility, maturity, and intrinsic value of the option. Delta is often employed in the calculation of appropriate hedging levels because it expresses the ratio of underlying contracts to option contracts required to establish a *neutral hedge*.

For instance, if an option has a delta of 0.33, a neutral hedge will require a hedge of 1/3, or 0.33, of an underlying contract for each option contract. If three option contracts are purchased, one underlying contract must be sold. That's why, when interpreted in this manner, the delta is sometimes referred to as *hedge ratio*: it specifies the number of underlying contracts that

- The buyer (seller) of a call is long (short),
- Or that the buyer (seller) of a put is short (long).

As the underlying asset—say, the stock market index—moves, the delta also changes. In the case of a call, a rise in the underlying asset that increases the probability of exercising sees to it that the delta rises. If the price of the underlying falls, the delta also falls, and the writer can sell part of his or her holding in the asset:

> Because delta gives the price change in the option for a 1 percent change in the underlying asset, the delta value of a position is used to estimate the value at risk for small changes in prices.

The fact is that as a metric, delta is fairly well understood by market players. As a result, the delta hedge is today the most common type of option replication. In terms of foreign exchange markets, for example, it is easy to visualize the change in the instrument's value for a unit change in the exchange rate—thereby constructing contracts so as to match the delta of the target option in a hedging operation.

Figure 10.2 presents an example of delta hedging in the options market. The ogive curve maps the change in the premium for the changing spot price of the underlying over a 30-day period. Experts contend that a static delta hedge can be unreliable, especially in volatile markets. For instance, the delta of a hedge might drift with movements in the spot exchange rate because of interest rate changes, balance-of-payments deterioration, or political events.

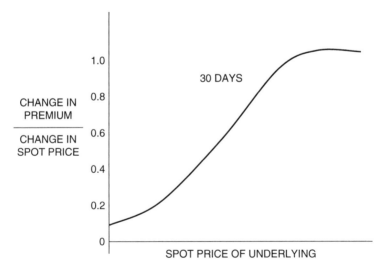

Figure 10.2 Delta hedging in the options market

This is one of the reasons why delta hedges are implemented with instruments such as forward contracts and currency futures contracts that are not sensitive to changes because of movements in the spot exchange rate. It is appropriate, however, to add that no method is foolproof.

An improvement to a static delta hedge is the dynamic hedge of which we briefly spoke in the preceding section, "The Greeks in a Nutshell." It is obtained by adding or subtracting to the forward or future position so as to track the changing delta of the target option—whether the factor affecting an option's delta is time, interest rates, exchange rates, or something else.

In conclusion, any type of hedging requires significant skill, and if improperly done, it can get financial analysts and traders into trouble. Not only must the calculation of hedges be analytical, factual, and documented but they must also be periodically adjusted for changes in operating conditions such as the drift in the option's delta and other factors that can turn a hedge on its head.

GAMMA HEDGING

There is another way of measuring the change in delta. This is done through *gamma*, which is the first derivative of delta and therefore the second derivative of the payoff function $F(x)$. Gamma, also known as the option's curvature, expresses the change in the delta of the option induced by a small change in the price of the underlying asset.

$$\frac{d^2F(x)}{dx^2} \qquad (10.2)$$

Gamma for options is analogous to convexity for bonds. While the target option may have a positive gamma, currency forward and futures contracts have gamma equal to zero. Among currency options, those with the shortest remaining time to expiration have the largest gamma (more on this later).

If an option has a delta of 75 and a gamma of 10, *then* the option's expected delta will be 85 if the underlier goes up 100 basis points; it will be 65 if the underlier goes down 100 basis points. Because gamma expresses *the rate of change*, with respect to the price of the underlying, the risk of delta changing is referred to as the *gamma risk*. This is a significant risk common to all options, part of what are considered higher-order risks.

To appreciate the importance of the second derivative of the payoff function $F(x)$, one should recall that the value of an option's delta is not a constant. For instance, in the case of currency exchange, it varies with the value of the currency. Therefore, the maintenance of a delta-neutral position requires important adjustments given that delta is sensitive to the currency's price. Gamma measures delta's sensitivity to changes, to the underlying contract's value.

• A *positive gamma* is a buy signal for calls and puts.

The significance of a positive gamma is that the delta of the position varies in the same sense as that of the currency. It increases when the price of the underlying increases, and drops when the payoff function drops.

• A *negative gamma*, in contrast, is a sell signal for calls and puts.

In this case, in order to remain delta neutral, the trader is obliged to buy the underlying currency if its price rises and sell if its price drops. In the case of both positive and negative gamma, its importance is greater when its absolute value is greater—because it measures the acceleration (or deceleration) of the option, telling how fast the option picks up or loses speed (hence delta) as the price of the underlying contract rises or falls.

Three approaches are used to *hedge gamma*. The simplest way is to buy back options identical to the ones that have been sold. It needs no explaining, however, that such back-to-back deals are not creating any profits, and therefore they are very rare in the over-the-counter market.

The second method is to buy deep-out-of-the-money options, a practice known as *buying the tails*. This applies to portfolios with at-the-money or slightly out-of-the-money options. The third approach is to do a horizontal spread (Chapter 9).

Typically, the characteristics of gamma discussed in the early paragraphs of this section permit making a *delta-gamma hedge*, which uses options near to expiration for convexity, taking a position in forward and futures contracts to match the delta of the target option. The effects of changes in the spot exchange rate on the option's delta are captured by gamma, which critically depends on the time remaining until expiration.

Practically, delta-gamma hedging produces no miracles, even if it is facilitated by the fact that close-to-expiration options can be easily found in the market. Hence, they can be nicely incorporated into a hedging strategy. In a delta-gamma hedge, for example, the trader may take a position in a short-lived call to match the gamma of the target longer-life option. Given that short-lived calls have much larger gamma than long-lived calls, few of them will be required.

The good news is that delta-neutral and gamma-neutral positions help in dynamic hedging. They practically mean that if the market moves against the writer, he or she is forced to move in the same direction as the market. The downside is that this amplifies the initial price volatility connected to the demand for derivative instruments.

This problem is amplified when there is an overwhelming amount of dynamic hedging in the same direction, with the result that price movements may become discontinuous—leading to financial dislocation where companies may suffer major losses. Essentially, while dynamic hedging is a protective strategy, it can have the effect of transferring risk by amplifying it. Eventually it hits the market players, particularly those who want to delta hedge in the same direction at the same time because

- The contrarians disappear from the market, and
- There are no takers on the other side of the trading equation.

The fact that under certain conditions hedging may turn out to be a greater exposure is not properly understood even by sophisticated traders and investors. Some of the instruments they use carry a 10-fold or greater multiple of normal risk. And there are some exotic types of instruments that seem to offer exceptional returns but really carry the seeds of a catastrophic financial loss. Sometimes what is supposed to be a sophisticated hedge turns into the exact opposite of a hedge.

THETA, KAPPA, RHO

A third way of measuring exposure is *theta*. It quantifies the loss of the option's computed value for each day with no movement in the price of the underlier. It makes sense to follow both *change* and *no change* in an option's price because both leave their footprint. Theta exposure is closely related to gamma exposure.

- The theta factor is sometimes referred to as the option's *time decay*.
- But in reality, it reflects upon price stability, rather than turbulence.

Theoretically, in hedging delta and gamma risk, theta exposure is hedged as well because all delta-gamma-neutral positions tend also to be theta neutral. However, many financial analysts consider this to be a weak proposition, and they depend on it a priori.

If the theta position is to be hedged, *then* this should be done by taking account of the anticipated change in the premium value of an option because of a change in time to expiration.

More precisely, we should

- Measure the decay in the time value of the option
- Show how its value changes from one day to the next, if all other variables stay the same

Theta is always negative; therefore, it benefits the writer and erodes the value held by the buyer of an option. It becomes zero at expiration of the option, decaying most rapidly toward the end of an option's life. The theta of a call option expressed as a function of the underlying price is presented in Figure 10.3.

As the section "The Greeks in a Nutshell" brought to the reader's attention, *kappa* expresses the sensitivity of an option's computed value to small changes in volatility affecting a given position. An option with a kappa of 0.20 can be expected to gain (lose) 0.20 in theoretical value for each percentage point increase (decrease) in volatility.

If kappa is high, *then* an option's value is sensitive to small changes in volatility.

If kappa is low, *then* changes in volatility have little impact on the option's value.

Kappa values range between zero and infinity, declining as the option's expiration approaches. Such values impact on the option's premium. Longer dated options have a higher kappa because they

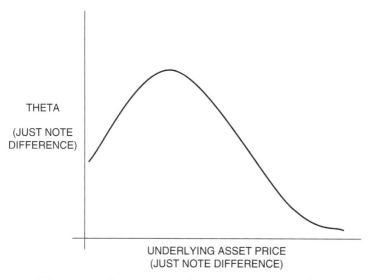

THETA

(JUST NOTE
DIFFERENCE)

UNDERLYING ASSET PRICE
(JUST NOTE DIFFERENCE)

Figure 10.3 Theta of a call option as a function of the underlying price

are more sensitive to changes in *implied volatility*. Kappa-neutral positions, if they ever exist, are supposed to make investors indifferent to shifts in volatility parameters.

Rho reflects the option's carrying cost. It gives the change in the option price and premium per 1 percent change in *interest rate*. Some traders think that since interest rates are relatively unimportant in the evaluation of options on futures, rho is also the least important of the option sensitivities. This is not necessarily true given the fact that the role played by interest rates in determining an option's premium is complex and varies from one type of option to the next.

• The relation between stock option premiums and interest rates is positive.
• In contrast, the relation between options on futures and interest rates is negative.

In many cases, the use of rho can be quite helpful in risk control. With currency options, for example, there are two separate interest rates to be measured—one of the base currency; the other of the quoted currency—because the forward exchange rate depends on the ratio between the two interest rates. The intrinsic value component will change, and it is important to know about the direction and magnitude of impact.

Last but not least, since all options have a degree of exposure to carrying costs, *weights* need to be set in a portfolio for their estimated neutralities in delta, gamma, theta, kappa, and rho. Weights are, however, subjective and change with time. Therefore, they must not only be chosen carefully but also be adjusted carefully.

CHAPTER 11

Credit Risk and Market Risk with Options

SELLING MARKET RISK AND BUYING CREDIT RISK

The preceding chapters provided plenty of reference to the fact that the value of options is significantly affected by movements in the underlying, whether this is interest rates, currency rates, equities, indexes, commodities, or something else. Therefore, a sound risk management policy requires steady and realistic estimates of profit and loss at two levels of reference:

1. An instrument-specific, detailed approach able to capture exposure position by position.

For exchange-traded options, this is done easily by marking-to-market. In contrast, options traded over the counter have no active market—hence the need to mark-to-model while assuming model risk.

2. A portfolio-level evaluation, which may be based on algorithmic approximation and must be available on request in real time.

Issue No. 1 is not necessarily prerequisite to issue No. 2 as the latter basically targets *credit equivalence* of market risk positions. This job will be typically done through demodulation of the notional principal amount (Chapter 2), the hypothesis being that in the computational process, minor errors or deviations will cancel themselves out.

The portfolio positions may be *hedged* (Chapter 4), with the aim to neutralize exposure; or they may be *unhedged*, designed deliberately to assume an exposure because of profits that will likely result. With hedged positions, the investor is vulnerable to the creditworthiness of the counterparty and its ability and willingness to carry out its obligations. Therefore, one way of looking at hedged transactions is that we

- Buy protection from market risk, and
- Pay for it by assuming credit risk.

The option's buyer is exposed to market risk as long as his or her asset is out-of-the-money. If it is at-the-money, the position is at the edge between profit and loss. But at the moment the option is in-the-money, the buyer faces credit risk even if the market risk is latent.

In the background of the switch from primarily market risk to primarily credit risk lies the fact that the holder of the option is confronted with delivery risk. In the case of the writer's default, he faces a dual exposure: the loss of the premium he has paid to the writer, and the loss of the financial gain he is entitled to in case he decides to exercise an in-the-money option. Four different types of tests should be performed to reveal the portfolios' secrets in terms of the aforementioned type of exposure:

1. *Scenario writing*, based on historical or hypothetical information elements
2. *Sensitivity analysis*, typically by symmetrically varying the values of a specific factor, or factors
3. *Statistical inference under conditions*, targeting *tail events* that may turn portfolio positions on their head
4. *Drills*, which amount to a worst-case analysis under severe market conditions

For credit risk management purposes, a valid guideline is provided by the mid-July 2005 accord between the Basel Committee and the International Organization of Securities Commissions (IOSCO) in connection to trading-related exposures and treatment of double-default effects. Its rules supplement certain aspects of Basel II and of the 1996 market risk amendment, by addressing five issues:

1. Treatment of counterparty risk for over-the-counter derivatives, repurchase agreements, and securities financing transactions
2. Handling double-default effects (wrong-way risk) for covered exposures, relating to trading book and banking book
3. Short-term-maturity adjustments in the internal ratings–based (IRB) approach under Basel II, for some trading book–related items
4. Improvements to the current trading book regime, especially with respect to treatment of specific risks
5. Design of a specific capital treatment for unsettled and failed transactions

Contrary to the credit exposure faced by the buyer, once the option's seller receives his premium, he is no longer dependent on the buyer for future performance as the counterparty. Hence, the seller faces no credit risk, though he continues being exposed to market risk until the buyer exercises his legal rights or the option expires.

Option sellers, however, have a challenging task in managing their portfolio in two complementary ways: the options that they wrote and their hedges in connection to those options. Here is a list of critical questions that should be asked in analyzing the options book:

- Are we a net buyer or net seller of optionsl Do we have a preference in maturities? In the type of option we buy or write?
- How does our net premium compare to what we lost with options last week? last month? last year? the last five years?
- Do we have a sound mechanism to check volatility smiles? forward volatility calculations? third parties' advice on volatility projections?
- Have we detected cases of mispricing? If yes, what action has been taken? If no, have we examined if there is option mispricing in our portfolio?

- Do we know if there is a concentration of strikes in our option book? What's the top management policy on this issue? If there exists a management policy, has it been observed during the last week? month? year? five years?

Beyond those more general queries, valid for all types of options, each instrument has its own characteristics that must be the subject of attention. For instance, investors in yield-based debt options run the risk that reported yields may be in error. The values disseminated by the authority of the options markets will usually be averages of dealer quotations or prices.

- It is possible that errors could be made in the gathering or averaging of values.
- It is as well most likely that averages are misleading figures because the spread of price distribution is not reported and nothing is known about confidence intervals (Chapter 6).

A trader or investor who buys or sells an option at a premium based on an erroneous or unreliable yield value is bound by the trade and has no remedy under the rules of the options markets. Similarly, market players who exercise options or are assigned exercises based on erroneous or unreliable yields will ordinarily be required to make settlement on the basis of the value initially given by the reporting authority, even if a corrected value is subsequently announced.

Offsetting risk under these conditions is most difficult. Furthermore, in addition to market risk resulting from averages and, in certain cases, from misquotations of market prices, there is the case that the credit risk, too, may be mispriced. This typically happens when the risk appetite among investors is growing (see the section "GM's Put Options for Fiat Auto: A Case Study" later in the chapter) or when there is plain misjudgment of counterparty exposure.

MARKET RISK CONTROL IN A NUTSHELL

Practically all of the cases of exposure made so far in connection to options concerned market risk that, theoretically at least, should have been enough. Still, to provide a common frame of reference, it is wise to take a quick look at the origins and underlying market risk factors (as it will also be done in the later section "Credit Risk Control in a Nutshell" with credit risk). In addition, we will briefly examine the link between asset prices and monetary developments feeding into market risk.

The *market risk* interesting us in this section is that of exposure to losses associated with off-balance-sheet positions because of movements in the market price of the underlying, including interest rates, currency exchange rates, equity values, and prices of other commodities. *General market risk* is the risk of a general market movement arising from, say, a change in interest rates or in official economic policy. *Specific market risk* concerns a given commodity that may move in a way contrary to general market trend.

Historically, some securities have tended to be highly sensitive to variables that, though they may be influencing the market generally, particularly impact certain securities. Evidently, it is to be expected that because of their specific characteristics, different securities exhibit different levels of market risk. Additionally,

- A security's sensitivity to market influences may change over time.
- The same security may be exposed to event risk much more than other securities or the market as a whole.

As we have already seen, the typical answer to market risk control is hedging. However, the aftermath of many hedges may be difficult to calculate; or a trader may think he has a hedge and some time down the line find that he doesn't have it. As the preceding chapters have shown, there are a great many reasons why options are difficult derivatives to hedge. For example, they are also

- Fast-moving targets
- A rapidly growing segment of present-day financial business

These two reasons see to it that part of market risk is the so-called *valuation risk*, which addresses the possibility that the profits of a transaction may be misstated or the amount of assumed exposure underrated. With a change in volatility, valuation assumptions can change, affecting profits and losses.

Misjudgments can happen not only with longer-term projections but as well with short-term derivatives contracts, which are readily priced because they tend to trade in a liquid market. It needs no explaining that valuation difficulties are just so much tougher if the derivatives are exotic. The difficulty is compounded because mathematical models must include an estimate of what the volatility of the underlying *will be*—in connection to a contract's most complex figures over the longer term.

A similar statement is valid about forwards because a forward (Chapter 2) obliges one party to buy and the other to sell the underlying at a specified time and price, but the market price can be quite different when the exercise time comes. As the careful reader will recall from previous examples, asymmetry is another major reason for the complexity of market risk control. In the case of an option-based derivative, the prices of the option and the underlying don't change in a linear fashion. Rather, much depends on the

- Option's exercise price
- Time remaining to expiration
- Volatility of the underlying
- Link between macroeconomic developments and asset prices

From the viewpoint of macroeconomics and of monetary policy, boom and bust cycles in asset prices pose significant challenges for central bankers who should not only identify underlying sources of volatility but also come forward with policy response. In turn, this policy response impacts on market prices, particularly the prices of those assets that are the most leveraged and would lead (or might lead) to an asset price bubble.

Theoretically, economists must be able to distinguish between fundamental and exceptional sources of asset price spikes. Practically, this is a very difficult task because estimates of the "right prices" are surrounded by a high degree of uncertainty, while at the same time boom and bust cycles in prices can be very damaging, leading to

- Greater market risk
- Macroeconomic instability

There are several reasons why monetary and market price developments tend to correlate. One reason is that both react to macroeconomic influences, including cyclical shocks to the economy. Strong money and credit growth may be indicative of a very lax monetary policy that fuels price changes in the market. Another important reason is that monetary policy and market prices are self-reinforcing variables whose impact may be both instantaneous and longer term.

Therefore, the analysis of monetary developments and evolution of credit are very useful in studying the pattern of market risk. Incorrectly, many people (including bankers) believe that market risk can be managed by frequently marking a portfolio to market or to model. This is not at all true. Model risk left aside, present-day approaches to marking-to-model

- Abstract from macroeconomic realities
- Tend to assume a functioning market, which is not the case in panics or other extreme conditions

Yet it is in the case of tail events and of panics that a given portfolio may become nearly worthless overnight. Even *if* it were possible to mark-to-market all derivative instruments in a portfolio, it would not be enough. Such practice has to be accompanied by thoroughly established procedures and technology that assures that this is done ad hoc, essentially amounting to *real-time risk assessment* enriched by experimentation through simulation. Only then is it possible that the resulting valuations can become the basis of an appropriate hedging strategy, including the ability to

- Enter into offsetting transactions
- Take opposite positions in underlyings
- Close out positions in full understanding of the risk and return

As far as market risk is concerned, the greater is the range of financial instruments available for hedging and position taking, the faster must grow the expertise in the control of exposure and in economic capital allocation. Internal capital allocation against market risk is still done through obsolete policies and systems whose use has become counterproductive.

An example of obsolete procedures is that of determining the degree of exposure on the basis of the need to cover risks arising from movement of prices from their mean values by 1 or 2 standard deviations. This approach tends to forget about the effect of tail events because of extreme price changes, even if it implies that riskier transactions face a higher capital assessment.

GM'S PUT OPTIONS FOR FIAT AUTO: A CASE STUDY

In the year 2000 General Motors and Fiat made an alliance that gave the Italian manufacturer the option to sell its holding in Fiat Auto to GM over a period of 5 to 10 years, the prolonged exercise time ranging from January 25, 2005, to July 24, 2010. A short historical flashback helps in appreciating the sense of this option, its market risk, and disastrous aftermath.

The GM-Fiat deal did not work in the same way as would a traditional option with a premium established in advance. What really happened in 2000 is that General Motors bought 20 percent of Fiat Auto, along with a put option on the rest of Fiat's equity in the motor vehicle business unit. But in 2005, this option to buy Fiat Auto turned around to haunt GM. Besieged by myriad other problems, the No. 1 auto manufacturer in the world had neither the money nor the will to buy Fiat Auto.

In mid-December 2004, the top brass of both GM and Fiat met at Lake Konstanz to find a compromise on the execution of the put option or, alternatively, to value its financial impact if GM decided to opt out of it. No matter what theorists say about put options, Fiat was asking for compensation if GM moved away from the responsibilities it had assumed in 2000.

On December 15, 2004, as these negotiations were underway, most analysts said that both companies wanted to reach an agreement, but there was a major difference of opinion on its price: Fiat was asking between $1 billion and $2 billion, while GM, which contested the validity of the option, was offering between $500 million and $1 billion. It became known in no time that the Konstanz meeting ended without results, which would lead to two possible solutions:

- Renewed negotiations below the top management level, or
- Court action, which would have been the case anyway if these new negotiations failed.

The irony is that even with an early expectation of a cash flow from GM into Fiat's coffers through a settlement, the Italian company's low credit standing had improved. Evidently, failure of the negotiations would have opposite effects on GM and Fiat. As both companies were aware of the negative market response, in the end, in a mid-February 2005 settlement, Fiat managed to get from GM $2.1 billion in compensation that

- Improved its financial staying power
- Because of its good management at the helm, set it on a path to recovery

True enough, 2000 to December 2004 was a time full of perils for General Motors, which wanted to downsize its Opel operations in Germany by 12,000 jobs and to downsize its operations in Sweden that had come from an ill-studied acquisition in the go-go 1990s. In the aftermath, contrary to its year 2000 plans, the world's then No. 1 automaker had scant interest or management time to acquire Fiat Auto.

Rumor had it that all GM wanted from Fiat Auto, if it had bought Fiat, was its gasoline-efficient motor vehicles. The rest was to be radically downsized. Nevertheless, it did not escape the attention of GM management that downsizing Fiat Auto would have meant a high cost in strikes with the result of paralyzing the Italian plants that would have been acquired.

To make matters worse, both companies had a low credit standing. GM had only a BBB– credit rating, the lowest of the investment grades, while at the time Fiat Auto's debt was considered to be at the level of junk bonds. The merger of a BBB– company and a BB– company would have produced only debt to be sold in the junk-bond market. This was in itself a big negative—over and above the fact that the acquisition of Fiat Auto by GM made very little sense in the first place. Put options don't always work the way books say that they do. Management risk and market risk make the difference.

CREDIT RISK CONTROL IN A NUTSHELL

As the careful reader will recall, credit risk is the possibility of loss incurred as a result of a counterparty's failing to meet its financial obligations. In the case of a borrower's default, the bank generally incurs a loss equal to the amount owed by the debtor, less any recoveries resulting from foreclosure, liquidation of collateral, or restructuring of the debtor company.

Credit risk exists with all lending products, commitments, letters of credit, and other more or less classical instruments of banking—as well as with counterparty exposure arising from derivative financial instruments and other sophisticated or complex transactions. At the root of credit exposure is typically the inability or unwillingness to face up to one's obligations. Therefore,

- Each counterparty to a transaction must be assigned a risk rating.
- Each transaction, too, must have associated to it a credit risk factor, based on its type and structure.

Because banks typically make more money by assuming credit risk rather than market risk and because loans are a credit institution's classical product line, there is a whole hierarchy of credit-screening procedures. These start with loans officers at the branch, and up the organization they involve senior credit managers and credit committees—which make credit decisions on major loans.

What is generally missing, however, is the measurement of counterparty risk embedded in combined credit and trading operations. Only the better-managed institutions have a system of establishing individual credit limits by counterparty *and* type of derivatives transaction—as well as a system for monitoring complex aspects of combined credit and market risk. Monitoring must be done intraday and exceptions reported ad hoc to senior management.

Derivatives are not the only instruments whose impact is felt on credit and trading relations associated with an entity's counterparties. Even some exposures resulting from rather classical types of loans are no longer what they used to be. Financial and technological developments have seen to it that

- Many loans are now made with little contact between the lender and the borrower.
- Loans are shuttled around the financial system, in a way similar to what is done with so many other financial products.

An interesting opinion of experts is that global investment and commercial banks have turned themselves into liquidity factories, making tradable instruments by securitizing them and selling them later on. The aftereffect is that while the banks' credit risk portfolios are more diversified than before, information on the creditworthiness of borrowers is scant.

Because credit exposure has been so widely spread, it is not surprising that banking crises are rare. In February 2007, the closure of a small bank near Pittsburgh was the first such incident in America since June 2004. At the same time, however, the fact that credit risk is more evenly spread does not mean the financial system as a whole is safer.

- It has become prone to less frequent, but more violent shocks.
- Financial aftershocks can easily spread from individual banks to the global financial landscape.

While these references are written in connection to the spreading of credit risk through securitized loans, options too can be influenced by and contribute to financial shocks given the market risk they represent for writers and credit risk for buyers—particularly under extreme conditions. As a result of relentless deal making between financial institutions, when liquidity dries up, the exposures the banks think they have outsourced to

- Hedge funds
- Insurance companies
- Pension funds

might return with a vengeance back into their books. These days credit risk is widely sold as a commodity through the explosion of *credit derivatives*, but protection buyers are wrong if they think they have been immunized from the risk of default. As for protection for the sellers underwriting the credit risks,

- In good times they get streams of income.
- But in bad times they are contractually obliged to make huge payouts.

Many central bankers, as well as banking industry experts, are now concerned that this dual ability of institutions to buy credit protection for their loans while also buying somebody else's securitized liabilities has led to a lowering of lending standards. Why double-check the accounting books if we are selling on the risk in a matter of days or even faster? and if we are buying securitized loans with opaque credit exposure?

The aftereffect of this change in proverbial due diligence became painfully evident in 2007, with the subprime crisis in the United States and Spain. To feed on the mortgage boom, finance companies lent to needy borrowers with poor credit records, creating the subprime mortgage market.

Whether or not "this" or "that" instrument was used to pass assumed credit risk to another market player, all past and still-active credit exposures to individual counterparties must be carefully monitored by credit officers, analysts, and risk managers. In addition, credit risk should be regularly supervised by the board's risk management committee taking into consideration

- Current market conditions
- Trends analyses
- Macroeconomics

Institutions that pay proper attention to credit risk are keen in recording periodic exposures, determining adequacy of the credit support provided through collateral, monitoring the value of securities, and notifying the counterparty of credit support shortfalls. It is as well wise to keep in mind that collateral can be a double-edged sword.

Eligibility of securities, thresholds, frequency of securities valuation, minimum acceptable amounts, permissible delays to cover, and other factors must be specified in advance through covenants to counterparties in derivatives transactions—rather than taking extra risks with covenant-light (*cov-lite*) policies.

In conclusion, one of the ironies with bending the risk control rules, and with "discharging" credit risk, is that at the same time banks sell off loans, they buy from other banks structured credit instruments. Few banks have trained themselves in how to use a rigorous substitution logic.

CREDIT IMPROVEMENT AND CREDIT DETERIORATION

The Basel II New Capital Adequacy Framework has had a dual aftermath. On one hand, there has been a positive effect: banks have more or less strengthened their risk management systems and procedures. On the other hand, however, they have also spread their risks in an effort to hold less capital against their loans. The originate and distribute (O&D) model used with subprime mortgages provides a real-life (but deadly) example. Here exactly lies the danger.

By focusing on the health of banks, the regulators have skipped over problems in less supervised realms of the financial system, like pension funds, hedge funds, and most particularly individual investors with less experience than banks in judging credit risk. In the banking industry itself, the reduction in capital adequacy has weakened the financial system.[1]

Another factor that led to credit deterioration lies in the fact that, with plenty of liquidity in the market, borrowers now call the shots. This raises nagging concerns about underwriting standards, leading to *leveraged lending*. All sorts of institutions are giving loans to borrowers with too much debt on their balance sheet and whose loans therefore should not be judged as investment grade by credit rating rules.

As a result, there is an urgent need for knowledge-enriched models able to mine the entity's credit exposure and flesh out *credit deterioration* on a permanent basis. Also, such models are needed to calculate capital at risk, request margin payments, and bring slippages of counterparties' loans into non-investment-grade status to management attention. Knowledge artifacts are also needed to track *credit improvement* by mining positive data on exposure.

In their contribution to credit risk control, expert systems capitalize on the fact that the financial stability of a company hinges, to a large degree, on its level of indebtedness, cash flow, and profitability.[2] Financial soundness is, to a significant degree, a good determinant of risk premium. A counterparty's financial staying power is approximated through the ratio of assets over liabilities with

- Assets taken at capitalization
- Liabilities assigned at book value

---

[1] Dimitris N. Chorafas, *Stress Testing for Risk Control under Basel II,* Elsevier, Oxford and Boston, 2007.

[2] Dimitris N. Chorafas and Heinrich Steinmann, *Expert Systems in Banking,* Macmillan, London, 1991.

Because the market is a tough critter, equity price movements reflect this ratio. The probability of default due to overindebtedness increases with the volatility of the firm's equity. These relationships are factored into the estimating approach by taking account of implied volatility of the share price, computed by using option prices. Nonrestricted tradability significantly influences the attractiveness of an investment.

Expert systems should as well be on hand to assess intraday whether a counterparty needs to come up with more securities as collateral to meet new, higher credit support requirements or to cover an adverse movement in the value of already deposited assets, compensate for currency exchange shortfalls, or respond to other events that lead to margin calls. Counterparties have to replenish their account by

- Transferring eligible assets
- Providing the bank with the power of attorney to draw assets from other accounts

The basic premise is that a rigorous credit quality process must assure not only early identification of possible changes in creditworthiness of clients but also an analysis of credit risk pricing through appropriate margins including regular asset and collateral quality reviews. Other important key credit risk factors are these:

- Business and economic conditions
- Historical experience with a given counterparty
- Compliance to regulatory requirements
- Concentrations of credit volume by industry, country, product, and credit rating

Steadily updated watch lists must be available interactively for all counterparties where adverse changes in creditworthiness could occur, with particular attention paid to the instruments being used. While credit derivatives help to mitigate certain credit exposures, they also engender their own risks.

Nothing is really secure in terms of counterparty risk. This should induce banks and bankers to continuously assess and improve their practices, from credit management policies to dynamic control of counterparty risk and the right pricing of all their instruments from loans to derivatives.

A different way of making this statement is that credit events that took place in the last two decades point to the fallacy of simplistic solutions when evaluating credit risk because many instruments considered "safe" really offer only a minimal amount of protection with wishful thinking filling the gap. Management should never be fooled by the idea that the good standing of a counterparty in the past means a good standing in the future because every business partner is exposed to the risk of

- Overextending his or her hand
- Running thin on management skill
- Draining its financial resources through some ill-calculated gambles

There may as well be national banking disasters, promoted by companies' overplaying their hands. For instance, by the late 1980s the Japanese banking system became awfully fragile precisely because of its wider and wider international expansion and the commitments that went along with it. The lessons to be learned from Japan's corporate world experiences were these:

- The evaluation of counterparty risk has become increasingly complex, owing to globalization and innovative financial instruments.
- Controlling the concentrations of credit risk is a major challenge, primarily because of a loose management policy in regard to profitable counterparties or industry sectors.

The need for monitoring and control actions is always present with derivatives transactions—their market risk and credit risk. It is much more difficult to follow counterparties internationally than nationally, as European banks found out the hard way by assuming a huge amount of credit risk with U.S. subprimes.

THE MISPRICING OF CREDIT RISK

The pricing of any industrial product and of any financial instrument has never been an exact science. Nevertheless, the nuts and bolts of a sound pricing process are to cover costs—including risks—and leave a profit, while tuning the asked price to a level established by the market to which the instrument appeals and that is affordable by its potential clients.

The fact that the pricing mechanism is not exact leaves the gates open for plenty of risks to sneak in. The one that will particularly concern us in this section is credit risk's mispricing. To make this discussion practical, the following section will discuss credit-risk-free debt options, and the section after that will discuss credit spreads and credit options.

Starting with the fundamentals, one of the challenges in the implementation of rational credit risk–based pricing policies with financial instruments lies in the fact that a wave of innovation in derivatives markets has produced sophisticated and complex products—with risk factors that are not well known, if they are known at all. For example, while the use of credit derivatives has exploded, giving investors in debt securities great flexibility, unknowns associated to novel debt products lead these same investors to ever-higher levels of

- Financial leverage
- Exposure at default

To make matters worse, in practically every jurisdiction, statistics centering on default likelihood are far more oriented toward bank loans than trading operations. The *annual default rate* is typically expressed as a percentage of formerly creditworthy enterprises that have become insolvent during the course of a given year. This rate is the percentage of defaults to the total number of companies certified as eligible for loans at start of the year.

This type of default information discounts the fact that many market players take loans to promote and support their trading activities. Therefore, the statistics being conveyed have little relevance to counterparty risk in trading operations, and they provide weak evidence, which leads to the mispricing of credit risk.

Contrary to views that prevailed as late as the first years of the twenty-first century, today several economists raise the question of whether the next downturn could be even worse than on previous occasions because of *mispriced credit risk* (see also in Chapter 14, the discussion on credit spreads). In the opinion of a growing number of experts, the increase in the level of exposure is being driven by the unusually high proportion of failure-prone companies rated triple C or lower, which is a non-investment-grade rating that is just a few notches above plain default.

- In 1990, in the United States the aforementioned rating category accounted for just 2 percent of junk-rated debt.
- In 2007, it made up almost 20 percent, and a notion that prevailed in the market was that nothing short of a crisis will keep it from growing.

This kind of crisis materialized in January to March 2007 with subprime lending in the housing industry in the United States. By mid-March 2007, an estimated 1.5 million families who did not otherwise qualify for mortgages but who were patronized by subprime lenders had defaulted or were about to default in their mortgages—and by so doing they brought down a couple of the major subprime lenders.

What particularly worries economists, analysts, and regulators is that the market is not pricing the triple-C risk into its demand for (higher) interest rates because it is misinterpreting default signals. The likelihood is that in an average low-default year, the market will experience between three or four junk-bond defaults. However, because 2006 saw no such defaults, bankers and investors widely and wrongly assumed that none would come in 2007—which proved to be wrong.

Experts suggest that, with all this flagrant mispricing, if only one major default occurs over the next six months (in the period following the time these lines were written), a spread of just 150 basis points would be sufficient to cover the associated loss. In contrast, more than one major default would see many investors bleeding. The mispricing of debt instruments takes no account of the fact that the extra basis points of bonds—junk, BBB, A, and AA compared to AAA—is in effect a cushion to absorb losses linked to credit spread widening:

If spreads widen, sellers of credit protection in the credit market will lose money, and

Then after this cushion is eaten away, these sellers of credit protection will be on the front line with their capital.

A risk scenario (but not worst case) will account for the fact that if equities begin to sell off due to a macroeconomic problem with inflation-led interest rates rising, the outcome for low-quality, high-yield credit is likely to be very negative, and eventually disastrous. The precedent for a worst-case scenario is the meltdown of the junk-bond market in the late 1980s.

American and European regulators are moreover expressing concerns that banks may be allowing hedge funds to increase their borrowing capacity, without proper measure of the assumed risk. One example is their use of collateral that in a financial crisis could lose its value rapidly (see also the section "GM's Put Options for Fiat Auto: A Case Study" earlier in the chapter). An additional factor is that, given the lower risk premiums in credit markets, it may no longer be prudent to assume that credit default swap contracts will be liquid when a credit risk adjustment comes.

Regulatory authorities and central banks have also found that certain firms are extending credit to counterparties whose business is characterized by not-so-liquid instruments. Because of these and similar facts, American regulators are now asking questions about offshore leveraged vehicles that allow U.S.-based banks to extend credit to hedge funds beyond the limits imposed by American law.

The fear among some regulators and knowledgeable market observers is that in a big market dislocation, hedge funds and other speculators investing in junk debt might be unable to sell those securities. This will increase the likelihood of widespread defaults. In fact, not only is there a possibility that credit risk is being seriously underpriced, but there is also a strong possibility that much trading in credit derivatives assumes that liquidity will remain when an adjustment in credit markets takes place—which is not at all true.

Questions connected to the ongoing mispricing of credit risk are of concern to every bank and every investor. They are also part of a broad new effort by the New York Federal Reserve, Securities and Exchange Commission (SEC), Office of the Comptroller of the Currency (OCC), Britain's Financial Services Authority, and continental European regulatory bodies to understand better and more accurately

- How much exposure large banks have to hedge funds
- Whether that could present a significant risk to the financial system, in the event of market disruption

As an example, experts worry about a spike in junk-bond default rates that is not priced in current instruments. In the late 1980s to the early 1990s, the global default rate on junk bonds zoomed to almost 13 percent. Nowadays it is estimated that even a less severe downturn can send defaults to nearly that level. In fact, several analysts think that a recession similar to the one that occurred in the early 1990s could push U.S. junk-rated default rates as high as 17 percent.

One of the problems with credit derivatives and other credit risk transfer mechanisms currently confronting central bankers is *embedded leverage* by which one's exposure is multiplied many times compared to the same investment in the underlying conventional security. According to financial industry experts, embedded leverage has expanded phenomenally, but at the same time

- It does not appear in balance sheets.
- Therefore, it is impossible to quantify it across the financial system.

Its effect is, however, felt, and this is the reason that no one can be sure how much capital must be set aside as insurance against embedded leverage going wrong. Additionally, mathematical models of risk, which are currently used to stress test derivatives,[3] give too much weight to the low volatility of 2004 to 2006, even though experimenters and risk controllers should know that it is incorrect to use the recent past as a guide to predicting the future.

CREDIT-RISK-FREE DEBT OPTIONS

Debt options approved for trading are of two kinds: price based and yield based. *Price-based options* are those that give their holders the right either to purchase or sell a specified underlying debt or to receive a cash settlement payment based on the value of an underlying debt. *Yield-based options* are cash settled, with the amount based on the difference between the exercise price and the value of an underlying yield.

---

[3] Chorafas, *Stress Testing for Risk Control under Basel II.*

The challenge of right pricing, of which we spoke in the earlier section "Credit Improvement and Credit Deterioration," is ever present. Investors who understand debt options appreciate that the key to their pricing is the relationship between *rates* and *yields*. These are the two ways of expressing return on debt securities:

- Coupon interest rates of a debt security reflect the return as percentage of that security's principal at par value.
- Yields express return (or, more precisely, projected return) as percentage of the amount invested.

Prices of debt securities move *inversely* to changes in rates. In the general case, declining rates on long-term bonds or money market instruments cause prices of outstanding debt securities to increase. In contrast, rising rates across a particular maturity see to it that prices of outstanding debt securities of that maturity decline. (Such decline is more important the further out is the maturity.)

Debt options on credit-risk-free instruments like U.S. Treasuries require the delivery of the underlying securities upon the exercise of the options. The exercise prices of these price-based options are expressed in terms of the prices of the underlying debt instrument relative to the exercise price of the option, which is their ultimate determinant.

With yield-based options, the value of the option is determined by the difference between the yield (or the yield complement) of the specified debt securities and exercise price. In assessing the effect of a change in interest rates or yields on the price of a debt instrument, it is always necessary to remember the nature of the relationship between

- An instrument's price and
- Its interest rate.

The designated maturity of the Treasury security from which the underlying yield is determined is a standardized term of every yield-based option. The underlying yield is derived from an outstanding security of designated maturity that has the longest remaining life. This means that newly auctioned securities having the longest remaining life will replace old issues on the first trading day following their auction. Therefore, the specific Treasury security from which the underlying yield is derived may change during the life of the option.

Many of the risks associated with debt options result from the character of markets in which the underlying debt instruments are issued and traded. Risks are also a result of the distinctive characteristics of these instruments themselves. Among the constraints involved in debt options is that the hours of their trading may not conform to the hours during which the underlying debt instruments are traded. To the extent that the options markets close before the markets for the underlying instruments close,

- Significant price and rate movements can take place in the underlying markets.
- Such price movements, however, cannot be reflected in the options markets and resulting pricing.

Any careful study of risk control procedures should account for the possibility of such movements, relating closing prices in the options markets to those in the underlying markets. A risk is that debt options may be exercised on the basis of price movements in the underlying security after the close of trading in the options markets when writers are no longer able to close out their short positions.

Furthermore, since trading interest in Treasury bonds and notes tends to center on the most recently auctioned issues, markets do not continually introduce options with new expiration months to replace expiring options on specific issues. Instead, the options introduced at the commencement of options trading in a specific issue are allowed to run their course, but

> Options trading in each specific issue of bonds or notes is phased out as new options are listed on more recent issues, although there may be options trading on more than one issue of bonds or notes at any given time.

Option contracts that are identical except for the principal amounts are not interchangeable. If a market lists different contract sizes on a particular issue of bonds or notes, a holder of a given number of smaller contracts could not close out his or her position by selling a lesser number of larger contracts with the same exercise price and expiration date, even though the amount of the underlying bonds or notes might be the same.

Exercise prices for Treasury bill options are based on annualized discount rates, computed as the discount from par at which a hypothetical 360-day Treasury bill could be purchased or sold. For reasons of consistency with other kinds of options, exercise prices are expressed as complements of discount rates (100 minus the annualized discount rate).

Exercise settlement values for yield-based options whose underlying yields are derived from Treasury securities are based on the spot yield for the security at a designated time on the last trading day of the option (as announced by the Federal Reserve Bank of New York). The aggregate cash settlement amount that the assigned writer of a yield-based option is obliged to pay the exercising option holder is the difference between

- The exercise price of the option, and
- The exercise settlement value of the underlying yield on the last trading day before expiration (as reported by a designated reporting authority).

This exercise settlement value is multiplied by the factor for the option, but different yield-based options may have different multipliers. One of the special features of yield-based options is that when the underlying yield is expressed in terms of a yield indicator, that indicator will represent a yield or discount multiplied by 10. When the underlying yield is expressed in terms of the complement of the yield, the yield complement will be stated simply as a decimal.

Given that exercises of yield-based options are settled in cash, option writers cannot fully provide in advance for their potential settlement obligations by acquiring and holding the underlying interest. Furthermore, the principal amount of Treasury securities needed to assure that an options position is fully covered will generally not remain constant throughout the life of the options but instead will fluctuate as a result of changes in yields and remaining time to maturity.

CREDIT SPREADS AND CREDIT OPTIONS

A *credit spread* is a spread in which the value of the option purchased exceeds the value of the option sold, or vice versa. The credit spread itself is a function of the grade of the asset being traded, compared to some other grade that serves as reference and is usually high. (More on credit spreads in Chapter 14.)

Credit spreads and other credit options are privately negotiated, over the counter between two counterparties. As such, they can be customized to meet the specific credit-related requirements—from hedging to other investment objectives.

As does any other option, a credit spread option grants the buyer the right, but not the obligation, to purchase a bond during a specified future exercise period at the contemporaneous market price or to receive an amount equal to the price implied by a strike spread specified in the contract. Spreads may be based on asset swap rates, government bond yields, or other prices. The exercise period may be

- A range of dates, with American options, or
- A single date, with European options.

Purchasing credit options enables investors to participate in price or credit spread movements, while risking no more than the option's premium. This, however, is not true of writers. Selling credit options can be a source of credit-related fee income, but it also carries unlimited risk, as is the typical case with options.

An investor could purchase a credit spread put to hedge the risk of widening spreads because he has written some notes. Or he may target a complex instrument because credit options provide the basis for building more exotic credit structures. Investors can use options on credit spreads to take a position on the relative performance of two different bonds without actually buying or selling either one. This instrument's design

- Strips out interest rate risk, and
- Focuses on pure credit risk.

In this manner, options on credit spreads permit investors to isolate credit risk from market risk and take a position relative to an asset's credit risk profile in the future. In a more general sense, credit spreads can be used to

- Earn premium income
- Profit from spread tightening or widening
- Buy securities on a forward basis when prices are favorable

The notion of credit spread is associated with bonds that are priced and traded at a spread over a benchmark instrument of comparable maturity. Most bonds denominated in U.S. dollars are priced at a spread over the current yield on 30-year Treasury bonds with similar maturities. Expressed in basis points,

- The yield differential, or spread, represents the risk premium.
- The market demands such premiums for holding the issuer's bonds that are not credit risk free (as discussed in the preceding section, "Credit-Risk-Free Debt Options").

Options referring to spreads over Treasury bonds, or some other defined benchmark credit, usually have maturities of between six months and two years. Their settlement can be in cash or through physical delivery of the underlying bond. On the option's exercise date, if the actual spread of the underlying bond is lower than the strike price, the option expires worthless. If it is higher, the writer delivers the bond and the investor pays a price whose yield spread over the benchmark equals the strike spread.

Thinking by analogy to other developments that took place in the past few years, it is likely that enterprising rocket scientists will use *undated debt* as the underlying for credit spreads. The trend toward very long dated or undated debt started in 2004 and 2005, as attested by the fact that some companies are issuing 50-year bonds and some companies are also drawing on the capital market through hybrid bonds.

Hybrid bonds are essentially subordinated debt securities that have maturities of up to 100 years, or they are perpetual and therefore *undated*. Such debt securities are counted by rating agencies as partial capital substitutes, but for their issuers they help to improve the debt ratio and other financial ratios. They also tend to lower the issuing company's financing costs particularly when clauses attached to them specify that

- The issuer can call in a hybrid bond after 10 years.
- Until the earliest call-in date, these bonds typically have a fixed interest rate, although thereafter they may have a floating interest rate.

This shift to a floating interest rate means that these bonds correspond more closely to 10-year bonds than to ultralong-period bonds such as 50-year bonds. Otherwise, however, investors may be locked into them for a long time. In 2005, bonds with maturity of 50 years were issued in Europe for the first time in nearly half a century. France and Britain both placed 50-year government bonds, and so did an Italian telecommunications company.

The curious thing is that although nobody can forecast ultralong, or even simply long, interest rates, such ultralong bonds were in great demand on the market, with demand exceeding supply. At the end of the day, investors will regret their 2005 euphoria.

PART FIVE

Futures, Forwards, and Swaps

CHAPTER 12

Futures and Forwards

FUTURES, FORWARDS, AND THE INVESTOR

In a spot transaction the agreed-upon price is paid immediately and the buyer takes possession of the asset. In futures and forwards the price is agreed in confirming the transaction, but payment occurs and delivery is taken some time down the line. As the reader will recall from the definition in Chapter 2, *futures* are traded on exchanges; *forwards* are bilateral over-the-counter contracts. Table 12.1 presents in a nutshell their characteristic differences.

Futures trades have been known since the early eighteenth century. Financial history books say that investors agreed on the share price of the Mississippi Company and made down payments for delivery at some future date. During the autumn of 1719, Mississippi shares officially traded in Paris for 10.00 livres, but they were sold in futures contracts for 15.00 livres.[1] A few months later, in December 1719, came the market crash, and the Mississippi Company went under.

In the boom market of 1719 in France, there was, as well, available an instrument equivalent to call options. Known as *call primes*, they permitted investors to pay a deposit of 1,000 livres for the right to buy a Mississippi Company share at 10,000 livres *if* its price shot past this target value. Plenty of means were available to investors to increase their gearing, but the stock market crisis that followed wiped out fortunes.

---

[1] Janet Gleeson, *The Moneymaker,* Bantam Books, London, 1999.

T A B L E   12.1

Ten Crucial Differences Characterizing Futures and Forward Contracts

Futures	Forwards
Standardized	Usually nonstandardized
Traded on exchanges	Bilateral agreements
Settled daily	Typically exercised at maturity
Buyer deposits a margin	Commitment depends on agreement
Buyer called to upgrade margin	Depends on agreement
Commission paid to broker	No broker involved
Price set by the market	Price fixed by the writer or common accord
Traded on items for which there is market demand	Developed and traded to fit the two parties
Offsetting by taking an opposite position	Thorough analysis needed for offsetting studies
Mainly market risk	Both market risk and credit risk

In the American commodities markets, futures originated in the 1860s. Today, commodities futures can be fairly sophisticated financial instruments, and they are still under steady evolution. For instance, *options on futures* is a development of the 1970s, more than a century after futures contracts began to be traded through futures exchanges. Comparing futures to options, we can say that

- *Futures* are leveraged *binding agreements*. They are exchange traded and specify a standard quantity with delivery to occur at a stipulated time and place.
- In contrast, options are a *conditional cover*. Their holder is not obliged to carry out the contract terms and will exercise the option only if she derives a profit from it. But she pays a price when she purchases the option.

Not only are commodity futures the original reference (more on this in the following section), but also until recently trading in the futures markets was dominated by commodities (wheat, soya, eggs, pork bellies, and so on). Since 1975, however, there has been a market for *financial futures* beginning with contracts such as certificates of deposit (CDs) and U.S. Treasury bills used by investors to hedge against interest rate risk.

As explained in Chapter 2, when compared to futures contracts, *forward* contracts are characterized by both similarities and differences, with a major difference being that forwards are bilateral agreements that are often customized. Historically, the development of the futures market followed that of the forwards market. According to economics historians, the forward market's origins were in the fact that, due to long transportation time, producers sought to avoid price risk by selling their grain *forward*, on a *to-arrive* basis.

With futures and forwards, the underlyings are assets like equities, bonds, physical commodities, or precious metals or logical commodities such as currencies, interest rates, and indexes. When buying or selling an underlying asset on the futures market, the trader or investor must supply a specified initial margin on agreement of the contract (see the following section). Usually, this is a relatively small percentage of the total value of contracted instruments, and, as such, it creates leveraging opportunities.

Calculated periodically during the life of the contract, the variation margin corresponds to the paper profit or loss arising from changes in the value of the contract or the underlying. In case of a paper loss, the variation margin can be several times as large as the initial margin, and, depending on market developments, it can keep on growing. When this happens, the broker calls on the investor, who is obliged to

- Deposit the required variation margin, and
- Cover the security dealer's losses accumulated in the contract.

The investor is entitled to close out the futures contract at any time prior to the expiration date, by selling his or her rights to the market. This, however, may represent financial loss. In case the contract is not closed out prior to expiration, it must be settled by the two parties. Settlement is achieved by either of two means:

- Physical delivery, which involves transferring the underlying asset for the full contracted value
- Cash payment, through which only the difference between contracted price and settlement price need be paid

Investors should be aware that, at least theoretically, there is no limit to how far the market value of the underlying can rise or fall. Hence, potential losses are unlimited, and (as stated) their size corresponds to the difference between the originally agreed price and the market's actual price at expiry. Leveraging sees to it that losses can substantially exceed margin requirements; therefore, futures and forwards lie in the twilight between speculating and hedging.

FUTURES AND MARGIN REQUIREMENTS

Futures are hedging instruments when a farmer, manufacturer, or merchant seeks price protection. A gold producer who wants to protect herself against fluctuations in the price of the precious metal will sell gold futures from part of her expected production throughput. Similarly, an importer of computer equipment who wants to avoid fluctuations in, say, the dollar-to-euro exchange rate, will buy dollars futures.

Investors who expect the stock market to go down will sell a stock index futures contract. Those who expect an easing in interest rates will likely buy *gilts* (government bonds) *futures*. Whether for trading, investment, or speculation, futures are typically traded on items for which there is sufficient demand in the market, and they are classified according to their underlying commodity or security:

- *Commodity futures* are based on grains, coffee, sugar, meats, or lumber.
- *Energy futures* are based on natural gas, crude oil, and crude oil derivatives (diesel fuel, gasoline, and so on).
- *Precious metals futures* are based on gold, silver, platinum, and palladium.

With a *stock index future*, the underlying security is a portfolio of shares reflecting a stock market index. For a *currency future*, the financial instrument is a given quantity of one currency to be exchanged for another currency. A currency futures contract is legally binding, reflecting the investor's interest to buy or sell standard quantities of money.

A quantity of a short-term financial instrument or of an interest rate on a standard quantity of a given currency underpins *money market futures*. However, currency futures and futures on money market deposits should not be confused. The latter concern T-bills, CDs, and short-term deposits or loans on Eurodollars and other strong currencies. Futures also exist on *bonds and notes* issued by sovereign governments such as U.S. Treasury bills, British gilts, and German bunds.

As these examples demonstrate, futures contracts provide the holder with an array of investment flavors and, therefore, the possibility to position himself or herself against the market through a legally binding contract that

- Concerns a certain standardized commodity, and
- Matures on a specified future date, at an agreed-upon price.

In exchange for the flexibility provided by this agreement to buy or sell an asset at a certain future date, on an organized exchange, and at a specified price, the buyer of the contract is subject to margin requirements. Notice that because margins are a small part of the contracts value, futures are leveraging instruments.

The term *margin* refers to a good-faith deposit of cash, securities, or other financial instruments required by a broker, futures exchange, or commodity exchange to ensure the buyer's performance. Though the margin represents a small amount of the total contract's worth, calls for additional margin are more or less a standard feature of futures contracts.

The hitch lies in the fact that margins are dynamic. Futures and options exchanges usually require traders to post *initial margins* when they enter into new contracts. Margin requirements, however, are subject to change as a result of

- Price changes
- Changes in volatility
- New regulatory requirements

Margin accounts are debited or credited by the broker to reflect changes in current market prices on the positions held. Holders of such positions must replenish the margin account if their margin falls below a minimum. Investors who lack liquidity to respond to calls for margin see their positions sold by the broker.

Margin requirements for all sorts of commodities are idiosyncratic. In the stock market, for example, *margin* refers to buying or selling stock short on credit. Margin customers are required to keep cash and/or securities on deposit with their brokers as collateral for their borrowings. In essence in a margin system,

- The investor borrows money from the broker to maintain his or her position, and
- The interest for that money is embedded in the futures price, which is subject to time decay (see Chapter 10).

No matter what the specific market in which they operate, investors who buy futures should always remember that for each trading day and for each contract, as the futures price changes, their margin accounts are adjusted to reflect gains or losses. The upside is that (normally) the investor can withdraw any balance in the margin account in excess of initial margin. The downside is that if the balance in the margin account falls below the maintenance margin, the investor receives a margin call and must immediately satisfy the broker's request.

Margins and other operations described in the preceding paragraphs further document that futures are standardized contracts, whose execution is guaranteed by the exchange that plays the role of a clearinghouse. As such, it specifies what is meant by a normalized amount, product quality, delivery option, and delivery date. The exchange also establishes limits on price moves of futures contracts.

FUTURES TRADING: A CASE STUDY WITH OIL

The futures markets have changed dramatically since the time when they were primarily agricultural in nature. As we briefly saw in the preceding sections, they have since expanded into a wide range of sophisticated financial instruments including interest rates, currencies, precious metals, stock market indexes, and energy products. *Energy futures* make an interesting case study.

The spot market for oil was created in 1969 by Philipp Brothers, then the world's largest metals trader. Marc Rich, one of Philipp Brothers' young and upcoming dealers, started selling small quantities of Iranian crude oil to independent refiners. This relatively minor operation got wind in its sails with the oil shocks of 1973 and 1979, which resulted in a shift in oil pricing

- Away from long-term contracts, and
- Toward the Rotterdam-based spot market.

The spot market inserted a financial middleman into the oil businesses' income streams. In the spot market one buys the oil only 24 to 48 hours before taking physical (spot) delivery, as contrasted to buying it 12 or more months in advance while the barrel of oil is still in the earth. (A barrel has 159 liters.)

The next step in the evolution of oil trading was the futures market, with two principal exchanges dominating oil futures trading: the London-based International Petroleum Exchange (IPE), established in 1980; and the New York Mercantile Exchange (NYMEX). The NYMEX is more than a century old, and it was also the first to start trading oil futures in 1983.

Also known as *paper oil*, oil futures contracts are in essence a claim against oil. Since the futures markets are leveraged, paper oil is far in excess of the volume of oil produced and delivered at oil terminals. Additionally, oil traders say that a futures contract may change hands 15 times before the underlying barrel of oil is pumped out of the earth—and sometimes much more than that.

Traders, investors, and speculators buy and sell on the NYMEX and IPE a horde of oil futures contracts, each one of them representing 1,000 barrels of oil. More than 10 million oil derivatives contracts are traded each month on the exchanges, and the leveraging associated with a futures contract pulls and pushes the oil price. If traders bet long, the price of a barrel will rise because bets pull up the price of the underlying.

> This happens with all underlying commodities, and as such, it magnifies price movements as well as helps in price discovery (discussed in the following section).

At the International Petroleum Exchange, for example, one can buy a futures contract on a margin of less than 4 percent, which represent 2,500 percent leverage. If the trader buys a single futures contract, representing 1,000 barrels of oil at, say, an oil price of $60 per barrel, then the contract represents $60,000—while paying $2,500 margin. Conversely, a margin of $60,000 will give the trader control over contracts worth almost $1.5 million.

Using leveraging and their market connection, a small group of players can control the world oil price. The daily turnover of Brent crude (North Sea oil quality) futures contracts on the IPE alone now approximates twice the global daily production of oil. This means that in spite of the fact that Brent crude represents a small fraction of the worldwide oil production, its futures determine the price of a big chunk of global oil production.

This example dramatizes the role of futures in a global investment perspective, and this role is steadily expanding. But futures trading can be quite demanding, and for this reason many investors are depending on professional services offered by full-time money managers. Acting as interfaces, they see to it that thousands of transactions are conducted each day on the exchanges without the participants' ever seeing, for instance, a gallon of heating oil.

By trading commodities by means of futures, an increasing number of investors are adding managed instruments to their portfolios. Frequently, these commodities tend to move independently of other asset classes, which sometimes helps in balancing a portfolio—given that conditions that are not necessarily favorable to stocks and bonds can be favorable for managed futures—and vice versa.

Speculators, too, buy a commodity if they anticipate a price increase or sell a commodity if they anticipate a price decrease. Futures provide them with leverage, but by buying and selling futures contracts in the hope of making a profit, they accept the risk associated with a price change that the producer or user of the commodity is trying to avoid. By hedging her position through a purchase or sale of futures, the producer (or user) of the commodity transfers her risk to an investor or speculator.

In a sense, managed futures are looked at as a process of diversifying portfolio assets in an attempt to distribute the risk. While losses may occur, diversification is a sound strategy for a portfolio, but it should be done in full appreciation of the exposure being assumed. Investors assume the risk that producers are trying to avoid. This difference in objectives and in risk appreciation is precisely what makes up the market.

Apart from willing buyers and willing sellers, a vital part of the futures market is the existence of dependable, properly regulated, and properly supervised exchanges, whose role is both to attract players and to execute orders. A futures market can be successful if there is a large number of participants who actively trade.

A *thin market* with relatively few participants will *not* be efficient, continuous, or liquid.

A market with a large number of buyers and sellers actively competing and trading with one another is one characterized by only small variations between bids and offers, as well as relatively small variations among subsequent transactions. If there are few participants in the market, the spread between bids and offers will be relatively wide, with large fluctuations between successive transactions, which is the pattern of an illiquid or volatile market.

Another factor for the success of a futures market is that the commodity must be one that is easily appreciated, graded, and standardized. This is essential in order for buyers to have confidence that the commodity that is delivered on a futures contract will be acceptable and (hopefully) profitable. Oil futures have been chosen as a case study precisely because the instrument fulfills such requirements.

PRICE DISCOVERY THROUGH FUTURES

Futures markets are free markets; therefore, they provide information about prices that help in price discovery connected to physical products and financial instruments. At least in theory, prices must accurately reflect relative costs of production and consumption. Therefore, it is very important to have access to a pricing mechanism that functions fairly well and provides reference on price targets.

In practice, price discovery is more complex than what theory suggests because supply, demand, and other factors enter the equation. Also, in practice, price discovery is enabled by the fact that, in the typical case a number of futures contracts on a given commodity are traded simultaneously even if each is calling for delivery of the commodity at a different time in the future.

The fact that prices in the futures market are the result of open and competitive trading in established exchanges means that they reflect the underlying supply and demand for a commodity. They also reflect expectations about what supply and demand for that commodity will be at various times in the future.

What is important is that this market system provides for the establishment of not one but many different futures prices for a given commodity at any given time. For instance, at any point in time there may be as many as two dozen futures contracts for gold being traded, each calling for delivery in 1 of the next 12 months.

This results in the establishment of a pattern of distinct prices, ranging from the price for near-term delivery to the price for distant delivery a year into the future.

This role of price discovery is a very important component of a free economy. As an example, if futures prices for oil are higher than the current spot price, this may indicate an expected increase in future spot prices for this commodity. This is, of course, a simplification because the futures price includes economic costs; on the other hand, it is true that the market mechanism can provide answers that would otherwise be elusive.

A reason why obtaining pragmatic answers in regard to prices is feasible is because futures markets serve basic economic functions. They facilitate capital formation, provide reasonable liquidity for transactions, assure a mechanism for the transfer of risk, see to it that transactions can be conducted with relative anonymity, and often become attractive ways for purchasing or selling.

Another interesting characteristic of price discovery through futures markets is that these prices are steadily and immediately disseminated to market players and to the public by automatic reporting systems. Thanks to information providers, futures markets are characterized by highly visible prices against which the current cash prices of dealers can be compared, which increases market efficiency by so much.

In its way, this both contrasts to and complements the cash prices system whereby different commodities are commonly traded in cash markets by dealers—that is, markets in which each dealer posts his or her own price. As it is to be expected, however, such prices often differ from one another because each dealer's customers are more or less unaware of existing price differences.

It is interesting as well that the pricing of futures pays attention to both the underlying's cash value and prevailing interest rates because it involves a *cost-of-carry valuation*. Futures are priced as a function of the

- Yield on the underlying asset
- Price of the underlying asset
- Time to expiration
- Investor expectations

The *cost of carry* is associated with the financing rate less something else; with equity futures, for example, this is the dividend rate. Notice that in this model interest rates are known but dividends are not always known. Also known is the current spot price, which is not true of the future spot price.

As a result of these considerations, the futures price is more than a linear variation of the spot price. It is adjusted for the foregoing parameters even if, in the general case, futures prices do not move far out of alignment with spot prices. This is due to arbitrage and delivery requirements.

Indivisible from the futures pricing and trades are the exchange settlement and delivery mechanisms. Commodity and currency futures are subject to physical delivery, though many are settled through cash transactions rather than through physical delivery. On the delivery day,

- The sellers of futures are the holders of short positions who must deliver.
- The recipients are the buyers of futures who hold the long positions.

All abide by contract specifications that define the underlying security or commodity, nominal amount, delivery date, and so on. At the same time, however, the able use of futures markets requires a thorough understanding of the factors influencing their prices. Precisely because the price of futures contracts is dynamic, investors must put in place a system of *cash deposits* and *margin requirements* (see the section "Futures and Margin Requirements" earlier in the chapter). These constitute the mechanism whose steady output requires the following:

- Steady monitoring of every inventoried position
- Uninterrupted information on paper profits and paper losses

On a daily basis, and preferably intraday, all positions must be revalued at their current *settlement price* by *marking-to-market*, keeping well under perspective the fact that margin requirements amount to a relatively small cash deposit while the futures contract represents a much larger notional amount of money.

In conclusion, because futures contracts are traded for delivery of an underlying commodity at various times in the future, they reflect current market expectations about future cash prices. Hence, the futures trading information elements about market expectations regarding the underlying commodity are assimilated to produce a single futures price for a target time period.

FORWARD CONTRACTS

The previous sections made the point that to create and sustain liquid markets, futures exchanges have introduced standardized contracts, centralized trading in a finite number of contracts, margin requirements, and carefully regulated and monitored trading. Also, to eliminate counterparty credit risk, clearing associations were created, guaranteeing contract performance through *delivery versus payment* (DVP).

In contrast to futures, *forwards* are bilateral agreements, they are traded over the counter (OTC), they are by majority custom-made, and they involve credit risk. The counterparties negotiate on the instrument's characteristics, type and quantity of the commodity to be delivered, and terms of the forward contract, which is usually not standardized but negotiated between the parties at trade time.

In many other respects, forward contracts are very similar to futures contracts, and their contractual provisions and obligations resemble those found in futures. But there are, as well, differences. For instance, contrary to futures, there are no margin requirements associated with forward contracts.

Customization aside, the reader should well appreciate that beyond market risk there exists *credit risk*, should the counterparty be unable or unwilling to face its obligations. This distinction is important not only because of the exposure it represents but also for the reason that it impacts on

- The nature of the contracting parties' obligations
- The contractual clauses associated to these obligations

Additionally, apart from the exposure to the risk of default or bad faith by the counterparty, forward contracts usually *lack liquidity*. Since they are usually customized and traded OTC, with few exceptions they cannot be bought and sold in a competitive, liquid, secondary market. The primary market, however, is vibrant. It has been estimated that more than $500 billion of both swaps and foreign currency forward contracts are written each year.

Customization, of course, has its advantages. It provides forward contracts with a certain flexibility that futures contracts do not have: they can be tailored precisely to the needs of the two parties, which can also agree on specific delivery requirements and procedures that best suit them. It is nevertheless possible that the terms of a forward contract can be standardized in ways emulating a futures contract. Therefore, the stronger distinction between futures and forwards is a *legal* one. The law distinguishes between forward and futures contracts on the basis of delivery:

> *If* delivery is intended and regularly occurs under a certain type of contractual arrangement,
>
> *Then* the instrument is likely to be considered a forward and not a futures contract.

In the United States, this criterion is consistent with the legislators' desire to permit off-exchange transactions between persons involved in a commercial cash commodity business, where deferred delivery of a commodity is an integral part of doing business. In a way, this reflects the fact that the main players in forward markets have been large and sophisticated commercial and investment banks, institutional investors, hedge funds, treasuries of large corporations, and brokers.

- A key reason why players in forward markets are mainly large participants is that all forward contracts entail significant credit risk.
- To minimize this exposure, contracting parties usually deal only with counterparties who enjoy an AAA or at least an AA credit rating.

Of the two parties involved in forwards in an OTC transaction, the purchaser of a forward assumes a long position. He or she agrees to buy the underlying asset on a certain specified future date for a specified price. The seller of the forward has a short position. He or she agrees to sell the asset on that same date for the same specified price. The counterparty with the short position delivers the contracted asset to the one with the long position, in return for the agreed delivery price. Thus,

Terminal value of a long position $= S - D$
Terminal value of a short position $= D - S$

where

$D =$ delivery price
$S =$ spot price at maturity

The price of futures fluctuates because they are exchange traded. In contrast, forwards are bilateral commitments to buy or sell an asset at a future date, so their price is determined when the deal is made (unless there is a secondary market for them which, as already stated, is unlikely). Though other commodities, too, may constitute the underlying, the majority of forward contracts are made on

- Interest rates
- Currency exchange

Interest rate agreements are bilateral contracts in which two parties agree on the interest rate to be paid on a notional principal amount (Chapter 2) of specified maturity, at a defined future time. Normally, no principal exchanges are involved, and the difference between the contracted rate and the prevailing rate is settled in cash.

Among forwards, interest rate contracts tend to have the longest maturity. This has both market risk and credit risk ramifications. In the longer term, the default probability even of an AA counterparty is not trivial. Furthermore, how a trader knows what will be the interest rates 20 or 30 years down the line is one of the financial mysteries. In currency exchange bilateral agreements, dealings between counterparties can be of two types:

- Foreign currency–*denominated* contracts
- Foreign currency *exchange* contracts

With foreign currency–denominated contracts, settlements are performed in a single currency. These include the popular *forward rate agreements* (FRAs, see the section "Forward Positions: An Example with FRAs" later in the chapter) that bet on the future interest rate in a foreign currency; *bonds* payable in a foreign currency; and commitments to sell goods or services for foreign currency.

The Commodity Futures Trading Commission (CFTC) classifies forex (foreign exchange) transactions mainly in accordance with their trading motives. Counterparties who use currency futures primarily to hedge open positions are said to be *commercial traders*, while all others (and particularly those with predominantly speculative motives) are classified as *noncommercial traders*. (According to the CFTC, the distinction between commercial and noncommercial traders is based on information supplied by the market participants themselves.[2])

With foreign currency contracts, obligations center around the exchange of currencies, with macroeconomic information interpreted primarily in the light of its impact on money market rates. Notice that while currency forward agreements constitute the bulk of foreign exchange trading, from the viewpoint of international investors, currency futures are often used to assess the current development in the global financial market.

Forwards are also written for other commodities. In all cases, the delivery price is the specified contract price, and it is unchanged throughout the contract's lifetime. The forward price is typically equal to the delivery price at the start of a contract, but it may be different from the delivery price thereafter. Settlement is done at maturity.

Like the purchase of a futures contract, a bilateral OTC agreement on a forward contract is a temporary substitute for a transaction in the cash market. Therefore, because neither contract is an asset to be purchased but rather an agreement to enter into a transaction at a later time, no money has to be exchanged at contractual time except for margin requirements of the futures contract.

FORWARD POSITIONS: AN EXAMPLE WITH FRAs

Futures, not forwards, were the first derivative foreign exchange instruments on record. Foreign currency futures were introduced in 1972 at the Chicago Mercantile Exchange (CME), following

---

[2] Deutsche Bundesbank, Monthly Report, Frankfurt, January 2007.

President Nixon's initiative to end the convertibility of the dollar into gold (which had been established through the Bretton Woods Agreement in 1944) and to let the dollar's exchange rate move freely in the foreign exchange market.

Financial historians look at the CME currency trades as the first financial futures contracts ever, antedating interest rate futures by three years.

The Bretton Woods Agreement, between America and Britain with Canada as junior partner, had established par values for the major world currencies, with the U.S. dollar pegged to gold at $35 per troy ounce. Because of this agreement,

- Currencies were permitted to fluctuate 1 percent above or below their par values.
- Central banks intervened to prevent greater departures from the par values.

However, by the 1970s, more than a quarter century after the end of World War II, the central banks found that their role had become very difficult to sustain.

The change to a floating-rate regime in the 1970s, in contrast to a fixed-rate currency exchange, has meant that currency values are permitted to change freely, to reflect the underlying private sector's demand and supply for currencies. This way, foreign currencies may be purchased or sold for future delivery in the international foreign exchange market among banks, money market dealers, and brokers.

The importance of a generally accepted currency exchange mechanism is better understood by keeping in mind that the inter-bank market is worldwide and wholesale. In it major banks trade with each other sometimes on behalf of their clients and in (many) other cases for proprietary trading reasons. In the spot market, transactions are executed now at today's price, with settlement typically taking place two business days later. In the forward market:

- Transactions are agreed upon today,
- But settlement will occur at a future specified date, at an agreed-upon price.

As the preceding section explained, this is characteristic of all forward markets and their instruments. Both the size of the contracts and their delivery dates are tailored to the individual needs of the counterparties. The contract prices are established by the bank or broker over the phone, with one counterparty or with a limited number of buyers and sellers. Participants are banks, brokers, treasuries of large companies, institutional funds, and commodity traders.

Commissions are set by the spread between buy and sell prices. There are no margins, but compensating bank balances may be required; and the clearing operation is undertaken by individual banks and brokers—on whose financial integrity rests the market's transparency and success. Moreover, this market is self-regulating.

Over the years, forward contracts have become a little more normalized than they were in the past, and they may provide a *right of offset*, or cash settlement, instead of requiring actual delivery. But while this type of forward contract bears substantial similarities to exchange-traded futures, in the general case it is not regulated by the authorities.

But there exist exceptions. For instance, American banks that are major participants in the forward market are regulated in various ways by the Federal Reserve Board, Comptroller of the Currency (OCC), Federal Deposit Insurance Corporation (FDIC), and other federal and state banking officials—even if banking supervisors do not regulate forward trading in foreign currencies.

In a similar manner, forward trading in foreign currencies is not regulated by a governmental agency in the country whose currency is being traded, though exchange control restrictions on the movement of foreign currencies are in effect in many nations. The bank engaged in foreign currency forwards generally acts as a principal in such a contractual transaction, and includes

- Its costs
- Its anticipated profit in the price it quotes for such a contract

Foreign currency futures and forwards provide a way for managing currency risk, and they can also be used to speculate on projected changes in exchange rates. However, exposures associated with investments in foreign countries, such as the purchase and sale of merchandise, building of factories, real estate investments, and others, have not only currency exchange risk but also interest rate risk inasmuch as loans may be contracted locally.

This interest rate risk is taken care of through *forward rate agreements* (FRAs). Explained in the simplest way possible, FRAs are contracts in which two counterparties agree on the interest rate to be paid on a notional deposit of specified maturity, at a given future time (usually 3, 6, or 12 months). Typically,

- The buyer believes that interest rates will be higher on the future fixing date than implied in the FRA.
- In contrast, in the opinion of the seller of the forward rate agreement, interest rates will be lower.

Normally, no principal exchanges are involved in an FRA, and the difference between the contracted rate and the prevailing rate is settled in cash. On the settlement day the party that loses pays to the party that wins the difference between the agreed contract rate and the official market fix. This difference is settled on the notional sum of the deal.

FRAs are foreign currency–denominated contracts, and they bet on the future interest rate in a foreign currency. But at the same time, as far as hedging or speculating in the global business arena is concerned, while FRAs and foreign exchange contracts are different, they act as twins:

- Settlement in a foreign currency–denominated contract is performed entirely in a single currency.
- In contrast, settlement in a foreign exchange contract involves an exchange of one currency for another.

One of the important uses of the FRA market is in helping to manage the floating-rate side of interest rate swap (IRS) positions. Hence, the two markets are not mutually independent. Another comparison that needs to be made is to interest rate futures. Up to a point, forward rate agreements are over-the-counter interest rate futures contracts. Compared with listed futures, they overcome several problems that typically confront the latter such as

- Fixed forward dates
- Contract specificity
- Margin calls
- Need to set up accounts and clearing facilities at exchanges

At the present time, when compared on an outstanding notional principal basis, the forward rate agreements market is about as large as the interest rate swaps market. Unlike listed interest rate futures contracts, however, FRAs involve credit risk.

SYNTHETIC FUTURES

Synthetic financial instruments were discussed in Chapter 2. Synthetic futures are created through two options. For instance, we can generate *synthetic long futures* through long call options and short put options with the same strike price. Conversely, *synthetic short options* are made by combining long puts with short calls with the same strike price.

By simultaneously buying a put option and selling the corresponding call option, a trader can construct a position analogous to a short sale in the futures market. A long or short position in interest rate futures can be used to create *synthetic securities* that have the same cash flows as alternative cash investments.

An example is the creation of a synthetic Treasury bill that might produce a higher or lower yield than an equivalent cash T-bill, depending on relative yields. The cash flows of the synthetic securities are the sum of cash flows on the spot and future positions used to create the security. A simple algorithm is the following:

Synthetic security = spot + futures

By combining short to long interest rate futures positions with positions in the underlying cash asset, it is possible to develop a variety of synthetic securities. Other synthetics can be generated by combining options and futures positions. For instance, a synthetic long call option is made by combining a long put option and a long futures option. A synthetic long put option is created by combining a long call option and a short futures option.

There are also synthetics made out of other synthetic instruments. A synthetic stock index future can be used to create a synthetic index future. The investor may purchase futures as a substitute for cash, investing the proceeds in a short-term credit product.

- If the position is held until the expiration of the futures contract, when cash and future prices converge, risk and return could be almost identical.

- But if the position is liquidated prior to the expiration, the synthetic index deal faces greater risks than a comparable cash index instrument.

Among the advantages of a long stocks position are dividends, as well as the fact that this operation is fairly simple. Disadvantages include higher initial costs, custodial costs, possible tracking error, and (under certain condition) market impact.

A similar statement is valid about commodities. For example, in a synthetic futures transaction on gold, the holder of a synthetic short future will profit if gold prices drop and incur losses if gold prices rise. A long position in gold call options combined with a short sale of gold futures creates price protection considered to be analogous to that gained through purchasing put options. The position holder will tend to profit from a decline in gold prices and will face a loss if the price of gold rises.

As these examples demonstrate, synthetic futures are proxies for short or long futures positions. One of the reasons stated by practitioners as to why synthetics may be more attractive than outright futures positions is that, other things equal, the synthetic product has the advantages of lower overall cost, lower custodial cost, no cash outlays, and lower margin requirements. Its disadvantages are greater price risk, rolling risk, and variation in the margin.

The pros say that a more potent reason for using synthetics is that they provide traders and investors with the possibility to develop new financial instruments that appeal to the market, even if those purchasing them do not quite understand their aftermath in case the market turns against their projections. As it cannot be repeated too often, the more sophisticated is the financial product, the greater is the required know-how and the higher the level of needed technology—not only to design and sell the instrument but also to permanently control its risks.

WARRANTS

Warrants is a subject that has much to do with options, and therefore, they should have been included in Part 4. However, it has been a deliberate choice to delay this discussion because equity and other warrants have futures-oriented features.

A *warrant* is a tradable instrument with the character of an option. Its holder has the right to purchase from, or sell to, the warrant issuer a quantity of financial products under specified conditions for a stated period of time. A company sometimes issues a warrant when raising new capital, with a plan to entice investors to acquire its underlying debt. In some instances warrants can be

- Stripped
- Valued
- Traded independently

Conversely, a warrant to equity attached to bond certificates gives the holder the right to purchase a share (or participation certificates) in the corporation issuing the bonds, within a stipulated period at a fixed price. Notice that the warrant might expire, but the bond continues being valid after the right has been exercised.

Conversely, the *equity* of a company can be defined as the sum of the value of all its common stock, preferred stock, and warrants. Company liabilities other than warrants can be viewed as options. The stockholders have the equivalent of an option on their company's assets (and, in cases, its produce). The common stock

- Is an option on the firm, and
- It can also be viewed as junior debt, subordinate to senior debt or other liabilities such as loans.

Warrants, which are exchange listed and traded, may give the holder the right to purchase a company's stock at a set strike price within a fixed time period, often more than one year. Such warrants are sold by the company itself, and require the issuance of new equity if an investor's warrant is in-the-money and exercise takes place.

In an effort to increase their annual returns, Dell, Intel, and Microsoft, among other companies, sell to investors put warrants on their own stock. For a limited period, the warrants give buyers the right, but not the obligation, to sell shares of stock back to the company at a set strike price below the market at the time they buy them.

Many financial analysts think that these transactions are ingenious because tax law makes any dealings that a company has in its own shares tax free. Such transactions also help the capital-intensive technology firms, whose operating costs are often too close to operating income to generate positive cash flows.

The hitch is that because the money received in such deals is not detailed on the income statement, it is unclear whether investors understand as well as company management does how much these sales can contribute to a company's financial position. Yet the proceeds show up on statements of cash flows that investors read.

- Companies that sell puts are betting that their shares won't fall to the options' strike price during the transaction's time frame.

If they are lucky, the put expires and the company keeps the money paid for it.

- In contrast, the buyers of the warrants are betting that the stock will fall.

Given that the company is obliged to buy back its shares from the outside investors if its stock drops below the strike price, the warrants are a potential liability, no matter how they are looked at or why they were issued. In contrast to options, the life cycle of a warrant is measured in years rather than months—hence its rate of variance can be substantial.

There are many reasons why modeling the fair value of warrants is more complex than it is for options. For instance, the exercise price can be paid using bonds of the company, even if they might be selling at that time at a discount. Or if the company is subject to a merger, adjustments made to its warrants may change their value. Serious valuation models for warrants examine the

- Underlying stock price and its volatility
- Life of the warrant
- Growth and earnings potential of the stock

They also account for the fact that warrant holders are not entitled to receive dividends if the underlying stock pays dividends and that if earnings dilution occurs, it will have an impact on the warrant's value—unless the warrant in reference has an antidilution clause, which protects the warrant holder from further dilution.

An interesting different class is *covered warrants*, which are not really warrants in a classical sense but third-party transactions in which a bank may write a warrant backed by the underlying stock of a given company. Covered warrants are exercisable into either

- Cash, or
- The underlying shares.

In this sense, covered warrants are securitized options on a given single stock, but they may also have as underlying a basket of stocks. Their aim is to offer investors the opportunity to gain exposure for a stock or a basket of stocks for less than the actual share price. Examples include American Depository Receipts (ADRs), debt instruments, emerging markets securities, and reverse floaters.

Although many covered warrant transactions are straightforward, there have been increasingly sophisticated structures brought to market in the past few years, with varying redemption features. With expiry dates of up to three years, covered warrants also offer much longer term exposure than equity options, which expire at dates of up to a year. The downside is that covered warrants can be highly illiquid.

In conclusion, in a general sense, a warrant may be traditional or covered. A traditional warrant is a right to subscribe for shares, debentures, other instruments, or government securities—exercisable against the original issuer of the securities. Warrants, however, often involve a high degree of gearing, and therefore a relatively small movement in the price of the underlying security results in the disproportionately large movement in the price of the warrant.

CHAPTER 13

Swaps

SWAPS DEFINED

A *swap* is a financial transaction in which two counterparties agree to exchange streams of payments over time, according to a predetermined rule applying to both of them. It is a legal agreement that specifies the notional principal amount, payments, and termination (maturity), as well as the terms of default.

A portfolio of swap agreements can be regarded as one of forward contracts—one for each payment date, and each written at same forward price. There are credit swaps, basis swaps, arrears reset structures, swaptions, and spreadlocks. There are also asset swaps including securitized asset swap/repackaging vehicles, gross market structures, physical commodities swaps, currency swaps, interest rate swaps, and others. Able swaps are contracted on the basis of a notional principal amount.

Some people tend to distinguish between asset and liability swaps. While the two are basically the same financial instrument, they are used for different reasons. Companies and investors use *liability swaps* to alter the profile of their interest payments. This is attractive when interest rates are expected to change. In contrast, an *asset swap* is employed to exchange one type of interest income for a different type of interest income.

- A *liability (coupon) swap* addresses the exchange of a stream of interest payments.
- An *asset swap* is used for the exchange of business income.

Interest rate swaps (IRSs, see "Interest Rate Swaps" and "Swap Spreads" later in the chapter) are transactions in which two counterparties exchange interest payment streams of different character, based on the underlying notional principal. IRSs can be fixed or callable, discount, premium, zero coupon, and amortizing. They can also be basis (time-decay) swaps as well as inverse floater/yield curve, leveraged, mortgage, and arrears swaps.

Standard terms and conditions for interest rate swaps are set by the International Swaps and Derivatives Association (ISDA). By country, local organizations, too, have a say on rules and contracts governing swaps. For instance, in Britain the British Bankers' Association Interest Rate Swaps (BBAIRS) are considered the standard for setting terms and conditions.

The three main types of IRSs are the following:

- *Basis swaps*, featuring one floating-rate index to another floating-rate index in the same currency
- *Coupon swaps*, with a fixed-rate to floating-rate contract in the same currency
- *Cross-currency interest rate swaps*, which may be set up with fixed rate in one currency to floating rate in another

More generally, the term *currency swap* refers to a group of financial instruments with which two counterparties exchange specific amounts of two different currencies at the outset and repay over time. Currency rate swaps can be classified into fixed and floating, puttable and callable, coupon, zero coupon, amortizing, forward start, leveraged, discount, premium, differential and quanto, and, most importantly, forward rate agreements (FRAs, Chapter 12).

Currency swaps were introduced in the 1970s, after the Smithsonian Agreement in 1971 that waived the fixed exchange rates that had been established in the Bretton Woods Agreement in 1944. In a currency swap, interest payments in the two currencies are exchanged over the life of the contract, and the principal amounts are repaid either at maturity or according to a predetermined amortization schedule. This is done according to a predetermined rule that reflects both

- The interest payments
- The amortization of the principal

Cash flows correspond to the principal amounts of two assets, or liabilities, that may or may not be equal in value. Also, it is possible to have coupon-only currency swaps with no exchange of principal. These are useful in hedging dual-currency liabilities where interest is paid in one currency and principal in another.

Currency swaps are also employed to convert a liability or an asset from one currency to another. They are as well useful in hedging dual-currency liabilities where the interest is paid in one currency and the principal in another. Depending upon whether the two sides of a currency swap pay a fixed or floating rate of interest, the transaction is classified as a fixed-fixed, fixed-floating, or floating-floating currency swap.

Hybrid swaps are cross-currency interest rates that combine elements of two types of swaps. A cross-currency coupon swap is a combination of a currency swap and an interest rate coupon swap, involving a simultaneous exchange of currencies and interest rate payments. Thus,

- One party pays a fixed rate on one currency's notional amount, and
- Receives a variable rate on the other currency's equivalent notional principal amount.

There are, as well, more complex versions such as *circus swaps*, which combine interest rates and currencies. Usually, with circus swaps fixed interest rates are used in both currencies.

The commodity swaps markets—which include energy, precious metals, and other physicals—differ from the other classes like interest rate swaps in two ways: The instruments are usually limited to futures contracts that cover a period of 1 year or less, while other types of swaps can reach 10 or even 30 years. Furthermore, rather than the treasurer, the main operator is the purchasing manager of the company.

One of the main players in *physical commodity swaps* are consumers of key commodities such as oil who (for example) cannot immediately offset an increase in their commodity costs with a like increase in their revenue. Other players are producers of commodities who use swaps because (for example) they cannot decrease their production cost when the price of the commodity they produce falls, and the problem is affecting their revenue. Still other players are speculators.

Other important swaps classes are *credit default swaps*, instruments that are fast rising in popularity (see "Credit Default Swaps" later in the chapter), and *equity swaps* such as index call swaps, index put-call swaps, equity-equity swaps, and an index with an embedded option. All these transactions require the full understanding of the swap dynamics, including the structuring of specific instruments, their pricing, and their application to the solution of individual asset and liability management problems.

PLAYERS, MILESTONES, AND FLAVORS OF STANDARD SWAPS

What many traders consider a *standard swap* involves the periodic receipt of a predetermined amount of the spot value of a unit of the commodity or financial instrument dealt with: interest rate, currency, or other asset. Typically, there is a regular exchange of payments over the term of the agreement, which can span over several years.

- As a financial contract between counterparties, the swap effectively fixes the price for a specified period of time.
- The parties agree to the length of the swap, the settlement periods within the swap, the quantities swapped per settlement period, and the price.

Unlike most other financial instruments, *swaps involve two-way payments*. This essentially adds up to a two-way possibility for profits but also a two-way exposure to risk. An aftereffect of two-way payments is that each party is exposed to the other in terms of

- Credit risk
- Market risk

Each party's financial staying power impacts on credit exposure, and this is true for all types of players in the swaps market. One of them is the *ultimate consumer* of swapped commodities, whether companies or investors. *Companies* have assets or liabilities to hedge. *Investors* (and speculators) usually enter the swaps market for profits.

Another class of swap players are the *market makers*. They provide liquidity by making two-way deals in swaps; and they usually hedge their swaps positions with instruments such as futures and

Treasuries. *Intermediaries* are still another class of players; they stand between two parties shielding the one from the other's credit risk. Intermediation may also be necessary for tax and other purposes.

The intermediaries are *brokers* in swap transactions who do not enter into the deals themselves. Their contribution is that of finding parties able and willing to execute swaps. Brokerage fees are paid up front, and they can be high, as they usually stand at the level of 0.01 percent of the notional principal amount, which may be quite large.

Milestones in swap transactions include the *trade* (or *effective*) *dates, interest payment dates,* and *maturity* or *termination dates.* The *effective date* of a swap is the date from which interest payments begin to accrue. A *reset date* (*fixing date*) is when the floating swap rate is reset. A swap typically *matures* with the last payment, according to established schedule.

A swap can also be terminated through a *buyout*, involving an up-front payment that reflects an adjustment made for prevailing market conditions. Another sort of termination is the *reversal*, whereby a new swap transaction offsets the original one. At each settlement period,

- One side pays the fixed price multiplied by the quantity of the commodity.
- The other party pays the then current spot price.

This structure is nearly identical in the different swap contracts briefly examined in the preceding section. Being a liquid instrument directly negotiated by two parties, the swap is subject to contractual terms and conditions that can be customized to meet each party's needs. The way to bet is that, for instance, with interest rate swaps, contractual clauses will use either of the following major swap patterns:

- Bullet
- Forward
- Appreciating
- Amortizing
- Roller coaster
- Zero coupon
- Off-market
- In arrears

As shown in Figure 13.1A, the *bullet interest rate swap* is one in which the notional amount does not vary over its lifetime. In a *forward start swap* (Figure 13.1B) the start date is delayed, and such delay may range from a few days to some years. Forward start swaps rely on basic compound interest for their pricing. The swap risk and swap reversal calculations are essentially annuities structures. Simplification of the otherwise complex notion of this type of swap helps

- In a better appreciation of the nature of the transaction
- In an improved understanding of the exposure involved

In an *appreciating swap* (Figure 13.1C), the notional principal amount increases in regular or irregular instruments over its life cycle. In contrast, in an *amortizing swap* (Figure 13.1D), the notional principal on which interest is calculated decreases in regular or irregular increments over its life.

A *roller-coaster swap* combines the appreciating and amortizing characteristics, with the notional principal amount fluctuating in increments. Appreciating, amortizing, and roller-coaster swaps

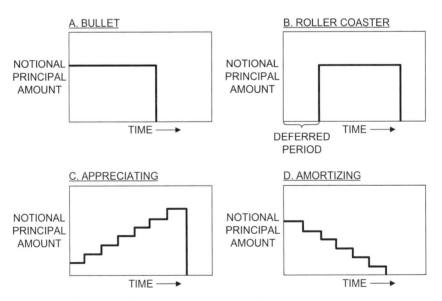

Figure 13.1 Different flavors of contractual clauses connected to interest rate swaps

need an algorithm able to provide an estimate of average lifespan. In a *zero-coupon swap*, a popular instrument, one counterparty will make the floating-rate payments at regular intervals, and the other counterparty will do a lump-sum payment usually on the maturity date. In a *reverse zero-coupon swap*, that lump-sum payment is paid up front.

With *off-market* swaps, the swap rate is set above or below the normal market rate. In return, the counterparty paying a lower rate (or the party receiving a higher rate) will make a lump-sum payment, usually up front. With *swap-in-arrears*, the floating rate is set at the *end* of the period, and corresponding amount is paid immediately. This flavor of swaps has lower quoted fixed rates if the yield curve's slope is upward.

INTEREST RATE SWAPS

Interest rate swaps (IRSs) were a development of the 1980s. Along with *credit default swaps* (CDSs), they are considered by many experts to be the most important new financial instrument of recent years. As the reader will recall from the first section, "Swaps Defined," IRSs involve an exchange of payments between two parties, with the amount of payment

- The same notional principal amount,
- But on a basis of a different interest rate.[1]

Notice that an interest rate swap does not involve a loan or actual exchange of principal. Technically, therefore, swap payments are not interest payments even if it is a rather usual practice to refer to them as such. Exchange of payments is specified by the swap agreement, common practice being six months or a year—but payments can as well be more frequent if this suits the needs of both parties.

Contrary to bonds, the contractual IRS agreement between the two parties specifies the exchange of a series of payments over a defined time frame. Though each party in a swap undertakes to make a payment to the other at specified intervals, in practice a single *net payment* is made from the one to the other party each time.

---

[1] The many aspects of interest rate risk are explained in Chapter 14.

This is like interest payments on a bank loan, with the added flavor that through the swap the risk characteristics can change; for instance, they can become floating-rate liabilities.

The default risk of one of the parties in the swap affects the swap rate, and thereby the swap spread. Other events, too, like the effects of emerging markets crises or financial turbulence can affect the swap spread. During the second half of 1999, the swap spread tended to increase, as concerns related to the Year 2000 problem influenced market psychology.

Credit risk and market risk are leading concerns of swap players. In terms of market risk, up to a point, the interest rate sensitivity, or duration, of a swap is similar to that of a bond: when interest rates move, the value of the swap also moves.

The pros say that growth in the market for interest rate swaps has improved the ability of bond issuers and, therefore, also of the central bank to modify the term structure of outstanding debt, without having to reenter the market to issue or repurchase debt instruments. At the same time, this also means that swap contracts can as well be used to replace longer-term fixed-income debt instruments by floating-rate debt.

One of the important applications of interest rate swaps is in benchmarking. Yields on longer-term government bonds (10-year and 30-year bonds) have long been used as benchmarks. Swap agreements add to the benchmarking toolkit because they allow a two-way evaluation because fixed- and floating-rate payments are exchanged between the two counterparties.

For instance, the difference in yield of a particular issue versus the yield at a similar maturity on the swap curve can be used for valuing a given bond. One way to proceed is by recomputing the fixed returns on corporate bonds into a floating rate via the swap market. This provides a comparison between securities with different

Maturity dates and interest rates.

The main task is one of calculating how many basis points two bonds deliver compared with money market deposits. Such practice reduces heterogeneous bonds to the value of their cash flows, eliminating at least some of the problems produced by the bonds' differences. Along the same line of references, a more sophisticated model will include cost of capital.

SWAP SPREADS

Concepts similar to those discussed in the preceding section in connection to interest rate swaps underpin the evaluation of the market's credit risk appetite by means of swap spreads. As an indicator, the swap spread conveys useful information on the likelihood of default and other factors. It is defined as the differential between

> The fixed rate on an interest rate contract, known as the *swap rate*, and the yield on a credit-risk-free government bond with a comparable time to maturity.

Assuming that market players entering into a swap are *risk neutral* and have the same degree of creditworthiness, the fixed swap rate is determined as the rate equating the present value of expected floating-rate payments with the present value of future fixed-rate payments.

Factors such as the steepness of the yield curve and the expected changes in future differentials between the short-term money market rate used in swap agreements and the corresponding default-free interest rate influence the swap rate and therefore the swap spread—which is viewed as *a measure of credit risk*.

The principle is that although the higher-rated corporate issuer borrows at a lower cost than does the lower rated, there is credit risk associated to all issuers of debt instruments. Among Group of 10 (G-10) countries, government bonds of the United States, England, Germany, France, Holland, and Switzerland are considered credit risk free.

The lower bound for swap spreads is the spread over Treasuries paid by AA-rated issuers, but it may also be a spread under LIBOR commanded by them for floating-rate borrowing. There is practically no upper bound for lower credit borrowing, though various market forces establish upper bounds that are not strict.

- The swap spread can be expected to vary with changes in the aggregate likelihood of default, as perceived by the market.
- When the probability that any given firm will default is seen as having increased, other things being equal, the swap spread will tend to widen.

Additionally, since the likelihood of default typically increases in anticipation of, or during, a recession, the swap spread may also convey information about changes in expectations of future economic activity and/or perceived liquidity risk and other important market factors. In the opinion of many economists, variations in supply and demand of corporate and government bonds can as well induce temporary changes in swap spreads.

Notice that spreads don't exist only between corporate bonds and credit-risk-free government bonds but also between bonds issued by two different jurisdictions both of them being credit risk free. The developments in the interest rate differential between the United States and Euroland at the close of the twentieth century and first years of the twenty-first provide an example. According to several economists, the interest rate differential can be broken down into two components:

- One component reflects the difference in real interest rates required by investors for holding U.S. and Euroland bonds until they mature, interpreted as being related to relative growth prospects.
- The market factor underpinning the other component is the compensation for the average expected inflation rate in the respective economies, during the life of the debt instrument.

Prior to the advent of the euro, for example, relative pricing of nominal and index-based bonds provided indications as to likely sources of changes in interest rate differentials between bonds issued by the U.S. Treasury and by the French Treasury. While subject to different developments in France, indexed bond yields and breakeven inflation rates have been frequently used as proxies for changes in *expectations* regarding longer-term real rates and inflation perspectives.

As these references demonstrate, a factual analysis of interest rate swaps and their spreads requires an in-depth knowledge of swaps, hedging objectives, and fundamentals of a pricing methodology. The analyst must as well explore the potential of dynamic hedging (Chapter 4) and successfully apply experimental tools in full knowledge of risk management goals.

SWAPTIONS

In a process fairly similar to that of practically all financial instruments, swaps pricing is dynamic. Interest rate swap prices change as a function of changes in interest rates, as well as with the supply and demand prevailing in the market for fixed-rate and variable-rate swaps. Other things being equal, prices tend to increase as

- Interest rate volatility increases, and
- Less favorable credit factors are taken into account (see also Chapter 14).

Because a swap is a liquid instrument and a privately negotiated contract, there exist as well other criteria for its pricing. Its sensitivity to strike rate should be accounted for, as well as its sensitivity to duration. Other, more specific pricing criteria relate to the fact that it is possible to customize a swap trade to meet the particular needs of the counterparty (which is also one of the reasons for hybrid swaps).

The large number of flavors available with IRSs, and their steady multiplication, sees to it that pricing is in no way a monolithic business the way it might be deduced by looking at a histogram, like the one in Figure 13.2. The interest rate swap market is

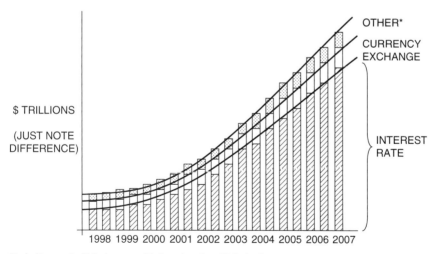

*Including equity-linked, commodity-based, and credit derivatives.

Figure 13.2 The rapid growth in OTC derivatives (nominal values, end-of-half-year data)

by far the largest derivatives market, with its different products largely customized and therefore individually priced.

In the background of the multiplication of different types of swaps have been not only the counterparties' requirements but also advances in swap technology. Like practically all other financial instruments, swaps can have derivatives such as callable swaps, puttable swaps, extendible swaps, capped and floored swaps, collared swaps, and swaptions (more on this later).

Swaptions are options on swaps. The differentiating characteristic of a swaption is that it gives its holder the right, but not the obligation, to enter into a swap agreement with the writer. Swaptions are over-the-counter instruments whose contracts terms specify the following:

- Notional principal amount
- Interest rate to be swapped by each party
- Frequency of swap payments
- Other terms, including maturity

Essentially, swaptions represent the right to enter into a swap. A *call option* gives its holder the possibility to receive a fixed and pay a floating interest rate. A *put swaption* gives its holder the right to enter into a swap, receiving a floating and paying a fixed interest rate.

- The fixed-interest-rate payer has the right to terminate a *callable swap* on or before the scheduled maturity date.
- In contrast, it is the floating-interest-rate payer who, at his or her discretion, can terminate a *puttable swap*.

In a callable swap, the fixed payer has the right, but not the obligation, to terminate it on or before the scheduled maturity. The floating-rate writer is compensated for this option by an up-front premium or increase in the fixed rate received. Usually, the buyer of a callable swap is a fixed-interest-rate payer who expects interest rates to fall.

In a puttable swap, the investor paying the floating rate has the right to terminate it. Payment for a puttable swap is made either by an up-front fee or by a reduction in the fixed rate received. *Extendible swaps* are similar to callable and puttable swaps. One of the players has the right to extend the swap beyond its stated maturity date, doing so according to a schedule.

In a *capped swap,* a ceiling rate is set on the floating side. *If* the index rises above this ceiling, *then* the floating-rate payer simply pays the ceiling rate. The party with floating rate either pays an up-front premium or receives a fixed rate lower than the market rate in return for the protection provided by the ceiling or cap. There is a lower limit for the floating rate in the *floored swap.* (See also the discussion of caps, floors, and collars in connection to options, in Chapter 7.)

Callable and puttable swaps can be seen as combinations of regular swaps and swaptions. A floating-rate borrower can limit the interest expense confronting him or her in any period by purchasing a cap:

- An *IRS cap* is a contract that has a contingent periodic cash flow.

If the prevailing floating-rate index is greater than the cap rate, *then* the cash flow is equal to the difference of the two rates. Other things being equal, the lower is the limit rate, the higher is the price of the cap contract. The opposite kind of protection is also possible.

- An *IRS floor* protects the lender from abrupt falls in interest rates.

The resulting cash flow is equal to the difference between the floor rate and prevailing rate applied to the notional principal amount. An *IRS collar* protects both ways, securing the trader or investor from worst-case interest rates whether they rise or fall. Floating-rate exposure might limit interest rate exposure by the investor's purchasing a cap, then financing the purchase by simultaneously selling a floor.

Swaptions are used by companies to monetize the call option owned by them into a callable bond issue. With American-style swaptions, the holder can choose the time that is most suitable to exercise them, but these cost more than European swaptions, which are exercisable only on the expiration date.

No matter which type they are, the contractual agreements to exchange specified cash flows, or commodities, between the two parties involved in the swap transaction can be

- At market
- Off market

- Above market
- Below market

At market is an interest rate swap in which no up-front pay-ment by either party is necessary. The alternative is an *off-market swap* with two variations: an above-market swap if the rate is greater than the at-market swap rate, with the fixed-interest-rate payer receiving an up-front premium; or a below-market swap if the fixed rate is below the at-market swap rate.

ASSET SWAPS AND EQUITY SWAPS

Basically, *asset swaps* are swaps tied to the assets of a balance sheet. Many experts consider them building blocks of derivatives from which a variety of different products evolved over time. With asset swaps, equity swaps, default swaps, and total swaps (*total return swaps*), the assets and liabilities are the underlying, or *reference*, securities.

Asset swaps are designed to change one or more attributes of the cash flow from an underlying asset. As such, they contrast to interest rate swaps and other swap types. Four characteristic fea-tures are outstanding among the many of these financial instru-ments:

- Creditworthiness
- Maturity
- Size
- Design

Chapter 11 looked into the many aspects of creditworthiness. Originally, maturities were in the three- to five-year range, but since the mid- to late 1990s there has been a push toward longer maturi-ties; this tends to increase the embedded risk. Also originally, typi-cal sizes of asset swaps were in the $5 million to $25 million level; but this too has changed. Corporate bonds now push toward the $100 million level, while Eurobonds tend to remain below the $15 million level.

The fourth important characteristic after creditworthiness, maturity, and size is design whose aim is to achieve the desired result in terms of credit, size, and maturity, as well as produce a

financial instrument appealing to the market. Design is a demanding task because participants in the asset swaps market may simultaneously be buyers and sellers. In this manner, lenders and
investors try to

- Improve portfolio diversification
- Gain exposure to credits, securities, and markets that may
  otherwise be difficult to access

Equity swaps are derivative instruments based on practically
the same notions as interest rate swaps, but they are used for different purposes. An equity (or index) swap is a contract, usually made
between an investor (or trader) and an institution, whereby the
individual agrees to pay the return over time (appreciation or
depreciation) on some stock to the bank, and the bank agrees to pay
the individual cash.

A two-way equity swap can be designed as a tandem of linked
forward transactions with strike and market prices compared at
periodic intervals. At each evaluation, the counterparties review the
level of, say, the index against the forward price and effect a payment in one direction or the other. In the aftermath of an interim
evaluation, the forward is reset to the current market level, and the
instrument continues until the next evaluation period.

The underlying of the swap may be an equity, basket of equities, or equity index. The premium may be paid up front as a cash
payment or through a series of periodic payments spread over the
life of the swap.

- An equity swap is not a security, and until recently it was
  unregulated and nontaxable.
- The investor who did not want to sell or could not sell the
  equities directly might effectively sell them by entering
  into an equity swap.

The ability to exchange the cash flow on one liability or asset for
that of another has had significant appeal. Even if the equity swap is
not a totally new type of product, it has provided a new way to

- Better understand how financial markets work
- Better appreciate embedded value with a certain amount
  of clarity

A reason why institutions go for equity swaps is that they are seeking upside or downside exposure to, or to the contrary, hedging of, their equity portfolios. Maturities typically range from one to five years, though there are also longer or shorter terms.

The institution pays the investor cash through the equity swap, while over time he or she would pay the bank the total return, which means the dividends plus the price appreciation on the stock. Between the lines of this reference lies the fact that anyone who wants to sell shares without recognizing capital gains and paying capital gains tax is welcome to use an equity swap because it is not deemed a sale since the investor still owns the underlying stock.

The downside is that a transaction designed as a series of multiple forwards with periodic settlement does not allow the instrument's intrinsic value to build up significantly, even if an equity swap is a leveraged instrument. On the other hand, the good news for the investor is that such structure lowers the amount of risk embedded in this transaction.

The credit institution or broker who enters into an equity swap stands to gain because it faces little or no market risk from the equity swap if it hedges its exposure to the stock payments from the investor by selling short. If the price of the stock declines, the institution will owe a correspondingly lower payment on its short sale. Even so, however, it still assumes an amount of exposure.

One of the flavors to be brought to the reader's attention is the *forward equity swap* practiced by real estate investments trusts (REITs). What REITs do is to borrow money to buy properties on the bet that they will be able to later sell the stock to pay the loans back. With this and similar plays, the financial sector's commercial paper has been zooming.

Increases in leveraging, however, cannot go on forever. The first sign that this process is unsustainable in the longer term came when the financial sector doubled the amount of its liabilities in the short space of one year: 1998. In the second quarter of 1998 alone, the combination of financial sector bonds and asset-backed securities grew by over $600 billion, an amount equal to 8 percent of the American economy. Leveraging has financed the stock market boom and supported the bubble in capital spending in the year 2000 as much of the business expansion was run on credit; and leveraging is behind the subprime mortgage bubble which burst July–August 2007.

One of the ironies of leveraging is that the more they borrow, the more corporations lose cash flow, which forces them to borrow even more. Eventually there comes a point where even larger components of the debt are not serviceable from profits. Even the reduction in the Federal Reserve funds rate is of little effect because declines in interest rates do not help profits when the economy is sitting on top of a capital investment bubble. Capital spending slowed after 2000, no matter what the level of interest rates was; and the mortgage market will take time to recover even with low interest rates.

TOTAL RETURN SWAPS

The preceding section brought to the reader's attention the fact that asset swaps are instruments for hedging in that they transfer the risk to somebody else. But they can also be used for leveraging, as many investors do with total return swaps whose structure allows counterparties to effectively go long or short on the reference asset.

A *total return swap* is a synthetic financial product. It is an agreement in which the total return of an underlying credit-sensitive asset, or basket of assets, is exchanged for some other cash flow. Usually this is tied to the LIBOR or to the return of other credit-sensitive assets. No principal amounts are exchanged, and no physical change of ownership occurs in connection to this transaction. When return is based on two reference assets or two baskets of assets,

> *If* at least one of these reference assets is a *credit-sensitive* instrument,
>
> *Then* the total return swap is a *credit derivative*.

One of the interesting aspects of credit risk–oriented swaps is that companies that have available credit lines but are unable to lend or invest because of balance sheet constraints can sell default swaps (or *differential swaps*). They do so using up some of their excess credit without breaching balance sheet limits, but because it cannot be repeated too often, this process is far from being free of risk.

Typically, two parties enter into a total return swap in order to exchange all the economic risks associated with a given security without transferring the security itself. The receiver and holder of the swap will be long of the total economic risk of a security or portfolio and will receive positive cash flows on that asset. This may be coupons or dividends, plus any appreciation in capital value.

The financing leg of the transaction can be structured with caps and floors on a floating interest rate, to control financing costs. The maturity of the total return swap need not match that of the underlying, and the swap can typically be terminated at any time. At termination, several structures permit the user to purchase the reference asset at its initial market price, instead of a cash settlement of the swap.

A total return swap may involve mortgage-backed securities (MBSs) in which an investor receives the total return on a *principal-only* (PO) *strip*. The investor may purchase a cap on the financing leg of the transaction, protecting the return on the trade from adverse movements in short-term rates.

Another type of total return swap involves corporate bonds. Thus, for instance, the buyer finances a BB-rated corporate bond and receives the total return on the bond and pays the LIBOR plus a spread. The structure allows the investor to finance an asset for which there is no traditional repurchase agreement market.

As instruments that permit investors to shorten an asset synthetically, total return swaps may be appealing to insurance companies, hedge funds, or corporate treasurers wanting to put their cash to work on a leveraged basis. As the foregoing examples document, total return swaps permit an investor to receive or pay the total economic return of an asset without actually buying or selling the asset itself. The algorithm is fairly simple:

- One party is synthetically long, and
- The other party is synthetically short on the underlying.

Many investors and companies interested in total return swaps are lenders who want to reduce their exposure to an asset without removing it from their balance sheet. By keeping the asset on their books, they may avoid jeopardizing relationships with borrowers and breaching client confidentiality since loan documentation remains in-house.

One variation of the total return swap is the *secured loan trust* (SLT) *note*, originally offered by Chase Manhattan to appeal to the geared market for loans. This is a series of notes in which an investor leverages exposure to a pool of sub-investment-grade loans. Pros see an advantage in the fact that total return swap payers do not have to hold the asset on their balance sheets.

The pros also add that another advantage is that total return swaps lock in financing rates and effectively create repurchase agreements in markets where repos may not exist. Also, they avoid the clearing, financing, and execution costs associated with an outright purchase; and the instrument's flexibility allows investors to isolate a spread of directional view, by taking action in a single transaction.

Though there are reasons to be found behind the stated benefits, it would be wrong to believe that with total return swaps companies and investors can have a free lunch. As a basic rule, the more beneficial an instrument seems to be to its holder, the greater are the risks associated with it and the greater are the skills required to make profits on it.

CREDIT DEFAULT SWAPS

A *credit default swap* (CDS) transfers credit risk associated with a particular borrower from the protection buyer to the protection seller. Since 2000, this is a market with exponential growth, as shown in Figure 13.3. Credit default swaps are *credit derivatives*, and they permit investors to trade credit risk separately from other types of risk. The *credit event*, which may be the bankruptcy of the reference entity, restructuring of its debt under unfavorable terms to the lender, or failure to meet scheduled debt repayments, must be properly specified in the CDS contract.

A simple form of a bilateral credit derivatives deal is that of two parties agreeing to exchange predetermined cash flows associated with a given credit event, over a defined maturity. Typically, the financial instrument provides default protection to the originator who is the *credit risk seller*. Most CDS contracts are based on physical settlement. The swap works through a net transfer from one party to the other credit risk exposure of the reference entity's debt, equal to the difference between

- Face value and
- Market value.

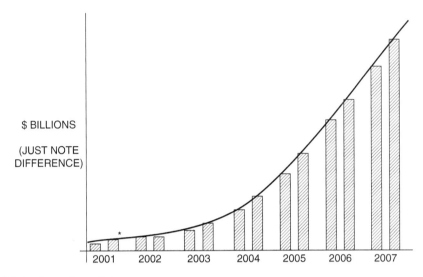

*First and second semesters.
Figure 13.3 Nominal amounts of credit default swaps outstanding

The growth of the credit derivatives market, and its success, depends on finding counterparties willing and able to assume the unbundled credit risk in exchange for a cash flow. Insurance companies and other entities provide that protection against a fee, and by so doing, they assume significant amounts of credit risk.

By transferring credit risk from the protection buyer to the protection seller, credit default swaps make it possible to short a loan. Moreover, these instruments, which involve their own credit risk, help in price discovery. As many analysts believe, the pricing of default swaps can reveal a great deal of market information about expected credit risk.

The whole concept behind an active market in credit default swaps can be encapsulated in one sentence: Lenders are capitalizing on the revolution in the marketplace for credit. Because of credit derivatives, banks are both able to buy credit risk and sell it short. Many credit institutions now want to be at the forefront of that business. Here are, in a nutshell, the mechanics:

- The CDS enables two parties to swap the credit risk associated with a reference security, or portfolio, without transferring the security itself.

- The *credit risk buyer* receives a fee from the credit risk seller. In exchange, the holder makes a payment if some reference security, or portfolio, experiences a credit event.

The reference asset can be any loan or security, or basket of loans or securities in a currency; and the swap can match or be shorter than the timeframe of the reference asset. The periodic payment depends, in large part, on the reference credit. Under this perspective, credit default swaps are a mechanism for distributing the default risk of securities and loans.

- They are tailored to specific needs, and
- Therefore they are highly customized.

The so-called *plain vanilla version* of credit derivatives is a credit swap whereby the protection buyer pays the protection seller a fixed recurring amount in exchange for a payment contingent upon a future credit event *if* that event takes place. Depending on the amount involved in the credit swap, this helps to cover part or all of credit loss pursuant to default. These are known as *ordinary CDS contracts*.

More sophisticated instruments like *fixed recovery CDSs*, also known as *digital default swaps,* allow investors to separate recovery and default risk. Their characteristic is that the counterparties agree upon a recovery rate that they will use after a credit event. A fixed recovery CDS buyer makes periodic payments to the seller, who provides protection to the buyer in case a credit event occurs.

In contrast, with *recovery locks*, or simple recovery swaps, no cash flows are exchanged prior to a credit event. If a credit event occurs, the seller delivers a defaulted obligation to the buyer in exchange for a preagreed fixed payment (specified in the contract) that represents the recovery value. Recovery swaps

- Are quoted in terms of percentages of the notional amount
- Express the fixed recovery value that is exchanged after a credit event

The CDS market in consumer credit came to life when dealers agreed on a standard contract applying credit default swaps, already widely used in the corporate bond market, to the pools of home, auto, or credit card loans—known as *asset-backed securities* (ABSs). Applied to the housing market, credit default swaps are derivatives that rise and fall in value based on the likelihood that homeowners will pay back their mortgages. As such, they are an instrument of interest to investors who want to bet against financially stretched homeowners.

Like an insurance policy, a CDS permits its holder investors to protect themselves against defaults on packaged pools of home loans. The insurance pays off if the homeowners miss payments on loans. Hence premiums tend to rise when homeowners' credit starts to look shaky. Trading has focused mainly on home-equity securities backed by adjustable-rate loans to people with subprime credit. This class has grown in recent years as mortgage lenders have offered easy financing to high-credit-risk borrowers.

As the early 2007 events with subprime credit demonstrate, *this* CDS market has yet to be tested by a wave of defaults. (By late 2006 subprime defaults stood at 13 percent, which is appreciable, but not dramatic.) Jurisprudence is important because even in the relatively mature market for credit default swaps on corporate bonds, payouts are frequently disputed. Some experts think that subprime mortgage–backed securities disparities can open a Pandora's box of litigation.

DIFFERENTIAL SWAPS

The eight previous sections provided plenty of evidence that swaps range in design from straightforward to fairly complex structures, some of which can be simplified by taking them apart, evaluating their cash flows, and studying them in terms of yield as well as present and future values. Essentially this means reverse engineering their structure, leading to a series of elements that have to be recombined by modeling the total product.

Reverse engineering and recombining are more difficult to do with leveraged swaps, which generate a payoff by magnifying the movement of the underlying such as a reference index. First and foremost, it is necessary to identify the degree of leverage inherent in the transaction, which is apparent in certain cases but is generally opaque. It takes lots of skill and experience to decompose the transaction into individual swaps components.

An interesting case of a complex and leveraged instrument is the *differential swap* (*diff swap*) whose interest rate references are based on floating rates in two different currencies but are payable on a net basis in a single currency. This structure is similar to a union of an interest rate swap and a swap emulating quanto options, and it has found a clientele among investors and intermediaries who try to capitalize on the movement in foreign currency rates without assuming foreign exchange exposure. Diff swaps have been linked to

- Financial instruments that offer foreign indexes paid in a base currency
- Indexed amortizing rate swaps, designed for such events as prepayments on a mortgage book

The pros say that even if diff swaps are complex, some positions offset others. Hedging is usually done on a portfolio basis, rather than deal by deal; and a bank with a large currency option book might have access to a hedging tool without paying inordinate market premiums.

On the other hand, contrarians think that even houses with large books might have trouble if extreme interest rate volatility makes hazardous the resetting of the interest rate leg in a swap. Under certain conditions, even a one-day mismatch, normally small in risk management terms, can have a big impact on exposure.

Contrarians also state that it is difficult to find convincing examples of an investor's assets or liabilities position that can be made safer by a differential swap. And the user who hopes to do a diff swap favorable to his or her investment position must have a view on the yield curve differential with another currency and hence an economic viewpoint.

Some specialists further suggest that many not-so-knowledgeable traders and investors are putting diff swaps on their books without really understanding the risks they are taking. For instance, they fail to appreciate that if they get a futures contract rolling over when rates are reset from, say, 5 to 7 percent, they can get huge changes in their hedge and also get burned.

Even with smaller interest rate fluctuations, too often risk control presupposes constant dynamic hedging on the trader's side. In contrast, the dynamics might be slightly different for users of diff

swaps because they have no foreign exchange risk since all payments are made in a single base currency. Thus,

- Their exposure is the differential between interest rates in
  the home market and in the market of the second currency.
- A frequently made bet is that this differential will narrow
  more slowly than forward rates or yield curves imply.

The main users of differential swaps are U.S. fund managers
and Japanese insurance companies, driven by high-current-yield
requirements from their retail client base. Such deals allow entities
forbidden to use other derivatives or foreign currency instruments
to take on some foreign exposure. Other users are investors who
want to express separately their

- Interest rate view
- Global foreign exchange view

Some European banks and brokers doubt whether diff swaps
are really a promising new hedging technology. They feel that differential swaps have taken the idea of derivatives too far from
underlying commercial needs. And they also suggest that the risk
and cost of this extra hedging is not balanced with potential profit.

RISKS ASSUMED WITH SWAPS

One of the ways swaps contribute to portfolio management is gap
reduction and duration shortening. They permit investors to sell
long-term assets and invest in shorter-term maturities. Other contributions are the exchange of fixed and floating interest rates, and
cross-currency exchanges (as described in the first section, "Swaps
Defined"). Unavoidably, however, they also involve risks:

- *Market risk*, specifically interest rate risk, is the leading
  concern of swap players.
- *Credit risk* is also present, mainly for the interest payment
  that is involved.
- *Legal risk* has many origins, one of them being the tax treatment of swaps, which varies from one country to another.
  The swaps payments may be deductible, but the costs of
  arranging a swap and the up-front commissions may not be.

- *Mismatch risk* refers to the position of the swap dealer who has two offsetting swaps hedging each other that are not exactly matched. Examples of such differences are these:
  - Maturity
  - Timing
  - Floating-rate index
  - Frequency of payments

Mismatch risks are not always given the attention they are worth. Whether arranged for customers of the bank or for proprietary trading, identifying matching requirements is an inexact process in regard to the amounts, fixed or flexible interest rates, and timing of swaps. Players willing to take on the exposure of possibly unmatched amounts in their own swaps books should have a first-class risk control system that

- Provides them with timely and accurate information
- Permits them to exercise at all times rigorous risk control

Even if all swaps are executed under ISDA master swap agreements, containing mutual credit downgrade provisions that sustain the ability to require assignment or termination in the event that either party is downgraded below A3 (under Moody's ratings) or A– (under S&P and Fitch), and even if more credit latitude is permitted for only those transactions having original maturities shorter than one year (because of their lower exposure), there is a significant amount of risk involved in swaps. As the reader is already aware, unlike most other financial instruments,

Swaps involve two-way payments, and therefore they feature a two-way exposure.

Each party is exposed to the other in terms of credit risk, and *credit risk* is an integral part of a swap transaction. The pros say that credit risk with swaps is small compared to that of a loan because only interest payments are involved, not the principal amount. Moreover, with swaps there is usually an offset arrangement such that in the event of the default by one party, the other is no longer required to continue making payments on the swap.

Contrarians say this argument conveniently forgets that in some swap structures, the credit risk can be significant. An example is zero-coupon swaps, where one party makes all the payments before the other makes any. Hence, it is better to look at the credit risk of a swap *as if it were a loan*.

The risk that counterparties will be unwilling or financially unable to make payments according to the terms of the agreements, whether these are swaps, purchased options, or forwards, should never be discounted. Gross market values of probable future receipts is one way to measure this risk—a process meaningful only in the context of net credit exposure to individual counterparties.

As the careful reader will recall, an AAA, or at least an AA, credit rating is all important in the market for over-the-counter derivatives, in which banks provide customized swaps and other deals for corporate customers. In swaps transactions, especially longer date currency and interest deals, which can cover a period of as much as 10 to 15 years, companies can assume significant exposures in regard to their counterparties.

Dealers in the OTC market are also beginning to demand collateral from counterparties. These arrangements are sometimes linked to the credit ratings on the parties involved so that as its credit ratings fall, a party may be expected to place more collateral against its own exposure. Besides the fact that counterparty risk is omnipresent, and all swaps, purchased options, and forwards must be carried out within the creditworthiness constraints in mind, swaps exposure also involves market risk, such as interest rate risk as well as other types.

Indeed, *interest rate risk* is a major concern of swap players. The interest rate sensitivity, or duration, of a swap is similar to that of a bond: when interest rates move, the value of the swap also changes. All swap dealers with unmatched swap positions in their portfolio are exposed to market risk, and they should use dynamic hedging, which requires significant know-how and high technology (more on interest rate risk in Chapter 14).

Interest Rate Risk Management through Derivatives

BEING AHEAD OF THE INTEREST RATE CURVE

Current interest rates, implied interest rates, contract terms and maturities—all impact on the term structure of interest rates and play an important role in shaping the *yield curve*. Moreover, given that hard currencies are international in scope and trading is done 24 hours per day, they offer an opportunity to make money in both bull and bear markets around the world, provided that one knows how to take advantage of yield curves:

- The *spot yield curve* on an interest rate product maps the yield in the cash market on that product, at a particular time.
- The *forward yield curve* describes what the market is predicting the current yield curve will look like at some point forward in time.

Interest rate risk is the risk that changes in the market interest rates might adversely affect a bank's financial condition because of their effect on its banking book, as well as on its trading book. Credit institutions and investors are exposed to interest rate risk whenever the interest-related sensitivity of their assets does not match the sensitivity of their liabilities and off-balance-sheet positions.

For instance, for a bank whose liabilities reprice faster than its assets, a rise in interest rates reduces the net interest income by increasing the cost of funds relative to its yield on assets. Changes in interest rates may affect not only an institution's current earnings but also its future earnings and the economic value of its capital.

If a bank has liabilities with interest rates that change faster than those on its assets,

Then, when interest rates rise, its net present value will decline.

The structure of a yield curve is usually but not always upward sloping. Yield curves can also be flat or downward sloping, depending on monetary policy and economic conditions. They may as well have a more uneven form, upward sloping over some maturities but being flat over other maturities.

The example in Figure 14.1 is that of a smoothly upward sloping yield curve. In contrast, the example in Figure 14.2 characterizing the euro's implied forward yield on April 11, 2007, is more complex. It involves a sharp rise in interest rate, backwardation, and then a smoother rise. *Backwardation* is a negative spread, or inverted yield curve, typically interpreted as signaling the probability of a recession.

Most economists underline the importance of studying the yield curve that represents the *term structure of interest rates*. This

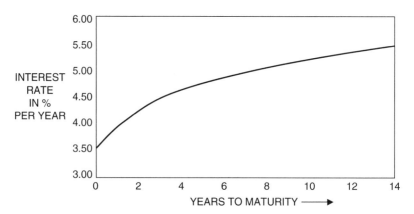

Figure 14.1 Implied forward yield curve of French government bonds on April 17, 1998

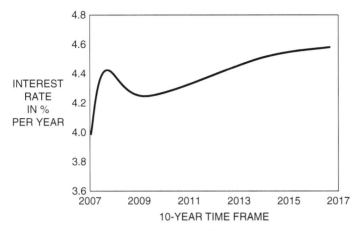

Figure 14.2 Implied forward yield curve of Euroland's interest rates on April 11, 2007

describes the relationship between the *yield to maturity* and the maturity of a given fixed-income position, typically represented by a plot of yields on risk-free securities issued by Group of 10 governments, with different terms to maturity at a given time.

This reference is used by investors, commercial bankers, and central bankers. Traders know that they must be ahead of the yield curve. The principle with all investment classes is this: Never forget why you invest. The next crucial question is, How? One of the important characteristics of institutional investors, for example, is that their activity tends to combine in the same person both views inherent in investments:

- The short-term trader and broker viewpoint
- The longer-term assets manager viewpoint

Several experts are using the concept of a *holding period* as a measure of an investor's steadiness and, in certain cases, of performance. Evaluating gains and losses resulting from investment decisions solely on a calendar-year basis is arbitrary. What one really wants to know is what the odds are for profitable performance over a holding period of a chosen length, with both risk and return as part of the picture.

The holding period and the investor's *time horizon* correlate. Many things can take place even over a short time horizon. While the bloodbath in bonds that occurred during February to April 1994 was due to the fact that the Fed raised interest rates several times in a row, falling rates can be just as deadly for some investments. A year later, in mid-July 1995, on Wall Street, some observers speculated that Salomon Brothers' proprietary house traders, some of whom were paid $30 million in 1994, lost money betting in the mortgage-backed bond market.

Mortgage-backed securities performed poorly as falling rates raised concern that mortgage refinancings would increase, shortening the lives of mortgage bonds and restraining gains. Basically, there are two types interest rate risk, each with its own challenges:

1. One is associated with optionality characterizing products that have defined cash flows like fixed-rate mortgages.

Living with fixed interest rates is relatively easy if volatility is low. Neither is this job difficult from a hedging perspective, except for the fact that there can be significant optionality embedded in the products and also in the process of selling them through securitization. The problem with optionality is that it is not always rationally exercised.

2. The other type of interest rate risk is associated with products that do not have any defined cash flows.

This is the case with many current account, savings, and credit card products as well as with certain forms of capital. In this connection, market behavior is the key driver. Such behavior is hard to model, though we can always develop patterns. The question is the level of confidence (Chapter 6) these master. A higher level of confidence is a function of our ability to foretell implied volatility.

Depending, on the composition of the bank's or the investor's portfolio, interest rate risk may be significant. A study done by the Bank of International Settlements (BIS) suggests that for the measurement of interest rate risk, credit institutions should classify interest rate–sensitive assets, liabilities, and off-balance-sheet instruments according to their

- Maturities, or
- Repricing characteristics.

This calls for a method for slotting various instruments into their bands, followed by the need to compute duration-weighted assets and liabilities, subject to certain adjustments. For a bank with high-duration (long-lived) assets relative to low-duration (short-lived) liabilities, the result of this computation provides an indicator of the degree to which the institution's value would be affected by a rise or fall in interest rates:

- Adversely in the case of a rise
- Positively in the case of a fall

Other things being equal, such a bank would find that, if sold as a going concern, its value would be different than it was prior to a change in the rates. It should, however, be appreciated that while the aforementioned computation is necessary for risk management purposes, a fair amount of interest rate mismatching constitutes a more or less normal feature of banking. Therefore, particular emphasis must be placed on inputs and outputs that are *outliers*. What constitutes an outlier must be interpreted against risk control norms established by the board.

THE TERM STRUCTURE OF INTEREST RATES

The preceding sections made the point that the term structure of interest rates is an important source of information for central banks, commercial banks, and investors. An indicator is the difference between a long-term and a short-term interest rate *term spread*, with statistics provided by historical yields of 10-year and 30-year Treasuries or other G-10 credit-risk-free government bonds.

Figure 14.3 brings into perspective a century of historical U.S. 10-year T-note yields. As the reader can easily observe, nominal 10-year dollar yields have spiked several times, with the highest spike in early 1980s as the inflationary thesis gained acceptance and the Fed moved against inflation the big way. As Figure 14.4 shows, two decades later, in early 2003, the interest rate of the 10-year Treasury note had bottomed.

What Figures 14.3 and 14.4 have brought to the reader's attention is the macroscopic view of interest rates. In reality the shape and level of the yield curve change from moment to moment because of the market's expectations about the monetary policy of the central bank and the interest rates' own market behavior.

The so-called *expectations theory* states that the spot interest rate on a long-term bond will equal an average of the short-term spot

Figure 14.3 Ten-year U.S. Treasury note yields during the twentieth century

interest rates that are expected to occur over the life of the long-term bond. Arbitrage

- Assures that, on the average, for different maturities the expected return will follow the above rule.
- Sees to it that the current forward rate on a specific instrument is equal to the future spot rate on that instrument.

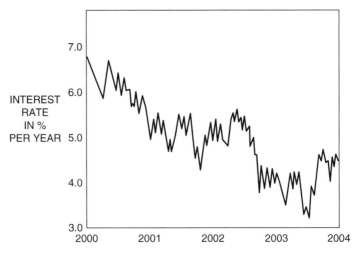

Figure 14.4 Ten-year U.S. Treasury note yields during the first four years of the twenty-first century

A large positive term spread may indicate that the market anticipates an increase in short-term interest rates because of a more positive outlook for economic growth. However, the yield curve also includes unobservable risks that are likely to vary over time, cumulatively known as *term premiums*—a term defined as the difference between

> The yield on a long-term bond and the expected average value of the short-term interest rate until the maturity of the debt instrument.

> Traders know that the "average" is a poor guide for day-to-day dealing, risk management, and hedging decisions. In contrast, the term spread tends to be a relatively good predictor of future economic activity over business-cycle horizons that are more or less well understood.

- Widening of this spread heralds an acceleration of economic growth.
- Narrowing of this spread indicates an incoming slowdown of macroeconomic factors.

From a monetary policy viewpoint, the term structure is of interest as an indicator of the market's expectations regarding interest rates and inflation rates. Its slope can provide information about the expected changes in both variables. The term structure is also important to investors because it reflects market expectations.

One could say that embedded in the current yield curve are forward curves for a whole family of forward times. A one-year forward curve suggests what the market is predicting the yield curve will look like in one year; a three-year forward curve maps what the market curve will look like over three years, and so on. Such estimates on forward-yield-curve shapes are based on current trading, with yield volatility being implied by current rates and market trends. There are formulas for

- Calculating forward rates for different maturities
- Deriving the resulting forward curve over the chosen period of time

However, a halo effect is unavoidable. *If* today's yield curve is steep, *then* the forward curve may be higher and steeper. But if today's yield curve is flat, the forward curve may also tend to be flat. Because the forward curve tends to magnify the shape of current interest rate trends, contrarians bet against the forward yield curve.

Other things being equal, interest rate calculation is simpler and less exposed to error in regard to securities providing one payment only, as is the case, for instance, with zero-coupon bonds. On the other hand, if a number of payments accrues during the life of the debt security, the computation of the rate of return on individual payments becomes more complex—with the rate of return on individual payments depending on the time of payment.

The prices of zero-coupon bonds can be used to calculate interest rates for respective maturities relatively easily since the only unknown variable is the price equation of the bonds. This is not possible for coupon bonds if the time to maturity is more than one year because payments accrue at different times.

While in computing the yield to maturity, all payment flows are discounted to current values at the same rate; in estimating the term structure of interest rates, each payment flow is discounted at an interest rate that varies depending on the reinvestment date and period. In principle, a continuous term structure would be observable directly in the bond market *if* a quotation for a risk-free, zero-coupon bond existed for each maturity. But in practice, there is only a small number of such bonds, which limits the number of observations.

For instance, while government bonds issued by the Group of 10 countries have a negligible default risk and hence are close to being risk-free bonds, they are mostly coupon bonds—not zero-coupon bonds. There are, however, computation algorithms to get around this problem, within the realm of computational finance.

To make feasible an accurate calculation of interest rates, individual payments have to be discounted not at constant but at maturity-related interest rates. Because the algorithm for the price of the coupon bond contains several variables, most of them unknown, interest rates have to be calculated iteratively.

- Theoretical yields to maturity are computed from a prespecified term structure and compared with that observed on bonds outstanding.
- The theoretical term structure is then varied until the calculated yields to maturity are more or less identical with the actually observed yield on bonds outstanding.

In the general case, there is a trade-off between the smoothness of the yield curve and its ability to fit observed data. Some of the existing models require that the parameters of specific interest rate function are estimated daily, based on the prices of government bonds, such as Treasuries. They also imply the use of nonlinear optimization techniques, with the criteria being the minimization of squared deviations of estimated yields to maturity.

THE CONTRIBUTION OF INTEREST RATE DERIVATIVES

Interest rate derivatives is a general term for financial instruments whose value is derived from the market price, a reference interest rate, or debt security. These derivative instruments include bond forwards, options, and interest rate swaps (see the following section, "Accounting for Interest Rate Derivatives"), making possible a significant amount of leverage. In terms of the notional principal amount, interest rate derivatives fall into three main classes. In order of magnitude, they are

- 76 percent swaps
- 14 percent options
- 10 percent forward rate agreements

Since their development in the late 1970s, interest rate derivatives have become important trading instruments in the financial markets as products used for risk management purposes. Under certain conditions, however, because interest rate derivatives are leveraged instruments, they may have a destabilizing impact on the financial markets.

There are many reasons behind the popularity of interest rate derivatives. Among the more important are the following:

- Transaction costs are lower than in the spot market.
- They tie up much less capital than do positions in the underlying assets.
- They can be used for hedging and to take on risks intentionally.
- They can be employed quite effectively for tax optimization reasons.

One of the positive effects of the interest rate derivatives markets is that they make it possible to separate a company's operational policy risks connected to an investment from the pure interest rate risk. This helps in making operating performance less dependent on factors outside its influence since, down to basics, interest rates are the domain of the central banks (and sometimes of governments). Moreover,

- Interest rate derivatives assist in making risk factors tradable.

In macroeconomic terms tradability is a precondition for the efficient allocation of assumed exposure, provided that market participants are in charge of their risks. Additionally,

- Using interest rate derivatives could be more cost effective than adjusting securities portfolios through buying and selling positions.

For instance, portfolio managers can hedge against interest through interest rate swaps; and, provided that they guess right the direction of interest rates, they could manage their portfolios' dependency on individual risk factors more quickly through derivatives.

For their part, credit institutions can manage the potential earnings effect of interest rate movements by using derivatives in their effort to control asset and liability mix. They could do so through the use of interest rate swaps and other instruments designated as hedges or capable of modifying the interest rate characteristics of specific assets or liabilities.

The able use of interest rate derivatives, however, has prerequisites. The qualification of such contracts must be evaluated for consistency with the bank's risk management strategy. This is the case with the use of derivatives in response to changing market conditions, as well as the characteristics and mix of the assets and liabilities in widespread circulation today. The swap, forward, or bought option position must be designated as effective in contributing to the firm's strategic plan.

Accounting and auditing principles must be fully observed (as discussed in the following section). Are amounts payable and receivable on interest rate swaps and options accrued according to contractual terms? Are they included in the related revenue and expense category as elements of yield on the associated instrument?

Compliance with accounting rules is a must. According to the U.S. GAAP and the IFRS, depending on management's intent, amounts paid or received over the life of futures contracts may be deferred until the contract is closed. On the other hand, contracts related to instruments that are carried at fair value should also be reported at fair value, with the amounts payable and receivable accounted for as an element of yield on the associated instrument.

If an interest rate derivative contract is terminated, any resulting gain or loss must be deferred and amortized over the original term of the agreement, provided that the effectiveness criteria have been met. If the underlying designated items are no longer held, or an anticipated transaction is no longer likely to occur, any previously unrecognized gain or loss on the derivative contract

- Needs to be recognized in earnings, and
- Needs to be accounted for at fair value with subsequent changes recognized in earnings.

Good governance requires steady management control. In the general case, open positions are closed by offsetting trades shortly prior to maturity, while fulfillment of futures contracts by delivery of the underlying is the exception. The effectiveness of all inventoried contracts should be evaluated not only on an initial and closing date but also on an ongoing basis.

If a contract is found to be ineffective,

Then it should no longer qualify as an *end-user position*.

Any excess gains and losses attributable to such ineffectiveness as well as subsequent changes in fair value must be recognized in the P&L calculations. Moreover, banks and investors should appreciate that while the impact of interest rate derivatives on the liquidity of the cash market is uncertain, as a rule the futures market withdraws transactions from the cash market.

Quite often, ambiguity arises from the fact that the futures market not only attracts transactions but also creates new trading opportunities in the underlying securities. But at the same time, the effect of derivative transactions on price formation depends on the level of information of the market players; poorly informed investors have a destabilizing impact.

ACCOUNTING FOR INTEREST RATE DERIVATIVES

Chapter 13 defined an *interest rate swap* as an agreement through which two parties exchange, at specified intervals, interest payment streams calculated on an established notional principal amount, with at least one stream based on a specified floating-rate index. It has been also brought to the reader's attention that certain contracts are combined interest rate and foreign currency swap transactions. (We will return to this issue in the following section in the discussion on internal interest rate swaps.)

The preceding section made the point that beyond what was stated in Chapter 13, there are as well available other derivative financial instruments for the management of interest rate risk, as well as for speculation. *Interest rate forward contracts* represent commitments either to purchase or sell at a specified future date a financial instrument for a specified price. Such derivative products may be settled in cash or through delivery.

Forward rate agreements (FRAs, see Chapter 12) are contracts with notional principal amounts that settle in cash at a specified future date based on the differential between a specified market interest rate and a fixed interest rate. They are utilized in trading activities and to manage interest rate exposure. According to the IFRS and U.S. GAAP, banks must mark gains and losses on these contracts in connection to their trading book.

In contrast, *if* management's intention is to keep such contracts to maturity, *then* gains and losses are deferred and amortized over the lives of the hedged assets or liabilities. But if assets and liabilities underlying these contracts are disposed of, then unamortized gains and losses are recognized in the income statement at the time of disposition.

In different terms, under both the U.S. GAAP and IFRS guidelines, disclosure of derivative financial instruments is separated into two classes based on the reasons that entities buy or write derivatives. Several experts have nevertheless suggested that the aforementioned two classes do not accurately reflect derivatives trading and that the disclosures would be more realistic if separated into three classes:

- Dealing proper
- Speculative position taking
- Risk management

Some regulatory authorities have considered this alternative, but they have been concerned about the difficulty in properly defining, and distinguishing between, dealing, speculative position taking, and risk management. This is particularly true as a variety of derivative instruments are used with all three classes, and they also feature both credit and market risk.

For instance, as the careful reader will recall, forward rate agreements have credit risk over and above market risk. The same is true of interest rate options bought, which expose the holder to credit risk to the extent that the seller may not be forthcoming in his or her contractually assumed obligations.

A callable and puttable floating-rate note (FRN) is an example of an interest rate option. Such instruments came to the market's attention in the late 1980s. Under a callable FRN, the issuer has the right to redeem the note prior to maturity. This is done at a prespecified price, often at par. Under a puttable FRN, the investor has the right to force early redemption. Because FRN coupons periodically reset to market interest rates, the credit risk of the writer is the primary driver of callable and puttable interest rate notes' market value.

In a more general sense, the Financial Accounting Standards Board (FASB) believes that fixed-rate loan commitments have characteristics similar to option contracts. They provide the holder with benefits from favorable movements in the price of an underlying asset or index, along with limited or no exposure to losses from unfavorable price movements.

But like option contracts, they subject the issuer to market risk. For this reason, the FASB has decided that those financial instruments should be included within the definition of derivative financial instrument and be subject to the disclosures required by the Statement of Financial Accounting Standards 119 (SFAS 119, the original regulation of derivatives, first of its kind in modern finance). By extension, variable-rate loan commitments and other variable-rate financial instruments may also include terms that subject the issuer to market risk.

INTERNAL INTEREST RATE SWAPS

In the 1990s, a discussion paper issued by the Basel Committee on Banking Supervision proposed a number of principles for the management of interest rate risk. This included not only procedures but also the role the board of directors and senior management must play in the control of interest rate exposure. This paper advised that

- The bank's board should examine and establish interest rate risk management policies, and
- It should be informed regularly about the interest rate exposure of the bank, including *what-if evaluations*.

Several steps are necessary to make this approach feasible. First, the bank's senior management should assure that appropriate systems and procedures are established to monitor, limit, and control interest rate risk. A basic prerequisite for this to happen is to establish the bank's risk management function such that it

- Reports directly to the board and top management
- Is independent of the business lines that assume credit, interest rate, and other risks

Banks that engage in large volumes of interest rate swap transactions and other significant off-balance-sheet interest rate arbitrage have to measure and control *basis risk* (see Chapter 1), assuring that the underlying obligations have the same maturity or interest rate rollover periods—even if the reference rates differ.

Moreover, board members, the CEO, and senior management must always remember that forward transactions, swaps, options, or futures can both reduce and increase exposure to interest rate risk. Different techniques are available for measurement purposes, from gap limits to risk factors and points—characterized by various degrees of complexity. And because all solutions make implicit and explicit assumptions that impact upon the results, these assumptions must be

- Clearly written
- Constantly reviewed
- Experimentally evaluated

The next basic step is to thoroughly study and steadily test the *hedging culture*. Swaps, options, and forward rate agreements may be entered into as a hedge against interest rate exposure; however, other very similar transactions may also be undertaken with the deliberate aim of increasing net interest rate exposures. If a bank acts as a market maker in these instruments, there may be an increase in both

- Interest rate risk
- Credit risk exposure

To guard against this likelihood, there should be in place a high-technology-supported system able to incorporate in real time the position risks arising both from on-balance-sheet and off-balance-sheet activities. As we saw on other occasions (Chapter 11), knowledge engineering can contribute quite significantly to the measurement of overall interest rate exposure for

- Any instrument
- Any counterparty
- Anywhere in the world

An important element in the implementation of a rigorous system of interest rate risk control is *internal interest rate swaps*. Their objective is to leave only credit risk in the banking book by transferring market risk to the trading book. This should be executed as a treasury function, centralizing all interest rate risk into a single position that can be laid off into the markets.

Figure 14.5 helps in explaining what the preceding paragraph suggested. Internal interest rate swaps take place between the banking book and trading book, with the objective to take market risk out of the loans book and put it into the trading book for hedging. In many jurisdictions, supervisory authorities support this practice as a tool for better internal risk management by the banks, but not for financial reporting reasons.

Here is an example on how this approach works. Say that a business unit (BU) is making five-year fixed-rate loans, but it is funding itself through a one-month LIBOR. By means of structuring the appropriate interest rate swap with the business unit, the bank's treasury can immunize the BU's loans from movements in

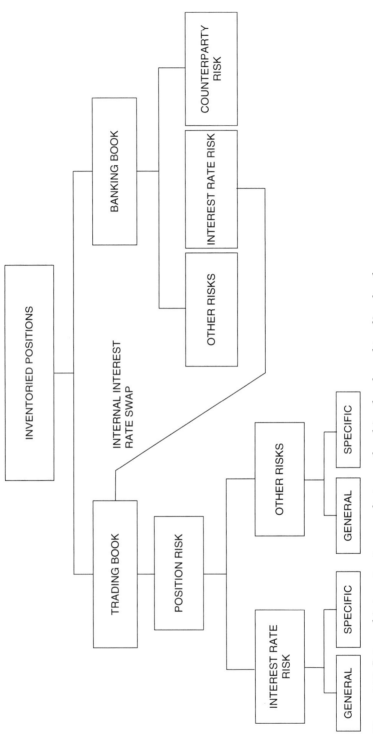

Figure 14.5 Internal interest rate swap between banking book and trading book

short-term interest rates.

- This leaves the business unit with an income stream that is the difference between the customer's rate and the five-year swap rate.
- The counterparty in this case is no longer a business unit but the business lending area of the credit institution.

This is a product pricing development. It observes a structure whereby the underlying pricing is overlaid with a network of swap transactions helping to protect the business unit against the profile of its interest rate risks.

The degree of sophistication used in connection to an interest rate risk control system varies among banks, but as a minimum, the chosen solution must be capable of capturing all the interest rate exposures in the banking book performing sensitivity analyses and permitting management to estimate the effect of a given change in interest rates, which will lead to hedging decisions.

A sound policy on interest rate swaps requires that the bank decide on a swap structure that needs to be of a perpetual nature, using rolling hedges that are reasonably simple. Depending on management's view of the yield curve, a bank can use interest rate swaps to match positions created by thousands of underlying customer accounts. To do so, it must

- Construct amortization profiles
- Adjust for anticipated early repayment as well as bad-debt events

In its fundamentals, this method is not too different from the one used with the option adjusted spread (OAS) in connection to securitization,[1] with the added requirement that one must anticipate new business currently being written, while the OAS is usually computed on an existing pool of mortgages or other assets.

- To deal with amortization profiles, banks typically construct aggregate positions from many underlying accounts.

---

[1] Dimitris N. Chorafas, *Financial Models and Simulation,* Macmillan, London, 1995.

- They hedge them on an aggregate basis by means of relevant amortization profiles, adjusted for early exercise and new business currently being written.

Modeling the different factors requires knowing the behavior pattern of loan holders—from mortgages to personal and business loans. Prepayment of loans can be studied through the Monte Carlo method. (There is as well a risk known as *pipeline*, due to the fact that a bank cannot effectively reprice all its mortgages or other loans every day with a new rate.)

As with every banking study, a most critical factor with financial interest rate swaps is accurate data. Constructing aggregate positions from thousands or millions of accounts requires a first-class database data-mining algorithm and any-to-any online access. It also relies heavily on data timeliness, accuracy, and integrity.

THE SYNERGY BETWEEN INTEREST RATES AND CURRENCY RATES

Bonds are a good proxy in explaining the concept of interest yield spreads and the hypotheses that go along with it—as well as its impact on currency exchange rates, and vice versa. Take the mid-1990s as an example. Italian bonds rose to new highs on expectations that Italy would be in on the first wave of single-currency participation in the euro (see also the last section in this chapter, especially the discussion of spreads in interest rates associated to credit risk).

As shown in Figure 14.6, the market's anticipations significantly narrowed the yield spread between German and Italian bonds, a surprising development given that in the mid-1990s the prospects of monetary union going ahead on time had worsened. Not only were France and Germany on a potential collision course about the single currency but also Germany was increasingly divided within itself, with the Bavarians digging their heels in against a weak euro.

On the other hand, as Figure 14.6 also shows, for nearly two years the markets had accepted the German mark–French franc union as more or less a fait accompli. Major European banks, however, warned that bond markets would be shaken by changes in

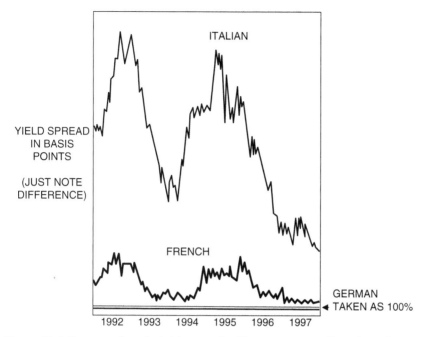

Figure 14.6 Ten-year bond yield spreads: German versus French and Italian

current currency sentiment, between then (mid-1990s) and the final stage of euro membership in the first years of the twenty-first century.

"Yield convergence is not a one-way road," the president of one of the leading banks said at the time, pointing out that if the euro agreements cracked, the German bonds would shoot up and the French would plummet—while France's socialist government would seize the opportunity to devalue. This was one of the statements by senior bankers that brought forward the synergy that exists between

- Interest rate risk
- Currency risk

Other statements made at the time went beyond yield spreads into currency spreads, pointing out that at times the two tend to correlate. Therefore, bankers and investors had to be most careful regarding their portfolio positions.

In an environment such as that of a new currency, like the euro, projected to bring under its fold a dozen other currencies, a main issue regarding a portfolio's composition is whether opposing interest rate positions in different currencies could be regarded as hedging one another. Or, rather, exposure is amplified.

A basic question is whether different currencies exhibit broadly similar interest rate movements with any degree of regularity; but the answer is far from simple. Exact measurement based on correlations of all rates in all involved currencies would be very complex and difficult to incorporate into a dependable model. A conservative solution is therefore

- To permit no offsetting between positions in different currencies, and
- To stick to this strategy even if it constitutes a worst-case approach.

Some analysts have advanced a different way of looking at the synergy of interest rate risk, based on the assumption that currency risks for both financial institutions and other companies are exposed to the potential cost of replacing the cash flow arising from financial instruments in their portfolio. Other things being equal, higher risk factors must be applied to those contracts that have currency exchange risk exposure over and above interest rate exposure—a statement that is valid all the way to the maturity of

- Interest rates
- Currency exchange hedges

Experts have suggested that when it comes to hedging, prudent management enters in derivative contracts *maturing within five years*. But specifically for currency exchange, conservative companies should see to it that *maturity does not exceed one year*. Table 14.1 presents the policy on maturities established by one of the better-known global companies in the food industry. In this table:

- *Interest rate contracts* include single-currency interest rate swaps, basis swaps, forward rate agreements and products with similar characteristics, interest rate futures, and interest rate options purchased.

TABLE 14.1

The Policy on Maturities on Interest Rate and Currency Exchange Hedging Followed by a Global Food Company

	With Maturity
Interest rate swaps for assets	5 years
Interest rate swaps for liabilities	5 years
Currency exchange forwards or assets	1 year
Currency exchange forwards or liabilities	2 years
Purchased options or assets	1 year

- *Currency-exchange-rate contracts* include cross-currency swaps, cross-currency interest rate swaps, outright forward exchange contracts, currency futures, and currency options purchased.

Several regulators advise that to calculate the credit equivalent amount of these instruments, a bank should add together the total replacement cost, obtained by marking-to-market of all its contracts with a positive value—along with an amount for potential future credit exposure that reflects the residual maturity of the contract, calculated as a percentage of the notional principal amount according to a matrix. One of the matrixes being used is shown in Table 14.2.

In the case of interest rate or cross-currency swaps arranged at off-market prices, some regulators require special treatment whereby the contract has been created in order to disguise a credit exposure to the counterparty. To measure the exchange rate exposure of contractually determined cash flows, it is advisable to

TABLE 14.2

A Matrix of the Residual Maturity of Interest Rate and Currency Rate Contracts

	Interest Rate Contracts	Currency Rate Contracts
Less than 1 year	Nil	1.0%
1 year and over	0.5%	5.0%

closely follow and monitor in real time all of the portfolio positions. This should be done through a *currency book* that

- Includes all affiliates and subsidiaries anywhere in the world
- Establishes the treasury's rights and obligations to a specific amount of currency over a specified time frame

Options, futures, forwards, swaps, and other derivatives in different currencies must be included in the cash flow estimate along with cash and receivables. Additionally, specific notice should be taken of the obligations to purchase or sell given currencies and the time at which they are to be received or delivered.

Interest rate exposure can be calculated in connection to commitments made for each currency by using a duration measure. Account should be taken of price elasticity in connection to contracted financial obligations, relative to changes in the interest rates. For options, the steady computation of *theta* (Chapter 10) by small increments is an advisable procedure. The same is true of duration measures for bonds, breaking up the projected cash flow stream over time, and calculating each discrete change and its effects on treasury positions.

INTEREST RATE RISK AND ITS MEASUREMENT

The better-managed financial institutions are developing sophisticated models to help themselves in getting a better appreciation of interest rate and currency exchange exposure, as well as an increased understanding of individual risks. Institutions that have adopted a systems approach identify several risk factors in an effort to model their exposure in a more accurate fashion. The downside for those banks that are behind in information technology development is that these risk factors

- Generate large matrixes of information elements
- Require a significant volume of calculation, which can be supported only by banks at the cutting edge of technology

One of the approaches followed by some of the leaders in the banking industry is that of identifying and managing risk points. A *risk point* represents the amount of gain or loss that would characterize each portfolio position in the aftermath of a given movement in interest rates or in currency exchange rates.

Some banks opt for a fixed movement—for instance, ± 1 percent. Others test the aftereffect of movements such as ± 100 and more basis points in conjunction with an overall risk point limit that is often sub-allocated to different trading desks and portfolio positions. One of the best examples of a simple and effective approach in evaluating the impact of interest rate risk has been developed by the Office of Thrift Supervision (OTS), which is the supervisory authority of the American Savings and Loans (S&Ls, thrifts, building societies).

After the events of the late 1980s and the wave of bankruptcies that shook the savings and loan industry, the Office of Thrift Supervision paid a great amount of attention to the interest rate exposure of the institutions it supervises. Of the regulated 1,119 S&Ls (essentially the more important), 90 percent file a daily report giving interest rate risk information, using a model compliant to OTS directives.

This model is the same for all reporting entities, and it integrates what-if hypotheses on the movement of interest rates; it also pays attention to maturity. The experimentation starts with current interest rates and changes them by 100, 200, 300, and 400 basis points up and down. The crucial adverse condition is at the shock level of ± 200 basis points.

The Office of Thrift Supervision runs the submitted results through a Monte Carlo simulation. It has also developed a standard reporting methodology for the savings and loans that distinguishes between operations made for trading reasons and those intended for risk management.

Only a few savings and loans are active participants in the derivatives market—typically 76 out of 1,119. As Timothy Stier of the OTS said during our meeting, "Once in a while we find a thrift who bought a reverse floater, but the majority of the savings and loans keep out of this market." Of prime importance, therefore, is interest rate risk control, and thanks to the OTS initiative, the thrifts have learned how to model

- Worst-case scenarios
- Sensitivity measurements
- Capital before shock calculations
- Capital after shock calculations

Sensitivity measurement and worst-case scenarios are important not only in the computation of capital requirements for offsetting interest rate risk but also for experimental purposes. For instance, in testing the empirical evidence that long and short positions of equal risk-weighted size are generally less risky as a pair than when considered individually.

Additionally, measures of expected volatility of future short-term and long-term interest rates can provide valuable information about the dispersion of market expectations or uncertainty regarding future interest rate developments. The use of implied volatility complements measures of expectations of future evolution of financial variables like forward interest rates and futures prices, by providing a weight of the uncertainty surrounding such expectations.

The better-governed credit institutions see to it that *trading* positions, including off-balance-sheet instruments held for trading purposes, and *nontrading* positions including off-balance-sheet instruments employed to hedge nontrading positions, are approached separately in measuring interest rate risk. A crucial question is how far should offsetting positions be recognized as hedges or partial hedges.

Also, should the recognition of hedges be dependent on the bank's policy of consciously managing its interest rate risk in an integrated manner? Or should marking-to-market also be an essential ingredient in such calculations? These are among the queries the Bank of International Settlements has been asking central banks to respond to by providing factual and documented answers. Theoretically, both the actual and notional, long and short positions in identical instruments with exactly the same

- Issuer
- Coupon
- Currency
- Maturity

should be fully matched and offsettable. Practically, due to crucial factors, among which is exchange risk, no offsetting can be done between positions in different currencies. In a globalized financial market, a universal measurement system and explicit measurement norms for interest rate risk are necessary to identify institutions that may be incurring extraordinarily large amounts of interest rate exposure.

INTEREST RATE SPREADS ASSOCIATED WITH CREDIT RISK

Investors became aware of the reemergence of major exposure due to credit risk following three events: the late 1980s meltdown of junk bonds and the bankruptcies of savings and loans (described in the preceding section); the mid-Asia market's downfall in 1997; and the Russian meltdown in 1998. All three led to a widening of spreads. Here is a brief analysis of the first two events.

Michael Milken based the success of his junk-bond business in the 1980s on the observation that the markets had historically exaggerated the risk attached to poor-quality credits. The so-called fallen-angels companies that were at some time in the past rather prosperous but had fallen on hard times

- Paid an excessive interest rate premium for their borrowing, or
- Were altogether shut out of mainstream credit markets.

According to Milken's book, this mispricing of risk had several consequences. One was that risky firms, and a number of start-ups or midsized companies, often had difficulties in borrowing enough money to pursue their ambitions. Another consequence was that there were significant advantages in the high credit ratings AAA, AA, and (to a lesser extent) A:

- These ratings facilitated access to loans at prices that were disproportionately cheaper than that available to weaker credits.
- In addition, what the weaker credits had to pay, if they could get a banking loan at all, was also well beyond the assumed credit risk.

Hence, by pioneering the high-yield but also higher-risk securities, Milken aimed to assure that credit became available even to much riskier borrowers. Competition did the rest, and competition saw to it that the yield on what became known as "junk bonds" was driven down, eventually leading to credit risk mispricing (see also Chapter 11).

At the high time of junk bonds in the 1980s, the spread between the interest rate paid on speculative-grade debit instruments and U.S. Treasuries had narrowed by nearly a full percentage point. This, however, did not mean that there were no shareholder benefits in a company with a strong balance sheet. Many, if not most, business activities require financial staying power:

- When they sensed its existence, capital markets took over from junk-bond financing.
- In addition, when companies with a weak capital base went under, the market thought again about credit risk, and interest rate spreads therefore widened.

Something similar took place with cheap credit in the 1990s, and it led to the East Asia crisis of 1997. Asian companies that bankers and investors thought had ring-fenced balance sheets drove themselves against the wall because of overleveraging, which drastically reduced their creditworthiness. The global market response that followed took two main forms:

- A broader knock-on effect affecting the whole of the bond market, almost independent of issuers
- A widening of interest rate spreads, which impacted financial institutions that were thought to have, directly or indirectly, exposure to East Asia and other emerging markets

Several analysts considered the general widening of spreads in the bond market as an example of *spread risk*. Others expressed the belief that the cases of East Asia (including South Korea) and eventually of Russia—as well as the LTCM virtual bankruptcy—were not only examples of how credit risk impact spreads but also of how a credit meltdown sees to it that profit forecasts

- Are sharply cut, or
- Revert to net losses for a lot of companies.

Spread risk and deteriorating credit risk correlate in that the former is a product of the latter. As credit risk mounts, the downgrading of the issuer, individually or as an industry, leads to spread risk, which increases by so much the pure cost of money:

- Spread risk is part of interest rate risk,
- But the top-most factor underpinning spread risk is credit risk.

To define spread risk in an accurate way, we must first analyze exactly what value credit risk is in a given transaction entered into with a counterparty. In the general case, the credit risk factor affecting the spread is a market estimate of the default probability of an issuer—whether this is a company issuing debt instruments or a sovereign backing a currency. Basically, this is a perceived likelihood, and it usually allows for partial recovery.

In both cases—interest rates and currency rates—spreads exhibit a mean reversion as they tend to oscillate around a mean value. But with currencies, the mean reversion pulls tend to happen with narrower parameters than those characterizing interest rates—unless there is a known and appreciated lender of last resort, as was the case in the late 1980s when the German central bank implicitly backed the Italian lira.

Spreads also tend to exhibit an upper boundary *as if* there were a natural tolerance. In the general case, for strong currencies, this upper boundary is roughly 2.2 times the mean value, though extreme events like a strong currency recovery establishes a trend breaking through this tolerance. In the early 1980s this happened with the U.S. dollar versus the other currencies of the Group of 10; and in the early 1990s the breakthrough characterized the dollar/yen exchange rate.

Because interest rate and currency rate events have to be analyzed and controlled, Tier 1 banks are increasingly interested monitoring spread risk, but very few have gone beyond a theoretical overview or have developed rigorous statistical tests. Yet we have the tools for monitoring and testing spread risk, looking to basis point sensitivities produced by different classes of instruments in our portfolio, such as

- Government bonds including bond futures
- Interest rate swaps and similar cash instruments like deposit futures
- Eurobonds and similar products
- Currency instruments, particularly of emerging countries

A good way to start is to look at changes in sensitivities within homogeneous time buckets. Taking debt instruments as an example, attention should then be paid to the rating of the bonds by independent agencies. Different ratings have different volatilities that lead to different spreads (The same is true of different currency–denominated bonds.) Using this information as a basis, it is wise to build simulators (simulation is a working analogy) and experimental procedures for stress testing. The challenge is to think out of the box, in the domain where real risks and returns typically lie.

INDEX

Dr. Dimitris N. Chorafas is an international management consultant. Since 1961, he has advised such eminent national and international banks as Union Bank of Switzerland, Bank Vontobel, Bank of Scotland, Bank Austria (Österreichische Länderbank), Erste Österreichische Spar-Kasse (First Austrian Bank), Commerzbank, Dresdner Bank, Credit Agricole, Credit Mobilier de Monaco, Socredit, Istituto Bancario Italiano, Banca Provinciale Lombarda, Credito Commerciale, Credito Emiliano, Banca Nazionale dell' Agricoltura, Demir Bank, and Mid Med Bank.

Dr. Chorafas has worked as a consultant to the top management of many multinational corporations, including General Electric/Bull, Univac, Honeywell, Olivetti, Digital Equipment, Nestlé, Omega, Italcementi, Worthington, AEG-Telefunken, Olympia, Osram, Antar, Pechiney, Compagnie Générale Transatlantique, Compagnie Française Thompson-Houston, National Iranian Oil Company, the American Management Association, and a host of other client firms in Europe and the United States.

A Fulbright scholar, Dr. Chorafas received his doctorate in mathematics and logic at the Sorbonne in Paris. He graduated from the National Technical University of Athens with a degree in electrical and mechanical engineering, has a Master of Science degree in computers from the University of California, Los Angeles, and has done postgraduate studies in banking and finance, operations research, production management, and biotechnology at UCLA, the University of Denver, and George Washington University.

Dr. Chorafas has been on the faculty of the Catholic University of America, Washington, DC (1956–1958). From 1962 to 1968 he chaired the Information Systems department, Centre d'Etudes Industrielles of the University of Geneva.

He has lectured as a visiting professor at Washington State University (Business Administration and Information Science), George Washington University, Georgia Institute of Technology, University of Florida, University of Vermont, University of Alberta (Canada), Technical University of Karlsruhe (Germany), Polish Academy of Sciences, Russian Academy of Sciences, and Ecole Polytechnique de Lausanne.

In his early career (1957–1960), Dr. Chorafas worked with IBM in mathematical simulators, systems engineering, and executive development in the United States and Europe. He was then director of management information systems with Booz, Allen & Hamilton International (1960–1961).

Equally familiar with the optimization of personnel and technology, his assignments have ranged from top-level company reorganization to market research, product planning, internal audit, and information systems design. For the last 45 years, he has acted as personal advisor to presidents of large corporations.

Dr. Chorafas is a recognized authority on strategic planning, risk management, internal controls, derivative financial instruments, management development, financial information systems, IT auditing, software policy, simulation, knowledge engineering, network design, database organization, system architecture, system integration, and corporate reorganization projects.

Over 8,000 banking, industrial, and government executives have participated in his seminars in the United States, England, Germany, France, Holland, Belgium, Denmark, Sweden, Finland, Italy, Spain, Austria, and Switzerland, as well as in Brazil, India, the Philippines, Indonesia, Hong Kong, and Singapore.

He is the author of 150 books published in 16 countries by McGraw-Hill, Prentice Hall, John Wiley, Irwin, Van Nostrand Reinhold, Academic Press, New York Institute of Finance, Institutional Investor, CRC-Auerbach, Macmillan/Palgrave, VRL, Lafferty, Euromoney, Butterworth-Heinemann, Elsevier and other publishers in France, Germany, Italy, Russia, Brazil, Japan, and China.

Dr. Chorafas is listed in *Who's Who in the World, Who's Who in Europe, Dictionary of International Biography, The Writer's Directory, Livre d'Or des Valeurs Humaines,* and *Men of Achievement.*